Studies on the European Union

Series Editor:
Wolfgang Wessels
Jean Monnet Chair for Political Science
University of Cologne

Volume 10

Maren Kreutler

Interest Group Coalitions in the European Union

An Analysis of (In)Formal Initiatives to Influence European Energy Policy

BLOOMSBURY

Die Deutsche Nationalbibliothek lists this publication in the
Deutsche Nationalbibliografie; detailed bibliographic data
is available in the Internet at http://dnb.d-nb.de

a.t.: Bochum, Univ., Diss., 2012, published with original title:
Maren Becker: The Formation of Coalitions in the European Union –
An Analysis of (In)Formal Initiatives to Influence European Energy Policy

ISBN: HB (Nomos)   978-3-8487-0600-6
        ePDF (Nomos)   978-3-8452-4848-6

British Library Cataloguing-in-Publication Data
A catalogue record for this book is available from the British Library.

ISBN: HB (Bloomsbury):   978-1-4742-2477-2
        ePDF (Bloomsbury):   978-1-4742-2476-5
        ePub (Bloomsbury):   978-1-4742-2475-8

Library of Congress Cataloging-in-Publication Data
Kreutler, Maren
Interest Group Coalitions in the European Union
An Analysis of (In)Formal Initiatives to Influence European Energy Policy
Maren Kreutler
211 p.
Includes bibliographic references.

ISBN   978-1-4742-2477-2   (hardcover Bloomsbury)
ISBN   978-1-4742-2476-5   (ebook (pdf) Bloomsbury)
ISBN   978-1-4742-2475-8   (ebook (epub) Bloomsbury)

1. Edition 2014
© Nomos Verlagsgesellschaft, Baden-Baden, Germany 2014. Printed and bound in Germany.

This work is subject to copyright. All rights reserved. No part of this publication may be reproduced or transmitted in any form or by any means, electronic or mechanical, including photocopying, re-cording, or any information storage or retrieval system, without prior permission in writing from the publishers. Under § 54 of the German Copyright Law where copies are made for other than private use a fee is payable to "Verwertungsgesellschaft Wort", Munich.

No responsibility for loss caused to any individual or organization acting on or refraining from action as a result of the material in this publication can be accepted by Nomos or the author.

Acknowledgements

First of all, I would like to express my thanks to my supervisors Prof. Dr. Rainer Eising (Ruhr-University Bochum) and Prof. Dr. Johannes Pollak (Institute for Advanced Studies (IHS) Vienna and Webster University Vienna), who have always been supportive. The points they required me to address have made this work significantly richer than it would have otherwise been. I could not have asked for better supervision.

I have been extremely fortunate in having very reliable colleagues at the IHS: Prof. Dr. Oliver Treib, Dr. Guido Tiemann and Dr. Manuela Caiani have all influenced my way of thinking. I would also like to express my thanks to my fellow PhD students at the IHS and at the Ruhr-University Bochum, especially Stefanie John, Sonja Lehringer and Florian Spohr, for their comments on the research design, and to Arthur Pitman from the Alpen-Adria University Klagenfurt for editing this thesis.

Moreover, special thanks go to Prof. Dr. Wolfgang Wessels and Nomos Verlagsgesellschaft for publishing this work and to the Austrian Political Science Association for partly funding this publication.

Furthermore, I owe a great debt to Gerold Kreutler, who has contributed a good deal to the completion of this work. He has not only given me valuable advice on the subject but also has made my life a lot more worthwhile and enjoyable.

Finally, this work could not have been completed without the support of my parents Sonja († 2006) and Volkhard Becker. Their constant trust in my abilities has encouraged me to pursue my own visions. And wherever these visions have led me, I have always known where to come home to.

Klagenfurt, May 2014   Maren Kreutler

Table of contents

List of abbreviations 13

Chapter 1. Introduction 17

1.1 The increasing significance of European energy policy 20
1.2 The theoretical contribution of this work 26
1.3 The methods applied in the empirical research 29
1.4 Outline of this work 30

Chapter 2. Recent developments in selected areas of European
 energy policy 33

2.1 The liberalization of the European energy market 35
2.2 The introduction of the Kyoto Protocol and the EU Emissions Trading
 Scheme (EU ETS) 39
2.3 The promotion of energy efficiency 48
2.4 The promotion of the use of renewable energy sources 55
2.5 Additional measures to ensure energy supply security 62
2.6 Conclusions 66

Chapter 3. The current state of research on interest group politics and
 related fields 69

3.1 Periods of research on the role of interest groups in the policy process 69
3.2 Literature on multi-level and network governance 72
3.3 Theories on coalition-formation 80
3.4 Approaches to collective action and social movements 87
3.5 The role of institutions in the policy process 91
3.6 Literature on actors' strategies to influence political decision-making 97
3.7 Studies on the determinants of the access and influence of interest
 groups 100

Table of contents

Chapter 4. Research design and case studies — 107

4.1 Research design — 107
4.1.1 The benefits of process-tracing case studies — 107
4.1.2 Case selection — 110
4.1.3 Variables and hypotheses derived from the theoretical background — 115
4.1.4 Data gathering tools: interviews and document analysis — 125
4.2 Case studies — 131
4.2.1 The policy process leading to the third liberalization package — 131
4.2.2 Interests and strategies regarding the inclusion of aviation in the EU ETS — 142
4.2.3 Developments related to the directive on the energy performance of buildings — 153
4.2.4 Coalition-formation concerning the role of biofuels in EU legislation — 165
4.2.5 The influence of coalitions on the receptiveness of the European institutions — 174

Chapter 5. Empirical results — 177

Chapter 6. Conclusions — 185

Literature — 189

List of tables

Table 1:	Registration of crude oil imports and deliveries in the European Union (EU 27) (intra + extra EU)	20
Table 2:	Key events regarding the liberalization of the EU energy market	36
Table 3:	Key events regarding the establishment of the EU ETS	45
Table 4:	Key developments regarding the increase of energy efficiency	51
Table 5:	National overall targets for the share of energy from renewable sources in gross final consumption of energy in 2020	57
Table 6:	Key events regarding the promotion of renewable energy sources	59
Table 7:	Key events regarding the security of energy supply	63
Table 8:	Core elements of ideal types of governance	75
Table 9:	Typology of network structures	77
Table 10:	Potential and type of policy change	77
Table 11:	Collective action processes	89
Table 12:	Core developments related to the third liberalization package	110
Table 13:	Core developments related to the inclusion of aviation in the EU ETS	111
Table 14:	Core developments related to the directive on the energy performance of buildings	112
Table 15:	Core developments related to the promotion of biofuels for transport	113
Table 16:	Types of interest representatives	125
Table 17:	Fields of interest	126
Table 18:	Categories of coalitions of European associations and/or NGOs	179

List of figures

Figure 1:	Impact of 1st-generation biofuels on agricultural prices in 2020	22
Figure 2:	EU-27 greenhouse gas emissions by sector and mode of transport, 2007	42
Figure 3:	EU-27 GHG emissions 1990-2008 (excluding LULUCF)	44
Figure 4:	Sectoral contributions to the potentials for increasing energy efficiency over time in relative terms	48
Figure 5:	Sectoral and overall growth of renewable energy in the European Union	58
Figure 6:	Estimated net imports of fossil fuels (baseline 2009)	62
Figure 7:	The domain of interaction-oriented policy research	93
Figure 8:	Central developments with regard to European energy policy, 1990 - 2010	109
Figure 9:	Measures to achieve a genuine single market	131
Figure 10:	First choice of economic instruments	141
Figure 11:	First choice of action other than economic instruments	142
Figure 12:	Opinion on the 1000m^2 total useful floor area threshold - Spreading on citizens, organizations and EU-wide organizations	154

List of abbreviations

ABI	Austrian Biofuels Institute
ACE	Architects' Council of Europe
ACEA	European Automobile Manufacturers' Association
ACER	Agency for the Cooperation of Energy Regulators
ACF	Advocacy Coalition Framework
AEA	Association of European Airlines
AEBIOM	European Biomass Association
AEF	Aviation Environment Federation
ASD	Aerospace and Defence Industries Association of Europe
ATAG	Air Transport Action Group
ATSOI	Association of the Transmission System Operators of Ireland
BING	European voice for the National trade associations representing the polyurethane insulation industry
BALTSO	Baltic Transmission System Operators
CAN-E	Climate Action Network Europe
CDM	Clean Development Mechanism
CEER	Council of European Energy Regulators
CEFA	Council for Environmentally Friendly Aviation
Cefic	European Chemical Industry Council
CEPI	Confederation of European Paper Industries
CEPMC	Council of European Producers of Materials for Construction
CH_4	Methane
CMP	Conference of the Parties serving as the Meeting of the Parties to the Kyoto Protocol
CO_2	Carbon dioxide
COP	Conference of the Parties to the Climate Change Convention
DG	Directorate-General
EADS	European Helicopter Association
EBAA	European Business Aviation Association
EBC	European Builders' Confederation
eBIO	European Bioethanol Fuel Association
EBAA	European Business Aviation Association
EBC	European Builders Confederation

Abbreviations

EC	European Commission
ECA	European Cargo Alliance
EEA	European Economic Area or European Express Association
EEB	European Environment Bureau
EEIF	Energy Efficiency Industrial Forum
EFTA	European Free Trade Association
ELC	European Lamp Companies Federation
ELFAA	European Low Fares Airline Association
ENGVA	European Natural Gas Vehicle Association
ENTSO-E	European Network of Transmission System Operators for Electricity
ENVI	Committee on the Environment, Public Health and Food Safety
EP	European Parliament
EPA	Energy Performance Certificates
EPBD	Energy Performance of Buildings Directive
EPC	Energy Performance Certificate
EPIA	European Photovoltaic Industry
ERA	European Regions Airline Association
EREC	European Renewable Energy Council
ERGEG	European Regulators' Group for Electricity and Gas
ET	Emissions Trading
ETI	European Transparency Initiative
ETS	Emissions Trading Scheme
ETSO	European Transmission System Operators
EU	European Union
EU ETS	European Union Emissions Trading Scheme
EUMEPS	European Manufacturers of Expanded Polystyrene
EURACOAL	European Association for Coal and Lignite
EURIMA	European Insulation Manufacturers Association
EuroACE	European Alliance of Companies for Energy Efficiency in Buildings
EUROGYPSUM	The voice of the European gypsum industry
EUROMETAUX	European Association of Metals
EUROPIA	European Petroleum Industry Association
EXIBA	European Extruded Polystyrene Insulation Board Association
FIEC	European Construction Industry Federation
FoEE	Friends of the Earth Europe
GHG	Greenhouse gas

Abbreviations

H_2O	Water
IACA	International Air Carrier Association
IATA	International Air Transport Association
IEA	International Energy Agency
IFEU	Institute for Energy and Environmental Research
IFIEC	Europe International Federation of Industrial Energy Consumers
IFN	International Friends of Nature
IOS	Institutional opportunity structures
IPCC	Intergovernmental Panel on Climate Change
ISO	Independent System Operator
ITO	Independent Transmission Operator
JIM	Joint Implementation Mechanism
JREC	Johannesburg Renewable Energy Coalition
MEP	Member of European Parliament
MLG	Multi-level Governance
NAP	National Allocation Plan (under EU ETS)
NORDEL	Organisation for the Nordic Transmission System Operators
N_2O	Nitrous oxide
OECD	Organization for Economic Cooperation and Development
OFID	OPEC Fund for International Development
OMC	Open Method of Coordination
O_3	Ozone
POS	Political opportunity structures
REEEP	Renewable Energy & Energy Efficiency Partnership
SEA	Single European Act
SME	Small and Medium-sized Enterprise
T&E	European Federation for Transport and Environment
TEU	Treaty on the European Union
TFEU	Treaty on the Functioning of the European Union
T&E	European Federation for Transport & Environment
TEU	Treaty on the European Union
TFEU	Treaty on the Functioning of the European Union
TSO	Transmission System Operator
UCTE	Union for the Coordination of the Transmission of Electricity
UEAPME	European Association of Craft, Small and Medium-sized Enterprises
U.E.P.A.	European Union of Ethanol Producers
UKTSOA	UK Transmission System Operators Association
UNEP	United Nations Environment Programme

Abbreviations

UNCED	UN Conference on Environment and Development
UNFCCC	United Nations Framework Convention on Climate Change
VAT	Value Added Tax
WMO	World Meteorological Organization
WWF	World Wide Fund for Nature
WWF-EPO	WWF European Policy Office

Chapter 1. Introduction

Political negotiations at the EU level are increasingly influenced by non-legislative private actors who seek access to policy-makers. During recent decades a vast number of national interest associations have established representations in Brussels in order to influence EU decisions. In addition, European associations have been founded to aggregate the interests of one or several sectors across Europe. In 2013, the European Parliament estimated that around 19,000 individual lobbyists (Library of the European Parliament, 2013) are involved in EU policy-making.

However, information on the number of lobbyists varies significantly depending on the sources used to count them. In order to make the European decision-making process more transparent with regard to the actors who are influencing the EU institutions and the particular interests they pursue, various attempts have been made to set up lobbying registers. By registering, organizations and individuals indicate that they are interested in contributing to the EU decision-making process and, thereby, follow certain rules and norms. The transparency register operated by the European Parliament and the European Commission currently[1] lists 6497 registrants.[2]

Berkhout and Lowery (2008) compared the data on interest organizations in the EU and considered to what extent the different sources (for example CONECCS[3], different directories published by Landmarks and Euroconfidential, or registers initiated by the EP and the Council) overlap. They found that »there seems to be surprisingly little overlap among most of the sources« (Berkhout and Lowery, 2008: 506) and that therefore scholars must be careful when drawing generalizations from them (see also Wonka, Baumgartner, Mahoney and Berkhout, 2009).

The validity of different types of registers cannot only be doubted with regard to the quantity of interest groups but also concerning the quality of the data provided. In the transparency register, primarily organizations and self-employed individuals are expected to set up a profile. Furthermore, some forms of collective activity, such as networks and platforms, are asked to register and name a responsible contact person. This presupposes that the »form of collective activity« has

---

1   As of April 5, 2014.
2   For the code of conduct see: http://ec.europa.eu/transparencyregister/info/about-register/codeOfConduct.do?locale=en [Accessed 05 April 2014].
3   The CONECCS database was closed in 2008 following the Green Paper European Transparency Initiative (COM (2007)127). Meanwhile, a voluntary register was launched by the European Parliament and the European Commission, which is available at: <http://ec.europa.eu/transparencyregister/info/homePage.do> [Accessed 27 August 2013].

17

reached a certain degree of formality, as a result of which a spokesperson has been selected who is authorized to speak on behalf of all actors involved. This, however, is not always the case. In recent years, the formation of informal coalitions between different kinds of actors seems to have emerged as a new phenomenon characterizing EU policy-making (Mahoney, C., 2008; Klüver, 2011). These coalitions can be identified by the joint actions of their members in the form of regular meetings in order coordinate the actors' positions and strategies, the joint formulation of a declaration on a specific goal to be attained or on a code of conduct to be observed, and/or the actors' joint submission of a position paper or report to policy-makers.[4] Associations and companies increasingly decide to pool forces and formulate a joint position paper on a particular policy issue to be submitted to EU decision-makers. While formal coalitions are more persistent over time and have established an administrative body to coordinate the interactions between the coalition members, these informal coalitions lack organizational structures, a letterhead and a spokesperson because they are usually formed to influence a single legislative initiative only. Therefore, they do not appear in any kind of register. This however contradicts some of the core principles the European Commission in its *White Paper on European Governance* emphasized as essential for more democratic governance:

> »Roles in the legislative and executive processes need to be clearer. Each of the EU Institutions must explain and take responsibility for what it does in Europe. But there is also a need for greater clarity and responsibility from Member States and all those involved in developing and implementing EU policy at whatever level« (COM(2001)428 final: 10).

In order to gain a complete picture of the actors involved in decision-making, informal coalitions must also be taken into account.

This work investigates why actors form different kinds of coalitions, which strategies these coalitions pursue to increase the receptiveness of the EU institutions and how persistent they are over time. When talking about actors, the focus clearly is on European associations and/or NGOs. The interactions between European associations and/or NGOs were analyzed because compared to national associations they are preferably consulted by the European institutions as they aggregate the EU-wide interests of a particular sector:

> »Policy makers undoubtedly benefit from the policy making simplification that results from dealing with coherent, representative, well-informed, effective, collective groups: the group can marshal arguments and determine priorities in a way that is useful for policy makers. This makes negotiation simpler« (Jordan, 1998: 46).

---

[4] For a more comprehensive discussion of the concept and its operationalization see Chapters 3 and 4.

This hypothesis is also supported by Eising (2009): »The EU institutions are dependent on the technical information and economic clout of firms and on the 'European encompassing interests' of Eurogroups and their members rather than on any 'domestic encompassing interest'« (Eising, 2009: 147). If European associations and/or NGOs form coalitions, they are even better able to communicate the »European encompassing interests«, because the coalition can unite different perspectives on a particular issue and translate them into a concrete policy position. In addition, coalitions are not only formed between European associations and/or NGOs that obviously share a large set of interests or norms. Rather, coalitions can be identified between actors that, at first glance, do not seem to have many interests or norms in common, such as environmental NGOs and some industry associations or the financial sector.

To be able to analyze the factors that determine cross-sector actor constellations and their interactions in the European multi-level system, the field of European energy policy was selected as an empirical background for the case studies. Energy issues increasingly affect a wide range of industry branches and individuals as well as different political and societal levels. Beyond that, the questions of energy supply security and the environmental consequences of energy production and consumption lie at the heart of the present EU agenda and are therefore increasingly the subject of debate among public and private actors.

On the basis of these considerations, the central research questions are:
Firstly, what are the factors leading to the formation of interest group coalitions in European energy policy? And secondly, what determines the strategies pursued by the coalition members to influence the EU policy process?

Finally, the impact of coalitions and different strategies adopted by the coalition members on the receptiveness of the European Commission, the European Parliament, and the Council of the European Union is assessed. This aspect has been included because it can be observed that although policy-makers seem to recognize the general need for further reforms in European energy policy, progress has only been mediocre. To name but two examples, liberalization efforts regarding the gas and electricity markets have not yet delivered the expected results and the EU is far from realizing its energy efficiency goals. The assumption is raised that coalitions of energy actors exist that are able to increase the receptiveness of European institutions and in this way shape the outcome of the decision-making process. Taking this aspect into account contributes to resolving the question under what conditions actors have an impact on the European decision-making process and under what circumstances they do not. For the analysis as a whole, however, due to related measurement problems this question is only of secondary relevance. Final conclusions on the influence of coalitions of European associations and/or NGOs on the receptiveness of EU institutions can hardly be drawn because they

Introduction

are based on the perception of the actors involved. In this work, on the one hand European associations and NGOs were asked to estimate their influence when acting as a coalition. On the other hand, MEPs and staff members from the European Commission and the Council were requested to assess the effectiveness of the strategies pursued by different coalitions.[5] However, as Dür (2008) emphasizes, one can only cautiously rely on results attained from such analyses, because »interest groups may have good reasons to either over-estimate it [their influence] - if they want to legitimate their existence vis-á-vis their members - or underestimate it - to avoid the creation of counter-lobbies that may affect their policy impact« (Dür, 2008: 1224). Nevertheless, the question of the impact of coalitions on the institutional receptiveness is not ignored and as a result, this work presents the tentative results gained on this issue, while at the same time indicating the methodological limitations.

From a theoretical perspective, the following approaches have guided this work: the Advocacy Coalitions Framework developed by Sabatier and Jenkins-Smith (1988; 1993; 1999; see also Sabatier and Weible, 2007) in order to explain policy change, the actor-centered institutionalism (Mayntz and Scharpf, 1995a; Scharpf, 1997), the concept of political opportunity structures (Kitschelt, 1986), and different approaches on interest groups' strategies (Baumgartner and Jones, 1991; Beyers, 2004; Mazey and Richardson, 1996). Before, however, the achievements and shortcoming of these approaches are discussed, the next section elaborates on why European energy policy is well suited to serve as background for answering the central research questions.

1.1 The increasing significance of European energy policy

> »Our interdependence, inside Europe and worldwide, has never been clearer. Tackling climate change, putting sustainable energy policies in place, helping our societies to face demographic change, rebuilding the world financial system, tackling the scourge of poverty; in today's complex world, we will only make progress if we join forces. That means we all have the responsibility to play our part: EU Institutions, Member States, civil society – at home and abroad« (Barroso, 2009: 13).

Energy-related questions are a core element of the present EU agenda. This is also emphasized in Barroso's guidelines for the European Commission 2010-2014 quoted above. In addition to the fight against climate change, combating poverty and the resolution of problems caused by demographic changes and worldwide financial turbulence, the development of sustainable energy policy is highlighted

---

5   For a more detailed description of the applied methodology see Chapter 4.

as a key theme. Indeed, societal and political actors have increasingly paid attention to energy issues in recent years. Pointvogel (2009) even speaks of an »unparalleled renaissance since the oil crises of the 1970s« (Pointvogel, 2009: 5704).

But how can the increasing significance of European energy policy be explained? Two key phrases best describe the challenges policy makers currently face: the *security of energy supply* and *climate change*. The security of energy supply entails the intensifying worldwide energy demand expected for the next 25 years as well as the EU's dependency on energy imports. In its *World Energy Outlook* (IEA, 2010), the International Energy Agency (IEA) developed two scenarios: the *Current Policies Scenario*, in which policies are assumed to remain the same as of mid-2010, and the *New Policies Scenario*, based on the assumption that national governments worldwide adhere to their recently made commitments. One of the main results was that:

»In the New Policies Scenario, world primary energy demand increases by 36% between 2008 and 2035, from around 12,300 million tonnes of oil equivalent (Mtoe) to over 16,700 Mtoe, or 1.2% per year on average« (IEA, 2010: 4).

According to the *Current Policies Scenario*, the demand may rise even higher, 1.4 per cent per year during the same period. A considerable share of this demand is attributed to non-OECD countries, above all China and India, which are projected to account for 93 per cent of the increase in energy demand. Although global demand for all energy sources is expected to increase, it is predicted that fossil fuels will be the most sought after, compared to renewable and nuclear power in both scenarios. Among the fossil fuels, crude oil in particular will remain a key energy source. However, high costs are expected for oil imports: it is assumed that end-users will have to pay $113 per barrel in 2035 (IEA, 2010: 5). As a result of the limited reserves of crude oil in the EU member states, the EU is a net importer. Regarding the origins of EU crude oil imports, Table 1 highlights the share imported from various regions (DG Energy, 2011), including intra-EU deliveries.

Table 1: Registration of crude oil imports and deliveries in the European Union (EU 27) (intra + extra EU) (DG Energy, 2011)

Registration of crude oil imports and deliveries in the European Union (EU 27) (intra + extra EU)	
Region	% of total imports
Middle East	13.38
Africa	22.56
FSU	40.88
Europe	21.05
America	2.14

The EU's dependence on imports from non-member countries is not only obvious when analyzing the demand for crude oil, but also when taking a look at its total energy needs. In 2008, more than half of the EU's gross inland energy requirements had to be satisfied using external sources (Eurostat, 2010). Imports originated primarily from Russia, Norway and some African countries, such as South Africa, Algeria and Libya. The dominance of a relatively small number of partners, however, makes the EU's energy supply increasingly insecure. Following the gas crisis between Russia and the Ukraine, scepticism has also emerged with regard to its dependency on gas imports.

The European Commission has expressed serious concern about this situation and has reacted with a variety of initiatives to ensure that the EU has access to an energy supply that meets the increasing demand. These include the diversification of energy suppliers and transport mechanisms, the development of an internal energy market, and the adoption of measures to enhance energy efficiency and to diversify the EU's energy mix. Energy efficiency and the production of energy from renewable sources, such as wind and solar power, geothermal energy, biomass, hydro-electric and tidal power, have thus emerged as potential solutions not only to the problem of supply security but also to that of climate change.

Climate change, as the second major challenge, has been linked to energy policy as a result of growing awareness that global warming is largely caused by human activities and that, consequently, human behavior must be modified in order to avoid negative consequences for the ecosystem (COM(2008)30 final). These range from extreme weather, flooding, and droughts to increases in malnutrition and the loss of biodiversity (IPCC, 2007). Policy-makers worldwide acknowledge that these problems cannot be solved at a national level, but rather that potential solutions have to be negotiated inter- or supranationally. One of the first initiatives in this regard was the adoption of the Kyoto Protocol which at the EU level is reflected in the European Union Emissions Trading Scheme (EU ETS). The Kyoto Protocol introduced three market-based instruments, namely Emissions Trading (ET), the Joint Implementation Mechanism (JIM), and the Clean Development Mechanism (CDM), which provide for the reduction of emissions through international cooperation. Additionally, energy efficiency has become an important issue within the European Union. The Green Paper on Energy Efficiency (COM(2005)265 final) published in June 2005 emphasized that the EU could reduce energy consumption by at least 20 per cent in a cost-effective manner and in this way contribute to environmental protection by reducing greenhouse gas emissions and at the same time lessening the EU's dependency on energy imports. This goal is coherent with the *20-20-20*-targets proposed by the European Commission in January 2008 (COM(2008)19 final; COM(2008)30 final). In addition to cutting greenhouse gas emissions by at least 20 per cent (below 1990 levels)[6] and reducing energy consumption by 20 per cent, the European Commission also suggested increasing the share of renewable energy in total EU energy consumption to 20 per cent. This third target clearly illustrates that European energy policy is determined by a variety of often conflicting interests. The production of biofuels, for example, does not only affect the renewable energy and various other industry sectors, but also areas such as agriculture, private consumption and health. Scientists (ABI, 2011; IEA, 2008; IFEU, 2004; OFID, 2009) have raised concerns regarding the implications of the production of 1st-generation biofuels (for example sugarcane and corn ethanol, oilseed rape and palm oil biodiesel) for the environment and malnutrition in developing countries. Ethanol and biodiesel production are assumed to have negative impacts on food security and food prices, scarce water resources, deforestation, and biodiversity (IEA, 2008: 6).

---

6   In 2011, the European Commission issued a proposal emphasizing the need for even more ambitious targets. Accordingly, greenhouse gas emissions are to be reduced by 80 to 95 per cent compared to 1990 until 2050 (COM(2011)112 final).

Introduction

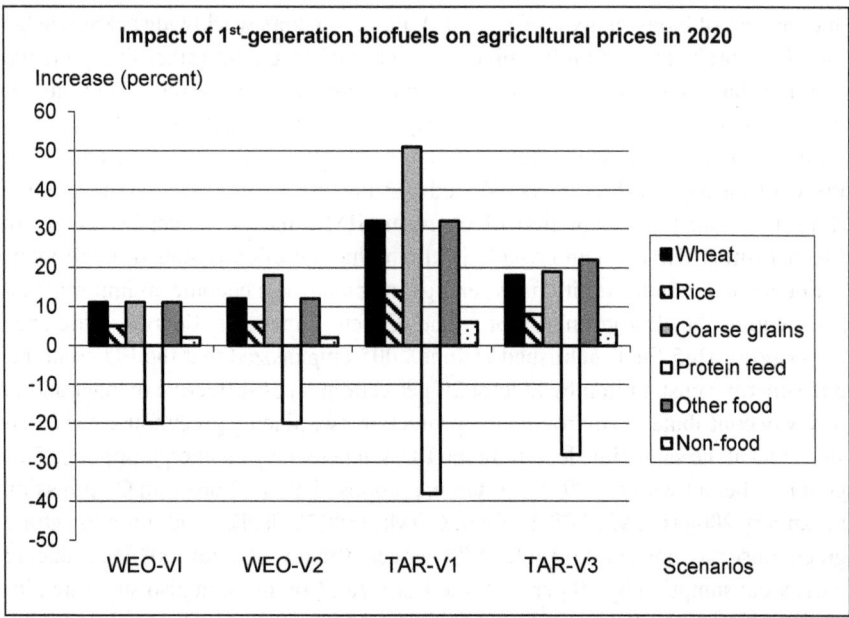

Figure 1: Impact of 1st-generation biofuels on agricultural prices in 2020[7] (OFID, 2009: 19)

Figure 1 illustrates the expected impact of 1st-generation biofuels on agricultural prices in 2020 according to different scenarios. On the basis of this data, a transi-

---

7   WEO-V1:"Assumes transport energy demand and regional biofuels use as projected by International Energy Agency (IEA) in its WEO 2008 Reference Scenario. Second generation conversion technologies become commercially available after 2015; deployment is gradual"; WEO-V2: "Assumes transport energy demand and regional biofuels use as projected by IEA in its WEO 2008 Reference Scenario. Assumes that due to delayed arrival of second-generation conversion technologies all biofuels production until 2030 is based on first-generation feedstocks";
TAR-V1: «Assumes transport energy demand as projected by IEA in its WEO 2008 Reference Scenario. Assumes that mandatory, voluntary or indicative targets for biofuels use announced by major developed and developing countries will be implemented by 2020, resulting in about twice the biofuels consumption compared to WEO 2008. Second-generation conversion technologies become commercially available after 2015; deployment is gradual (percentage as in WEO-V1)";
TAR-V3: «Assumes transport energy demand as projected by IEA in its WEO 2008 Reference Scenario. Assumes that mandatory, voluntary or indicative targets for biofuels use announced by major developed and developing countries will be implemented by 2020. Accelerated development of second-generation conversion technologies permits rapid deployment; 33 percent and 50 percent of biofuels use in developed countries from second-generation in 2020 and 2030 respectively" (OFID, 2009: 15).

tion to improved technologies is recommended as »many of the problems associated with 1st-generation biofuels can be addressed by the production of biofuels manufactured from agricultural and forest residues and from non-food crop feedstocks« (IEA, 2008: 6).

The remarks made here regarding the future of the EU's energy policy illustrate the fact that the targets proposed by the European Commission require comprehensive investments in the research and development of new technologies by several industrial sectors in the member states. Furthermore, these policies can threaten the international competitiveness of the respective industries and put them at a disadvantage compared to their competitors in non-EU countries with less strict rules. Especially in the current economic climate, many industries feel as if they have been put under severe pressure (European Alliance of Energy Intensive Industries, 2010). As a consequence, energy actors, including producers, consumers, technology providers, NGOs, specialized research institutes, and politicians concerned with energy issues, have to ensure that their own needs will be met. Therefore, they attempt to influence decisions on a) the priorities of European energy policy, and b) the allocation of scarce financial means. Influence on EU policy can be exerted during stakeholder consultations launched by the European Commission on decisive topics, but also by communicating their interests regularly in bi-lateral meetings with the European institutions. Moreover, energy actors are under pressure to acquire external funding in order to mitigate the financial burden of investment in research and development. The European Commission is aware of the need for financial backing and therefore is prepared to contribute:

> »Given the time scale for the development and dissemination of energy technology, the urgency of bringing new high-performance, low-carbon technologies to the European markets is more acute than ever. [...] Europe-wide coordination and collaboration should include the pooling of different funding sources. All stakeholders will be expected to contribute. The Commission will seek to leverage the EU budget to raise further the overall level of funding« (DG Energy, 2011a: 18).

The European Investment Bank (EIB), one of the world's largest multilateral financing institutions, which draws its resources primarily from the capital markets, is one potential provider of long-term finance for energy projects (EIB, 2009). Recognizing the high priority of energy on the EU's agenda, the EIB lending policy focuses on five areas: 1) renewable energy, 2) energy efficiency, 3) research, development and innovation (RDI) in energy, 4) security and diversification of internal supply, and 5) security of external supply and economic development. The investment required is estimated as follows:

> »In the coming years, large-scale investment will be necessary in Europe's energy market. First, there will be the need to replace a substantial number of existing power stations that will become obsolete in the period 2010-2030. Beyond this, in order to meet climate change commitments, the investment needed in renewables may amount to around EUR 600-700bn; the investment required in energy efficiency may well exceed this figure« (EIB, 2009: 3).

Introduction

After describing the reasons for the increasing importance of EU energy policy, the following section will elaborate on the theoretical contribution of this analysis regarding the role of different actors in the EU policy process. At the same time the shortcomings of the existing research will be revealed and it will be outlined how this work can fill these gaps.

1.2 The theoretical contribution of this work

As indicated above, the core assumption of this analysis is that European associations and/or NGOs form coalitions in order to influence European energy policy. The formation of a coalition requires that potential allies reach consensus on the policy issue they intend to shape. Consensus-seeking usually occurs during a very early stage of the policy process. From the perspective of European associations and NGOs[8], coalition-formation is expected to fulfil the following aims:

a) to identify and, if possible, resolve a conflict on a policy issue as early as possible;
b) to formulate a joint position to be submitted to the decision-makers;
c) to emphasize the representativeness and credibility of the arguments and in this way;
d) to increase the receptiveness of the European decision-makers.

The role of the informal norm of consensus in decision-making in the EU has often been discussed, especially with respect to decisions made in the Council (Heisenberg, 2005; Naurin and Lindahl, 2010). According to Naurin and Lindahl, consensus-seeking is the daily business of policy-making: »It is about getting things done and finding common ground and acceptable solutions to concrete problems, often in the face of overarching ideological agreement« (Naurin and Lindahl, 2010: 489). The same holds for the integration of interest groups into the policy process. Clearly, decision-making is a very time-consuming process. If European associations and NGOs achieve consensus on a policy issue currently being negotiated at the EU level and succeed in forming a coalition, they can save valuable time that European institutions would otherwise have to invest in identifying the stakeholders' common interests.

In the social sciences, valuable studies have been carried out on the formation of networks and coalitions as well as their role in policy-making. With their *Advocacy Coalition Framework* (ACF), Sabatier and his collaborators try to explain

---

8   As emphasized in several interviews conducted with European industry associations and NGOs.

policy change, taking into account the dominant relations between different types of actors at the political level. An advocacy coalition can be described as a coalition of various actors within a policy network who pursue a common aim based on a collectively shared belief system. Members of an advocacy coalition may be members of political parties, interest groups, elected politicians, experts, researchers or journalists. This means that membership is not restricted to any political or societal level and also goes beyond the dimensions of the so called *iron triangle* of legislators, agency officials and interest group representatives (Sabatier and Weible, 2007: 192). Advocacy coalitions in a policy field intend to influence the policy process and to translate the joint position into a specific policy outcome. Although the ACF provides valuable insights into actor constellations and interactions in the policy process, some aspects regarding the formation of coalitions and their strategies require more in-depth research:

1) Sabatier and Jenkins-Smith explain why coalitions are generally formed: »Within a policy subsystem, policy participants coordinate their strategies with allies in advocacy coalitions to influence policy« (Weible and Sabatier, 2007: 125). They also provide one answer to the question of what keeps the coalition members together. According to the ACF, individuals are assumed to be rationally motivated. However their rationality is bounded by limited cognitive abilities. Rather than mere rational considerations, joint belief systems determine their decision to join a particular coalition: »Advocacy coalitions include policy participants that both (1) share similar policy core beliefs and (2) engage in nontrivial degree of coordination« (Weible and Sabatier, 2007: 128). Policy core beliefs are described as »normative/empirical beliefs that span an entire subsystem« and include how a policy subsystem is perceived, for example its basic values, the effectiveness of the policy instruments applied, or the distribution of power between private and public actors (ibid: 127). The existence of a joint belief system has been analyzed in different case studies (Jenkins-Smith and St. Clair, 1993; Kübler, 2001; Sewell, 2005). What, however, has been widely neglected by the developers of the ACF as well as scholars who have applied the approach to empirical cases is the importance of short-term interests as an explanatory variable for the membership in coalitions. This analysis not only investigates the role of short-term interests regarding the decision to form or join a coalition, it also provides an answer to the question of whether the dominance of short-term interests or long-term belief systems has an impact on a coalition's persistence over time.
2) In social science research on EU policy-making it is widely acknowledged that establishing informal contacts with other stakeholders and decision-makers is a decisive element of a potentially successful lobbying strategy (Christiansen, Føllesdal, and Piattoni, 2003; Fairbrass and Jordan, 2003; Greven,

2005). However, comprehensive studies that go beyond the recognition that informal contacts exist are rare. Here light will be shed not only on formal, but also on informal forms of cooperation among European associations and/or NGOs concerned with energy-related questions. Although these coalitions lack formal organizational structures, it is assumed that they nevertheless are important players in the field of European energy policy.

3) There is also lack of knowledge on the question of why, under certain circumstances, no coalition is formed although the actors concerned with a policy field share a norm system or common interests. By identifying a set of variables responsible for the decision not to form or join a coalition, here it is revealed which obstacles may exist that prevent or at least complicate cooperation.

4) Weible and Sabatier (2007: 133) admit that, in the causal chain depicted by the ACF, explanations are missing with regard to »how advocacy coalitions use resources and venues«, though these missing links can be crucial for understanding what determines policy change. Valuable works exist on the function of resources and institutions in the policy-making process (Beyers, 2004; Eising, 2007). These studies focus on the strategies pursued by companies or associations and do not apply the assumptions to the level of coalitions. This work provides an answer to the questions of which role financial and human resources play in the strategies coalition members pursue to influence political decisions and which venues coalition members use to influence decision-makers during the various stages of the policy process.

5) In 1999, the ACF was revised in order to also include the characteristics of European corporatist regimes. A new variable labelled *coalition opportunity structures* was introduced, which describes »the degree of consensus needed for major policy change« and »the openness of political systems« (Sabatier and Weible, 2007: 200). This work contributes to the discussion on the role of institutions by testing the impact of *institutional opportunity structures* (Kitschelt, 1986; Tarrow, 1991), defined here as *institutional agendas, institutional rules* and *office-holders* on the formation of coalitions and the strategy choices made by the coalition members.

In order to analyze both the role of long-established norms and of short- and long-term interests in the formation and persistence of coalitions, the basic assumptions of the ACF about their model of the individual are complemented by a rationalist perspective. The intentional behavior of individuals is one of the major elements of the actor-centered institutionalism (Mayntz and Scharpf, 1995a; Scharpf, 1997). This approach is designed to explain past policy choices and is characterized by

»giving equal weight to the strategic actions and interactions of purposeful and resourceful individual and corporate actors and to the enabling, constraining, and shaping effects of given (but variable) institutional structures and institutionalized norms« (Scharpf, 1997: 34). In accordance with rational choice theory, actors are said to select the best strategies available to realize their preferences under the conditions determined by the institutional setting (Scharpf, 1997: 31).

The ACF and the actor-centered institutionalism are then combined with the literature on political opportunity structures, as all approaches take into account the effects of institutional structures on actors' perceptions and behavior. The theory of political opportunity structures (POS) was developed in the 1960s and 1970s as a part of research on collective action and social movements. Kitschelt defines POS as »specific configurations of resources, institutional arrangements and historical precedents for social mobilisation, which facilitate the development of protest movements in some instances and constrain them in others« (Kitschelt, 1986: 58). In Chapter 3, it will be elaborated more in detail on to what extent the three approaches complement each other.

1.3 The methods applied in the empirical research

The empirical research is based on qualitative and comparative case study methods. Qualitative analyses prove especially valuable when it comes to the study of a unique or a limited number of cases or when the possibility exists that more than one causal mechanism leads to the expected outcome (Hancké, 2009). This assumption is also raised here. Gerring describes the virtue of case studies as follows:

> »Their virtue is their ability to elucidate mechanisms connecting a particular X with a particular Y. By watching the progress of a single unit […] over time and by paying attention to variation within that case we can often observe, or at least intuit, a complex causal relationship at work« (Gerring, 2001: 215).

Among the case study methods Gerring distinguishes between the *extreme-case*, *typical-case*, *crucial-case*, and *counterfactual* analysis (Gerring, 2001, 215). For this work, crucial cases have been selected that can serve to »confirm or disconfirm an existing theory, or to suggest modifications in that theory« (ibid: 220). Here, cases are defined as the processes of the formation of coalitions between European associations and/or NGOs and the strategy choices made by the coalition members with regard to four crucial legislative acts of European energy policy (→ 4).

In order to test and further develop existing theories, process-tracing has been applied. Process-tracing can be characterized as a qualitative method to identify

Introduction

causal mechanisms between independent variables and the outcome, the dependent variable (George and Bennett, 2005: 206). The method has increasingly been used in the social sciences over the last two decades, especially with regard to the analysis of outcomes the occurrence of which could not be explained in terms of only two or three independent variables (Hall, 2003). To gather data, interviews were conducted with European associations and NGOs, different DGs of the European Commission, members of the European Parliament or their assistants and representatives from the Council of the European Union. In addition, a vast quantity of documents were analyzed, consisting of legislative acts and press releases issued by the European Union on core issues of European energy policy and of position papers submitted by a wide range of energy actors to EU policy-makers. Both tools serve to trace the process leading to the formation of coalitions and the formulation of different strategies pursued by the coalition members (→ 4).

1.4 Outline of this work

In Chapter 2, first of all the recent developments in European energy policy are summarized, thereby taking into account related global events. Within this field, the focus of the European Commission lies on five areas: the liberalization of the European energy market, the introduction of the Kyoto Protocol and the EU Emissions Trading Scheme (EU ETS), the promotion of energy efficiency, the use of renewable energy sources, and measures to ensure supply security. This summary mainly serves to identify the cases for the empirical analysis.

Chapter 3 provides an overview of the research on interest groups and related fields, while at the same time summarizing the theoretical approaches that serve as the background of this work. After presenting an overview on the different periods of research, approaches on multi-level and network governance as well as the formation of coalitions and social movements are revealed. Following this, the focus is shifted to the role of institutions in the policy process, in particular the implications of actor-centered institutionalism and the literature on political opportunity structures. Finally, related work on the strategies of interest groups and their potential influence on the EU policy process is highlighted.

Chapter 4 begins by describing the research design, thereby outlining the variables and theoretical hypotheses which have guided this work as well as the data gathering tools used. The hypotheses are then tested in four case studies. The analysis demonstrates that European associations and/or NGOs regularly form different types of coalitions in order to increase their influence on the receptiveness of the European Commission, the European Parliament and the Council. A categorization of the dominant coalitions participating in the policy process is presented.

As is revealed, the degree of formality of these coalitions depends on several variables, such as the existence of either common (short-term) interests or long-established norms as central motivation for cooperation or the reputation of the associations and/or NGOs involved. In addition, the potential of coalitions to increase the receptiveness of the European institutions is assessed. Attention is also paid to another important issue, namely why coalition-formation sometimes fails.

In Chapter 5 the empirical results are summarized. It is concluded that formal and informal coalitions of European associations and/or NGOs have become important players in the field of European energy policy. Nevertheless, compared to interest groups acting alone, coalitions are not able to increase the receptiveness of the European Commission, the European Parliament and the Council per se, but have to fulfil certain conditions in order to be successful.

Chapter 2. Recent developments in selected areas of European energy policy

At this point, some general introductory remarks must be made on the present state of European energy policy in EU law. The first steps to create a common European energy policy were undertaken during the early phases of the integration process. With the *Treaty establishing the European Coal and Steel Community* and the *Treaty establishing the European Atomic Energy Community*, energy issues were put at the heart of the Community. Nevertheless, the EU had not been assigned clear competencies in this field due to the fact that the member states regarded energy policy as a strategically important sector and remained resistant to transferring authority to the EU institutions (Eising, 2000: 195). Thus, the EU had to rely on the powers it possessed in other areas. These were on the one hand derived from areas like competition or environment policy in the framework of which the Council could adopt measures which affected national energy policies. On the other hand, powers were based on the establishment of the internal market (especially Art. 114 TFEU) and on the *flexibility clause* (Art. 352 TFEU), which under specific circumstances extended the potential scope for action (Pollak, Schubert and Slominski, 2010).

Despite the lack of explicit energy-related powers, the EU has increasingly advocated the establishment of a consistent policy to be applied in the member states. Following the rise of energy issues together with their far-reaching implications for the economy and environment on the member state level, a new legal title (Title XXI) on energy policy, going back to the constitutional treaty, was finally achieved with the adoption of the Lisbon Treaty. Article 194 states, that:

> »In the context of the establishment and functioning of the internal market and with regard for the need to preserve and improve the environment, Union policy on energy shall aim, in a spirit of solidarity between Member States, to:
> a) ensure the functioning of the energy market;
> b) ensure security of energy supply in the Union;
> c) promote energy efficiency and energy saving and the development of new and renewable forms of energy; and
> d) promote the interconnection of energy networks« (Art. 194 (1) TFEU).

Today, a large number of legislative acts concerned with European energy policy originate from the EU level. Therefore, it has to be clarified who actually has a say.

The European Commission was established as a supranational body which could act independently from the member states. It is the only institution that possesses the right to initiate legislation. After legislation is passed by the Council and the European Parliament, the European Commission has to surveil if the member states correctly apply EU law. Furthermore, with the entry into force of the Lisbon Treaty, the European Commission's executive power was strengthened. Within the European Commission, the Directorates-General (DGs) of greatest relevance for all issues related to the EU's energy policy are the DG for Energy (ENER), the DG for Climate Action (CLIMA), the DG for Competition (COMP), the DG for Mobility and Transport (MOVE), the DG for Enterprise and Industry (ENTR), and the DG for the Environment (ENV). The DG for Energy and the DG for Mobility and Transport were formed in 2010 following the appointment of the new Commission and, dividing the role of the former DG for Energy and Transport which had been responsible for all activities related to energy services and mobility. Although the policy fields are now quite separate on an administrative level, they are nevertheless closely related. This is apparent, for example, when one thinks of the importance of fuel prices for logistics companies or the amount of greenhouse gas emissions of the transport sector. The DG for Climate Action was established in February 2010 to handle climate-related topics which were previously the responsibility of the DG for the Environment. The DG for Competition has played a significant role with special attention to the internal market project. It is not surprising that the Commission has continually tried to strengthen the EU's role in energy policy in this area, as it is equipped with considerable competencies in competition policy. For instance, it can impose fines in case of violation against competition law (Art. 101ff. TFEU). In addition to the competences the Commission has in competition policy, the institution possesses further instruments to reach compliance. According to Art. 258 TFEU, the Commission has the duty to ensure that the member states correctly apply EU law.

Since the Maastricht Treaty entered into force in 1993 and introduced the co-decision procedure, the European Parliament's relevance in the decision-making process has increased. Its position was even more strengthened when the co-decision procedure became the 'ordinary legislative procedure' with the adoption of the Lisbon Treaty. Although the parliamentarians have often not been able to come to a coherent position in energy policy in the past, the EP generally advocates aspects concerning environmental and consumer protection and human rights policy more strongly than the Commission (Geden/Fischer 2008).

Within the institutional arrangement of the EU, the member states have at least two opportunities to articulate their interests: First, when the ordinary legislative procedure is applied (Pollak and Slominski, 2008) and, second, in the Council of the European Union (Transport, Telecommunications and Energy Council (TTE)).The Council has a huge impact on the policy process, because it is the

Liberalization

institution where the representative of the member states meet regularly and this is why it has been described as the EU's real "decision-making centre" (Wessels 1991). The Council in its various configurations consists of the ministers of the member state who discuss the subjects that are on the EU's agenda. The frequency of the Council's meetings depends on the configuration. Energy issues are dealt with in the Transport, Telecommunications and Energy Council (TTE), which exists since 2002 and meets roughly every two months.

In the following section, the most important developments in European energy policy are summarized. In doing so, global developments are taken into account, acknowledging that the discussion of energy and climate change issues cannot be limited to the European arena. At the same time, the legislative process leading to the EU's current policy is depicted. This summary will then serve to identify the cases (→ 4.1) for the empirical analysis.

2.1 The liberalization of the European energy market

Since the late 1990s the liberalization of the electricity and gas market has constituted a core element of the EU's agenda. The European Commission hoped that competition would increase, that prices would remain low and that the security of energy supply would be enhanced. Such a reform was to be realized at two levels: at a national level, member states were expected to adopt certain directives within a fixed time frame in order to open their own markets. At the EU level, the European Commission initiated measures to improve cross-border trading rules (Jamasb and Pollitt, 2005). The first directives were concerned with common rules for the internal electricity and natural gas markets (Dir. 96/92/EC and Dir. 98/30/EC), which came into force in February 1997 and August 1998. These legislative acts can be traced back to a Council Resolution from September 1986 on the Community's energy policy objectives. This document emphasized that the »adequate and secure availability of energy on a satisfactory economic basis remains a prerequisite for the pursuit of the economic and social objectives« (Council Resolution, 16 September 1986: 1). Three important directives adopted in the early 1990s further paved the way for this step: firstly, the *Council Directive concerning a Community procedure to improve the transparency of gas and electricity prices charged to industrial end-users* (Dir. 90/377/ EEC), followed by the *Council Directive on the transit of electricity through transmission grids* (Dir. 90/547/EEC), and thirdly the *Council Directive on the transit of natural gas through grids* (Dir. 91/296/EEC). In addition, the *White Paper Completing the Internal Market* of 1985 (COM(85)310) and the *Single European Act* of 1986 contributed to the establishment of an internal electricity and gas market, though not explicitly referring to the Community's energy policy.

The directives adopted in 1996 and 1998 aimed at a gradual liberalization of the market. The decision-making process was impeded by large disagreements, particularly between France, Germany and Great Britain; eight years of negotiations were required until an agreement was finally reached (Eising, 2002: 85). Directive 96/92/EC was concerned with the establishment of the internal electricity market and aimed to increase »efficiency in the production, transmission and distribution« while at the same time »reinforcing security of supply and the competitiveness of the European economy and respecting environmental protection« (Dir. 96/92/EC: 1). Similar principles were included in Directive 98/30/EC consisting of the rules for the internal market in natural gas. Both documents stipulated concrete goals to be achieved during the years to come, while at the same time leaving room for interpretation at the member state level. Thereby, the European Commission made concessions towards the member states, which however had the side effect of slowing down the establishment of an internal market (Pollak, Schubert and Slominski, 2010: 115 ff.). During its meeting in Lisbon in March 2000, the European Council decided to push through a second legislative package in order to speed up the liberalization process. These considerations resulted in Directive 2003/54/EC, again including the common rules for the internal market in electricity and Directive 2003/55/EC on common rules for the internal market in natural gas. Both acts repealed the previously adopted ones. The key issues of these directives were the unbundling of transmission and distribution system operators, and the unbundling of accounts (Dir. 2003/54/EC, Art. 10, 15, and 19; Dir. 2003/55/EC, Art. 9, 13, and 17). Furthermore, the access of third parties to transmission and distribution systems was addressed (Dir. 2003/54/EC, Art. 20; Dir. 2003/55/EC, Art. 18). Accordingly, the member states are requested to ensure that third parties can access transmission and distribution systems based on tariffs to be applied to all eligible customers. Furthermore, the Community's competition rules must be satisfied ensuring that no party is discriminated against. In addition to these directives, Regulation 1228/2003 specified the »conditions for access to the network for cross-border exchanges in electricity«. In 2009 the European Commission published its evaluation of the progress achieved with regard to the creation of an internal energy market. It was concluded that even four years after the deadline (July 1, 2004) the implementation of the second electricity and gas directives was still incomplete (COM(2009) 115 final). The responsibility for monitoring the progress of the member states was assigned to the European Regulators' Group for Electricity and Gas (ERGEG), which reported that some member states were still far from fully complying with the directives (COM(2009)115 final: 3). Further shortcomings existed in numerous areas, including: the still extremely concentrated gas and electricity wholesale and retail markets, the differences in gas and electricity prices between the member states, the incomplete implementation of unbundling measures, the provision of information on consumers' rights and choices, and the Community's ability to adequately react to a potential gas supply crises (COM (2009)115 final: 5ff).

Based on these insights, the European Commission initiated a third legislative package. Proposed in 2007, it entered into force in September 2009. As in previous years, two directives were simultaneously adopted for the gas and electricity market (Dir. 2009/72/EC; Dir. 2009/73/EC), which were intended to remove the remaining barriers. The member states were given 18 months (until March 2011) to implement it.

Three topics were central to this third legislative package (Pollak, Schubert and Slominski, 2010), with the first topic once again being the question of unbundling vertically integrated undertakings, as they were perceived as a major challenge to the opening of the gas and electricity markets. While former directives regarded the *legal unbundling* as sufficient, that means the legal separation of production and transmission, the legislative package of 2009 included the option of *ownership unbundling*. Ownership unbundling was already mentioned in the proposal of 2007 and was regarded by the European Commission as the most effective alternative for promoting investment, fair access, and transparency. Member countries are required to ensure that »the same person or persons are not entitled to exercise control over a generation or supply undertaking and, at the same time, exercise control or any right over a transmission system operator or transmission system« and vice versa (Dir. 2009/72/EC: 1; 2009/73/EC: 1). The second central aspect was related to the access of third parties, while the third topic dealt with the transfer of competencies to the Agency for the Cooperation of Energy Regulators (ACER, founded in 2010), an institution that was expected to assist the national regulatory authorities and eventually coordinate the work between them.[9] What should be noted here is that in contrast to those areas of European energy policy that are described in the following sub-chapters, the liberalization efforts have hardly been influenced by the general public or by environmental groups. This was the result of, on the one hand, a lack of resources on the part of the respective interest organizations, especially in the early days of the liberalization efforts, and, on the other hand, the minor involvement of the DG Environment in the political negotiations (Eising, 2000: 204). With regard to the research question underlying this work, the empirical analysis will show, if the fact that the general public and NGOs have demonstrated minor interest in the subject affected the formation of coalitions that were built to determine the rules of the internal market. Finally, Table 2 summarizes the key developments in the process of liberalizing the European energy market.

---

9 For more information visit: http://www.acer.europa.eu/portal/page/portal/ACER_HOME [Accessed 24 May, 2011].

Table 2: Key events regarding the liberalization of the EU energy market (DG Energy)

Date	Key events regarding the liberalization of the EU energy market
1985, June 14	COM(85)310 final: White Paper from the Commission to the European Council: Completing the internal market
1986, September 16	Council Resolution concerning new Community energy policy objectives for 1995 and convergence of the policies of the Member States (86/C 241/01)
1990, June 29	Council Directive 90/377/EEC concerning a Community procedure to improve the transparency of gas and electricity prices charged to industrial end-users
1990, October 29	Council Directive 90/547/EEC on the transit of electricity through transmission grids
1991, May 31	Council Directive 91/296/EEC on the transit of natural gas through grids
1996, December 19	Directive 96/92/EC of the European Parliament and of the Council concerning common rules for the internal market in electricity
1998, June 22	Directive 98/30/EC of the European Parliament and of the Council concerning common rules for the internal market in natural gas
2003, June 26	Directive 2003/54/EC of the European Parliament and of the Council concerning common rules for the internal market in electricity and repealing Directive 96/92/EC
2003, June 26	Directive 2003/55/EC of the European Parliament and of the Council concerning common rules for the internal market in natural gas
2003, June 26	Regulation (EC) No 1228/2003 of the European Parliament and of the Council on conditions for access to the network for cross-border exchanges in electricity
2005, September 28	Regulation (EC) No 1775/2005 of the European Parliament and of the Council of on conditions for access to the natural gas transmission networks
2006, March	COM(2006)105 final: Green Paper: A European strategy for sustainable, competitive and secure energy
2006, March-September	Public consultation: Green Paper: A European strategy for sustainable, competitive and secure energy
2007, January 10	COM(2006)841 final: Communication from the Commission to the Council and the European Parliament: »Prospects for the internal gas and electricity market«
2007, January 10	COM(2007)1 final: Communication from the Commission to the European Council and the European Parliament: An energy policy for Europe
2007, September 19	COM(2007)528 final: Proposal for a Directive of the European Parliament and of the Council amending Directive 2003/54/EC concerning common rules for the internal market in electricity

Liberalization of the European energy market

2007, September 19	COM(2007)529 final: Proposal for a Directive of the European Parliament and the Council amending Directive 2003/55/EC concerning rules for the internal market in natural gas
2008, October 22	Directive 2008/92/EC of the European Parliament and of the Council concerning a Community procedure to improve the transparency of gas and electricity prices charged to industrial end-users
2008, November 13	COM(2008)781 final: Communication from the Commission to the European Parliament, the Council, the European Economic and Social Committee and the Committee of the Regions: Second strategic energy review: an EU energy security and solidarity action plan
2009, July 13	Directive 2009/72/EC of the European Parliament and of the Council concerning common rules for the internal market in electricity
2009, July 13	Directive 2009/73/EC of the European Parliament and of the Council concerning common rules for the internal market in natural gas
2009, July 13	Regulation (EC) No 713/2009 of the European Parliament and of the Council establishing an Agency for the Cooperation of Energy Regulators
2009, July 13	Regulation (EC) No 714/2009 of the European Parliament and of the Council on conditions for access to the network for cross-border exchanges in electricity
2009, July 13	Regulation (EC) No 715/2009 of the European Parliament and of the Council on conditions for access to the natural gas transmission networks

2.2 The introduction of the Kyoto Protocol and the EU Emissions Trading Scheme (EU ETS)

Before the EU legislation regarding emissions trading is summarized, consideration must be given to the developments on a global level as the first decisive measures were initiated there. One of the core institutions concerned with the expected effects of climate change has been the Intergovernmental Panel on Climate Change (IPCC), which was established by the United Nations Environment Programme (UNEP) and the World Meteorological Organization (WMO) in 1988. Since then this organization has issued a number of scientific studies on the present state of climate change and its impact on the global environment as well as on worldwide socio-economic conditions. The first IPCC assessment report released in 1990 (IPCC, 1990) supported the propositions that had been made thus far mainly by ecologists on the causes of global warming. These assumed, among other things, that greenhouse gases produced by mankind were likely to accelerate the increase of global temperatures. According to an IPCC definition, global warming can be described as »a change of climate which is attributed directly or indirectly to human activity that alters the composition of the global atmosphere and which is, in addition to natural climate variability, observed over comparable time periods« (IPCC, 1995: 4). Greenhouse gases consist of the following gases: water vapour (H_2O), carbon dioxide (CO_2), methane (CH_4), nitrous oxide (N_2O), and ozone (O_3). Due to their heat-trapping effect they are considered to be the primary causes of global warming. H_2O is the most abundant greenhouse gas, although most discussions of climate change only refer CO_2 and CH_4. The CO_2 concentration in the atmosphere is largely the result of anthropogenic emissions originating mainly from fuel combustion. In contrast, agriculture, including animal and arable production, is one of the most decisive sources of CH_4 and N_2O. With regard to O_3, it can be differentiated between the stratospheric or »good« and the ground-level or »bad« ozone. While the former protects the earth from harmful ultraviolet rays, the latter forms as the result of a reaction between oxides of nitrogen and sunlight in the earth's lower atmosphere where it can reach toxic concentration.[10]

Sceptics state that the high CO_2 concentration in the atmosphere in addition to the rising temperatures which have been observed during the last decades can all be attributed to natural causes (Klein, Gupta, Cooper and Jansson, 2007). Others claim that a predicted global temperature increase of at least two degrees Celsius is the result of human activity and would have wide-ranging consequences, such as the retreat of glaciers, rising sea levels, extreme weather, or a loss in biodiversity (IPCC, 2007; UNFCCC 2007). This view in particular was supported by the IPCC. Indeed, the organization's first report greatly influenced people's perception of the topic. Most decisive for the development of an integrated global as well as European energy and climate change policy was, however, the fourth IPCC assessment report (IPCC, 2007), which was released in 2007. In its synthesis report the most important results are summarized:

1) The concentrations of CO_2, CH_4 and N_2O in the atmosphere have increased dramatically: »The atmospheric concentrations of CO_2 and CH_4 in 2005 exceed by far the natural range over the last 650,000 years« (IPCC, 2007: 37).
2) This increase is primarily the result of human activities since 1750 and »now far exceeds pre-industrial values determined from ice cores spanning many thousands of years. Global increases in CO_2 concentrations are due primarily to fossil fuel use, with land-use change providing a smaller yet significant contribution. It is very likely that the observed increase in CH_4 concentration

---

10 See: UNEP http://ozone.unep.org/ [Accessed 15 April 2011].

is predominantly due to agriculture and fossil fuel use. The increase in N_2O concentration is primarily a result of agriculture« (IPCC, 2007: 37).

3) Consequences of the increase of greenhouse gas concentrations in the atmosphere can be observed in global warming and its accompanying risks, as well as in extreme weather such as longer and more intense periods of drought, for example in the Mediterranean and parts of southern Africa and Asia, in the melting of glaciers and in rising sea levels (IPCC, 2007: 64-65).

Consequently, the emissions trading scheme, which relies on the same conclusions as the IPCC, was initiated by a separate UN institution. The United Nations Framework Convention on Climate Change (UNFCCC) is an international treaty that aims to reduce global warming. The UNFCCC was signed by a majority of countries in 1992, within the context of the UN Conference on Environment and Development (UNCED) in Rio de Janeiro and entered into force in March 1994. As opposed to the UNFCCC, which was based on the voluntary commitment of the states, the Kyoto Protocol was adopted in 1997 as a legally binding addition to the treaty. It entered into force in February 2005 after ratification in Russia. As of 2013, 191 states and the EU have signed and ratified the Kyoto Protocol.[11] To mitigate the effects of human activity on the global atmosphere, the Kyoto Protocol contains emissions targets for the so called Annex I countries. Accordingly, the industrialized countries that ratified the Kyoto Protocol agreed to reduce their greenhouse gas emissions by at least five per cent until 2012 compared to 1990 emissions. Countries with commitments under the Kyoto Protocol are expected to meet their obligations to reduce greenhouse gas emissions primarily through national measures. The protocol offers three market-based mechanisms, namely the Emissions Trading (ET), the Joint Implementation Mechanism (JIM), and the Clean Development Mechanism (CDM), which allowed the reduction of emissions through international cooperation. Article 17 of the Kyoto Protocol defines the mechanism of emissions trading:

> »The Conference of the Parties shall define the relevant principles, modalities, rules and guidelines, in particular for verification, reporting and accountability for emissions trading. The Parties included in Annex B may participate in emissions trading for the purposes of fulfilling their commitments under Article 3. Any such trading shall be supplemental to domestic actions for the purpose of meeting quantified emission limitation and reduction commitments under that Article« (United Nations, 1998: Article 17).

In the EU this mechanism is reflected in the European Union Emissions Trading Scheme (EU ETS), which was introduced in 2003 (Dir. 2003/87/EC, amending Council Dir. 96/61/EC; see also Dir. 2004/101/EC) and entered into force in 2005.

---

11 For the status of ratification see: http://unfccc.int/kyoto_protocol/status_of_ratification/items/2613.php [Accessed 05 April 2014].

The aim of the EU ETS was to assist the EU member states in meeting their individual obligations under the Kyoto Protocol. The central mechanism underlying the EU ETS is that the corporations, such as power stations, combustion plants, oil refineries and iron and steel works, as well as factories making cement, glass, lime, bricks, ceramics, pulp, paper and board[12] in each member state are allocated emission allowances within a certain limit. If a company keeps its emissions below the level originally allocated, it has the possibility to save the remaining amount for future needs or to sell it to others. The costs a company has to face in case it is short on allowances and, thus, has to buy additional ones on the market, serve as means of exerting pressure to reduce emissions. The total amount of emissions allowances is regularly reduced so that it is guaranteed that the greenhouse gas concentration in the atmosphere ultimately decreases. At the same time, the JIM and the CDM are also applied to the EU member states so that these can use the credits gained to minimize the costs resulting from compliance with the Kyoto targets. Essential to these mechanisms is that by allowing the industry to apply a bundle of measures to reduce overall emissions, the EU intended to not put its own emission-intensive sectors at a disadvantage compared to those countries that did not integrate the Kyoto Protocol into national legislation. In doing so, expensive investments could be avoided in the short term and the competitiveness of domestic branches was strengthened or at least sustained. In particular, this respected the needs of the energy-intensive industries, such as the iron, steel, lime or paper industry, which pursued a comprehensive lobbying strategy to redirect the attention of decision-makers in this regard (see for example European Alliance of Energy Intensive Industries, 2004).

Prior to the first phase starting in 2005, member states were expected to prepare National Allocation Plans (NAPs) that determined the quantity of CO_2 emissions granted to national energy and industry sectors for a certain period. By fixing the overall amount of CO_2 emissions, so it was assumed, scarcity was created and consequently companies were obliged to reduce their emissions (DG Environment, 2005). However, in the course of the first trading period from 2005 to 2007, all allowances were distributed for free as several countries had allocated more allowances to their industries than were actually needed. As a result, prices decreased from 30 Euros per ton to almost zero in early December 2007 (European Environment Agency, 2008: 8). For the second trading period from 2008 to 2012, the European Commission insisted on stricter rules concerning the total amount of allowances. The NAPs, which had to be submitted to the European Commission by the end of June 2006, had to be consistent with a catalogue of twelve principles

---

12 See DG Climate Action: http://ec.europa.eu/clima/policies/ets/index_en.htm [Accessed 24 May 2011].

that were postulated as necessary conditions for compliance with the Kyoto Protocol. If they did not meet these criteria, the Commission could reject the plan either partly or in total, which resulted in the suspension to start with the allocation of allowances to national industries (DG Environment, 2006). The NAPs submitted in the second round, however, again differed greatly from one another and threatened fair competition in the internal market. Thus, it was decided that beginning with 2012 allowances would be allocated at the EU level through fully harmonized standards (European Commission, 2008).

Since the Kyoto Protocol entered into force, negotiations on a treaty for the time following the first commitment period have been ongoing. The question of how to deal with greenhouse gas emissions after 2012 was discussed intensely during the United Nations Climate Change Conference in Bali in 2007 (COP 13). This led to the *Bali Roadmap*, which set the goal of finishing negotiations in Copenhagen at the end of 2009 (COP 15). As has become apparent in the meantime, this plan was too ambitious to be realized. So far, due to diverging interests of the nation states, no major breakthrough in the form of internationally binding rules has been reached. At the EU level, interests are more homogenous and as a result have produced concrete measures. In particular, additional sectors that were not affected by emissions trading, such as buildings, transport, agriculture and waste management, are now included in the scheme.

Within the transport sector, the inclusion of aviation was intensively discussed among the member states. In December 2006, following open stakeholder consultations throughout 2005, the European Commission issued a legislative proposal which included aviation in the EU ETS in order to incorporate the contribution of aircraft emissions to climate change into existing rules (COM(2006) 818 final). This initiative was based on the argument that technological developments in the aviation sector had been insufficient in reducing greenhouse gas emissions to the required extent and could not compensate for the growth in worldwide air traffic (COM(2006)818final: 2). According to an analysis conducted by the IPCC, global passenger air traffic was »projected to grow by about five per cent per year between 1990 and 2015, whereas total aviation fuel use - including passenger, freight, and military - is projected to increase by three per cent per year, over the same period, the difference being due largely to improved aircraft efficiency« (IPCC, 1999). It was assumed that traffic and emission growth could even approach a similar rate per year until 2050, although long-term scenarios were surely difficult to predict. In this way, measures taken by other industries to minimize the effects of greenhouse gas emissions on the global atmosphere would be undermined. The Association of European Airlines (AEA, 2006) pursued an intensive lobbying strategy against the proposal of the European Commission, stressing that the EU legislation would primarily affect European airlines to the benefit of other carriers. In addition, it claimed that, according to Eurocontrol data, the number of

European energy policy

flights taken each year would not increase as heavily as predicted by the European Commission (AEA, 2006).

Figure 2 demonstrates the share of greenhouse gas emissions in the transport and, in particular, the aviation sector compared to other branches.

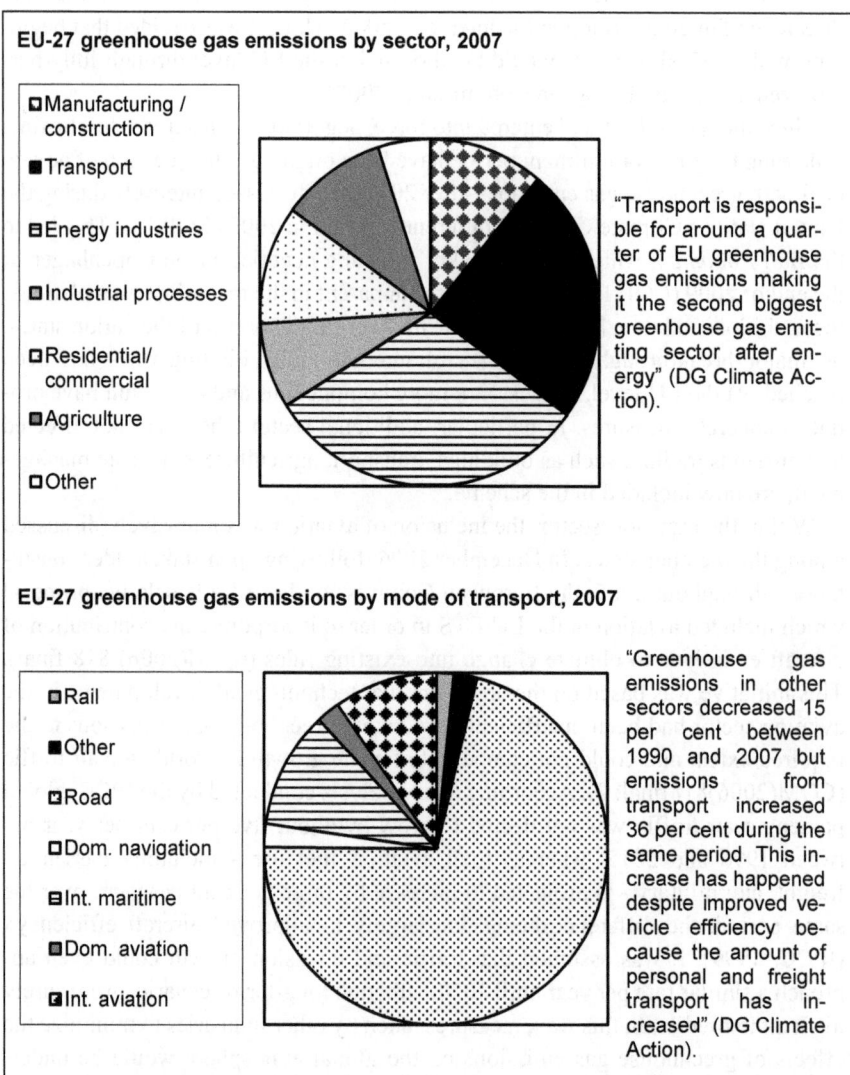

Figure 2: EU-27 greenhouse gas emissions by sector and mode of transport, 2007 (DG Climate Action)

Directive 2008/101/EC stipulated the inclusion of aviation in the EU ETS from 2012 onwards. Concerning the quantity of allowances to be traded, Article 3c states that for the period from January until December 2012, 97 per cent of the average 2004-2006 level of the aviation emissions are to be allocated to aircraft operators. For the period starting in January 2013, this amount is to be reduced to 95 per cent per year of the same value. In order to be able to track the actual amount of emissions resulting from aviation, the member states must ensure that each aircraft operator submits a monitoring plan to be approved by the responsible national authorities. Regarding the scope of the directive, as defined in Annex I, the rules will be applied to all flights that either depart from, or arrive at airports located within the territory of the European Union. This implies that airline operators which do not have their headquarters in one of the member states must also take part in the trading of emission allowances. Nevertheless, some activities will be excluded, namely:

- »flights performed exclusively for the transport, on official missions, of a reigning Monarch and his immediate family, Heads of State, Heads of Government and Government Ministers, of a country other than a Member State, [...]«;
- »military flights performed by military aircraft and customs and police flights«;
- »flights related to search and rescue, firefighting flights, humanitarian flights and emergency medical service flights [...]«; and
- »flights [...] performed by a commercial air transport operator operating either fewer than 243 flights per period for three consecutive four-month periods or flights with total annual emissions lower« than 10 000 tonnes per year« (Dir. 2008/101/EC, Annex 1c).

On the basis of the Agreement on the European Economic Area (EEA), which entered into force in 1994, not only the 27 EU members but also the three EFTA countries Iceland, Norway and Liechtenstein decided to include the EU ETS into their national legislation. The EEA agreement states that EU legislation can be included not only with regard to the establishment of the single market, but also in other important areas in which cooperation seems to be useful. Thus, the EU ETS was officially incorporated into the EEA agreement in 2007. This development was in accordance with the intention of the EU ETS to constitute a model that can also be introduced in other countries and subsequently be linked to the EU scheme (Agreement on the European Economic Area, 1994).

European energy policy

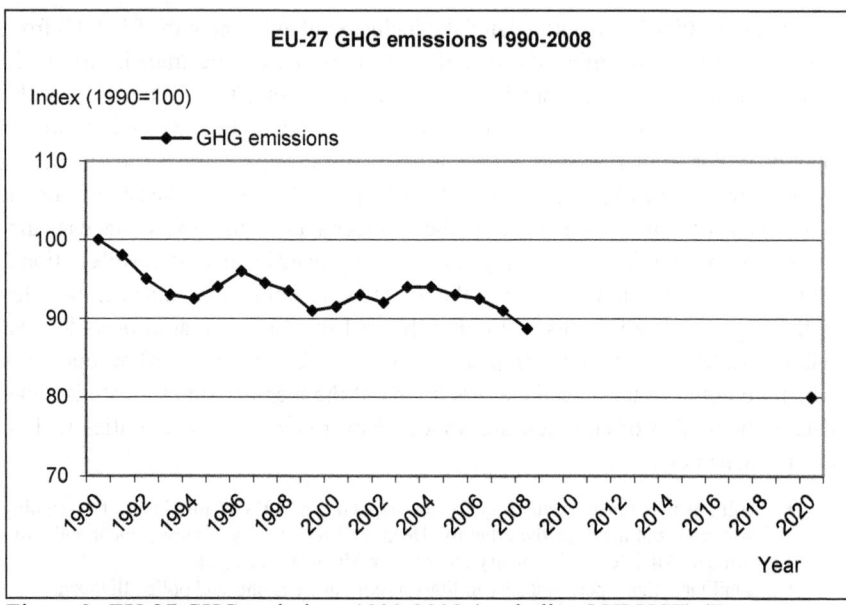

Figure 3: EU-27 GHG emissions 1990-2008 (excluding LULUCF) (European Environment Agency, 2010: 7)

What effect did the reductive greenhouse gas emission measures have in the EU? Figure 3 illustrates the development of greenhouse gas emissions between 1990 and 2008 with activities in the LULUCF sector (Land Use, Land-Use Change and Forestry) excluded[13]. The EU committed itself to an average reduction of greenhouse gas emissions by eight per cent compared to 1990 levels. This reduction target should be attained by 2012 and shared among the member states (*burden sharing*). It shows that in the EU-27 the GHG emissions in the respective period decreased by 11.3 per cent (627 million tonnes CO_2-equivalents) (European Environment Agency, 2010). For the EU-15, with obligations under the Kyoto Protocol, a decrease of only 6.5 per cent could be noted, which means that so far they have not yet reached their goal of an eight per cent reduction. The highest increase among the »old« member states could be observed in Spain (42.3 per cent, from 285.1 to 405.7 million tonnes). Nevertheless, also in Spain there is a tendency

---

13 Note: GHG emission data for the EU-27 as a whole; refer to domestic emissions (i.e. within its territory) and do not include emissions and removals from LULUCF; nor do they include emissions from international aviation and international maritime transport. CO2 emissions from biomass with energy recovery are reported as a Memorandum item according to UNFCCC Guidelines and not included in national totals. In addition, no adjustments for temperature variations or electricity trade are considered. The global warming potentials are those from the 1996 revised IPCC Guidelines for National Greenhouse Gas Inventories (EEA Technical report, No 6/2010).

towards a reduction of GHG emissions, depicted by a decrease of 7.5 per cent between 2007 and 2008. Austria was also not able to meet the Kyoto targets with GHG emissions increasing by 10.8 per cent. In contrast, Germany, achieving a reduction of 22.2 per cent by 2008, is often cited as leading example (European Environment Agency, 2010: 10). In 2008 it was decided to reduce GHG emissions even by 20 per cent by the year 2020 (COM(2008)19 final; COM(2008)30), which is shown in Figure 3.

Finally, Table 3 summarizes the crucial developments in the process of establishing an EU ETS, taking into account related global events.

Table 3: Key events regarding the establishment of the EU ETS (DG Climate Action)

Date	Key events regarding the establishment of the EU ETS
1990, August	First IPCC assessment report
1992, June 12	UNFCCC signed in Rio de Janeiro (entered into force March 1994)
1997, December 11	Kyoto Protocol adopted as binding addition to the UNFCCC treaty
1999, May 19	COM(1999)230 final: Communication from the Commission to the Council and the European Parliament: Preparing for implementation of the Kyoto Protocol
2000, March 8	COM(2000)87 final: Green Paper on greenhouse gas emissions trading within the European Union
2001, July	6th UN Conference of the Parties to the Climate Change Convention (COP 6, part 2), Bonn: agreements on details of Kyoto Protocol
2001, September	Public consultation with stakeholders
2001, October 23	COM(2001)581: Proposal for a Directive establishing a scheme for greenhouse gas emission allowance trading within the Community and amending Council Directive 96/61/EC
2002, November 27	COM(2002)680: Amended Proposal for a Directive establishing a scheme for greenhouse gas emission allowance trading within the Community
2003, October 13	Directive 2003/87/EC establishing a scheme for greenhouse gas emission allowance trading within the Community
2004, October 27	Directive 2004/101/EC establishing a scheme for greenhouse gas emission allowance trading within the Community
2005, February 16	Kyoto Protocol entered into force
2005, March-May	Public consultation: Reducing the climate change impact of aviation (DG Environment)
2005, July	Johannesburg Renewable Energy Coalition: Roadmap 2005-2007
2005, September 27	COM(2005)459 final: Communication from the Commission outlining plans to reduce the impact of aviation on climate change

2005, November	11th UN Conference of the Parties to the Climate Change Convention (COP 11) and 1st Meeting of the Parties to the Kyoto Protocol (CMP 1) in Montréal
2006, March 8	COM(2006)105 final: Green Paper: A European strategy for sustainable, competitive and secure energy
2006, March-June	Public consultation: Green Paper: A European strategy for sustainable, competitive and secure energy
2006, December 20	COM(2006)818 final: Proposal for a Directive so as to include aviation activities in the scheme for greenhouse gas emission allowance trading
2007, November	Fourth assessment report of the IPCC
2007, December	13th UN Conference of the Parties to the Climate Change Convention (COP 13) and 3rd Meeting of the Parties to the Kyoto Protocol (CMP 3) in Bali
2008, January 23	COM(2008)16 final: Proposal for a Directive of the European Parliament and the Council amending Directive 2003/87/EC so as to improve and extend the greenhouse gas emission allowance trading system of the Community
2008, August-October	Public consultation: Towards a comprehensive and ambitious post 2012 climate change agreement
2008, November 19	Directive 2008/101/EC to include aviation in the EU Emissions Trading Scheme (entered into force February 2, 2009)
2009, April 23	Directive 2009/29/EC amending Directive 2003/87/EC so as to improve and extend the greenhouse gas emission allowance trading scheme
2009, August	End of public consultation on the future of the EU ETS
2009, December	15th UN Conference of the Parties to the Climate Change Convention (COP 15) and 5th Meeting of the Parties to the Kyoto Protocol (CMP 5) in Copenhagen
2010, November	16th UN Conference of the Parties to the Climate Change Convention (COP 16) and 6th Meeting of the Parties to the Kyoto Protocol (CMP 6) in Cancún

2.3 The promotion of energy efficiency

One of the core documents regarding energy efficiency in the EU is the *Green Paper on Energy Efficiency* (COM(2005)265 final) published in June 2005 and based on the results drawn from scientific studies, conducted for example by the Wuppertal Institute or the WWF. These results illustrated that the EU could reduce energy consumption by at least 20 per cent in a way that is not exceedingly cost-intensive for the respective industries. Furthermore, the increase in energy efficiency would contribute to environmental protection by reducing both greenhouse gas emissions and the EU's dependence on energy imports. Finally, due to necessary investment in the renewable energy sector, the creation of new jobs was expected. On the basis of the green paper, all interested parties were asked to participate in an open consultation by submitting position papers. In this way, the European Commission hoped to identify where and how obstacles could be overcome and savings realized. The European Commissioners also clearly stated which measures were generally intended (COM(2005)265 final: 21ff). First of all, huge potential was seen in the buildings sector[14], with energy to be saved with the introduction of energy performance certification for all buildings exceeding 50 m² at the time when they are built, sold, or rented out, accompanied by recommendations on how efficiency improvements could be made in a cost-effective manner. In addition, the application of these rules to buildings under major renovation was also considered. A second measure was concerned with lighting, as it was assumed that energy-saving electric bulbs would use »five times less current« than standard ones (COM(2005)265 final: 22). This view was supported in two meetings held by the Ecodesign Regulatory Committee in 2008, during which the member states called for a draft regulation on how to improve energy efficiency in households. As a result, the European Commission adopted two regulations, which stipulated that incandescent light bulbs have to be replaced by energy-saving alternatives by the end of 2012 (Commission Regulation (EC) No 244/2009, (EC) No 245/2009). The European Commission also analyzed other domestic appliances and suggested certain requirements for heating, cooling, and electric motors in households. Finally, the fuel consumption of vehicles was identified as an area in which energy savings could be realized to a large extent, especially in the context of the growing number of private cars and motorcycles. The European Commission stressed its aim of reducing average CO_2 emissions to an amount of 120g/km for all new automobiles entering the EU market (COM(2005)265 final: 23). Additionally, one of the biggest challenges to reducing energy consumption in the transport sector lies in the provision of reliable and convenient public transport facilities which convince passengers to abstain from using their cars (IEA, 2010). Figure 4 highlights the estimated potential of different sectors to contributing to an increase in energy efficiency.

---

14 The Green Paper was not the first initiative in this field. Already in 2002 a directive had been adopted on the energy performance of buildings (Directive 2002/91/EC). This legislative act similar to the subsequent ones relied on the voluntary compliance with standards.

European energy policy

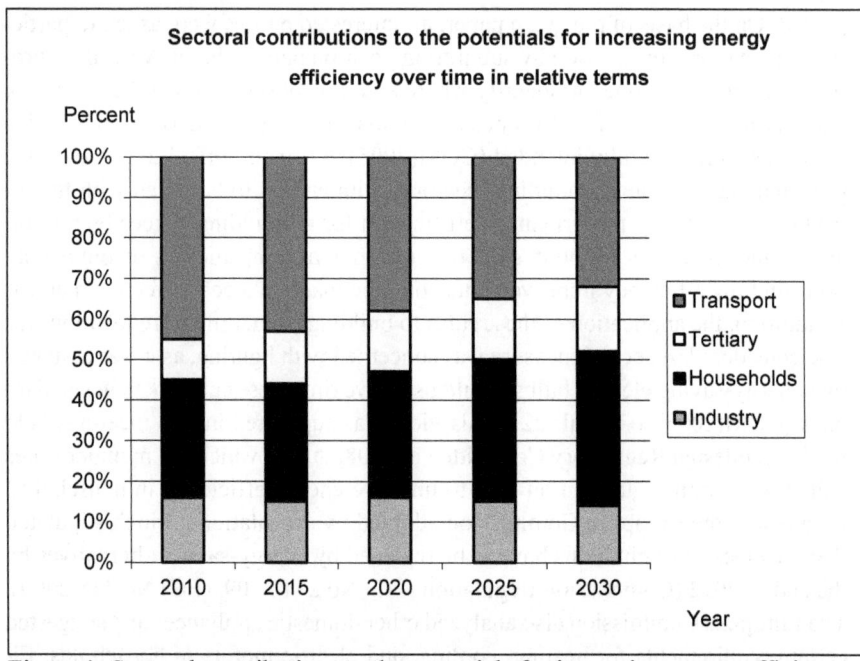

Figure 4: Sectoral contributions to the potentials for increasing energy efficiency over time in relative terms (Fraunhofer ISI et al., 2009: 10)

The public consultation on the *Green Paper on energy efficiency* confirmed the European Commission's assumptions on where energy savings could best be realized. Accordingly, energy efficiency in the buildings sector was considered to be the »top priority« (COM(2006)545 final), especially in the long term, as these measures often take time to become effective. This was followed by the transport sector. In both contexts, the majority of the stakeholders participating in the public consultation (72.4 per cent) were in favor of fiscal incentives at the EU level. These would increase the demand for energy-efficient products and thus stimulate the industry to focus on the production of such goods (European Commission, 2009: 17). Furthermore, the application of policy instruments at the national, regional, and local levels was called for. Consequently, the *Action Plan for Energy Efficiency*, released in October 2006, also intended to mobilize »the general public«, in order to draw people's attention to their own consumption habits (COM(2006)545 final: 4). Concretely, the following priorities were highlighted:

- to develop an »updated and dynamic appliance and equipment labeling and minimum performance standards«;
- to establish minimum »building performance requirements and very low energy buildings (passive houses)«;

50

Energy efficiency

- to make »power generation and distribution more efficient«,
- to improve »fuel efficiency of cars«;
- to facilitate »appropriate financing of energy efficiency investments for small and medium enterprises and Energy Service Companies«;
- to spur »energy efficiency in the new member states«;
- to facilitate a »coherent use of taxation«;
- to raise »energy efficiency awareness«;
- to improve »energy efficiency in built-up areas«; and
- to foster »energy efficiency worldwide«.

By introducing these measures, the European Commission expected the first notable effects within a period of three to six years; the scope of which was then to be evaluated in regularly conducted Strategic Energy Reviews.

Although the green paper and the action plan on energy efficiency described above clearly constituted important steps in reducing energy consumption, the European Council summit held in March 2007 was even more decisive. It was described by private as well as public actors as a historical success on the way to establishing advanced environmental protection. For instance, German chancellor Merkel stated that the summit would »lead to a real change in our behavior towards energy supplies« (Bundesregierung, 2007) while the European Renewable Energy Council, the umbrella organization of the European renewable energy industry, welcomed »this clear signal for changing our energy supply structure« (EREC, 2007).

In general, the Spring European Council under the German presidency focussed on three topics as part of the Lisbon Strategy, namely economic growth and employment, better regulation, and an innovative energy policy (Council of the European Union, 2007: 1). However, these three issues were not regarded in isolation from each other. Instead, the European Commission was invited to submit new proposals encompassing all subfields. Due to the widely acknowledged fact that industrial greenhouse gas emissions are the primary cause of climate change, the Presidency Conclusions called for an integrated energy and climate change policy which balances the need for immediate action in order to ensure environmental sustainability with the concerns of different industry sectors regarding the cost-efficiency and competitiveness of the available technologies. Based on the European Commission's Communication *An Energy Policy for Europe* (COM(2007)1 final), the Council additionally adopted a comprehensive *Energy Action Plan* for the following two years. This action plan addressed the following issues:

1) the necessity to increase competition, ensure effective regulation, and encourage investment in the internal market for gas and electricity in order to foster its efficient operation and completion;

2) the effects of potential crises on the security of energy supply and possible reactions;
3) the development of an agreement on how to approach external energy policy, for example through intensifying bilateral relations with other countries and regions;
4) the need to fix concrete targets for energy efficiency improvements and the increasing share of renewable energies and biofuels;
5) and finally, the development of a European Strategic Energy Technology plan to be examined at the European Council meeting in 2008.
(Council of the European Union, 2007: 16ff.)

Concerning climate change, the most important proposals were summarized under the easy to remember slogan *20-20-20 until 2020* as presented by the European Commission in January 2008 (COM(2008)19 final; COM(2008)30 final). This implies that greenhouse gas emissions should be reduced by at least 20 per cent and up to 30 per cent in case of an international agreement »committing other developed countries to comparable emission reductions and economically more advanced developing countries to contributing adequately according to their responsibilities and respective capabilities« (COM(2008)30 final: 2). Furthermore, the EU should increase the share of renewable energy in total EU energy consumption by 20 per cent as well as reduce energy consumption by 20 per cent in order to meet the efficiency goals. These objectives are to be realized by the year 2020.

Crucially, to create an environment of institutional certainty, binding targets had to be formulated for the European Union as a whole. Most of the proposals fell under Article 175 TEC (192 TFEU), which provided the EU with competences in the field of environment policy. Each member state was, however, free to select those instruments that were best suited to realizing these goals without putting its national economy at a disadvantage. Nevertheless, the European Commission recently criticized that »the EU is on course to achieve only half of the 20 per cent objectives« (COM(2011)109 final: 2). Restricted access to financial support and a lack of awareness of the potential for reducing energy consumption aggravated by insufficient commitment in some sectors were identified as being the main barriers to the implementation of EU law in the member states (COM(2008)772 final). Therefore the *Energy Efficiency Plan 2011* was developed, which included measures to close these gaps. As announced in the document, these will be implemented through specific legislative instruments, such as the revision of the directives on energy services and combined heat and power (Dir. 2006/32/EC, Dir. 2004/8/EC). The European Commission also stressed that if the member states fail to develop appropriate strategies for ensuring a 20 per cent reduction in energy consumption by 2020, binding targets for each member will be formulated at the

Energy efficiency

EU level after 2013, taking into account individual starting points (COM(2011)109 final: 3).

Despite the obvious advantages of reducing energy consumption for the environment, some critics also claim that the introduction of energy-efficiency standards might paradoxically lead to an increase in industrial emissions. These direct rebounds can be described as an *income effect* (for consumers) and the *substitution effect*: the use of energy-efficient appliances increases the consumers' income due to the lower amount of energy consumed. Consequently, consumers can use the additional income to buy other goods and services. Ultimately, the production of goods needed to meet the higher demand leads to an increase in emissions (Breakthrough Institute, 2011). Finally, table 4 summarizes the key developments with regard to energy efficiency.

Table 4: Key developments regarding the increase of energy efficiency (DG Energy)

Date	Key developments regarding the increase of energy efficiency
1992, May 21	Council Directive 92/42/EEC on efficiency requirements for new hot-water boilers fired with liquid or gaseous fuels
1992, September 22	Council Directive 92/75/EEC on the indication by labelling and standard product information of the consumption of energy and other resources by household appliances
1993, September 13	Council Directive 93/76/EEC to limit carbon dioxide emissions by improving energy efficiency (SAVE)
1996, September 3	Directive 96/57/EC of the European Parliament and of the Council on energy efficiency requirements for household electric refrigerators, freezers and combinations thereof
2000, April 26	COM(2000)247 final: Communication from the Commission to the Council, the European Parliament, the Economic and Social Committee and the Committee of the Regions: Action Plan to improve energy efficiency in the EC
2000, September 18	Directive 2000/55/EC of the European Parliament and of the Council on energy efficiency requirements for ballasts for fluorescent lighting
2002, December 16	Directive 2002/91/EC of the European Parliament and of the Council on the energy performance of buildings and its amendments
2005, June 22	COM(2005)265 final: Green Paper energy efficiency or doing more with less
2005, June-2006, March	Public consultation: Green Paper on energy efficiency or doing more with less COM(2005)265 final
2006, March 8	COM(2006)105 final: Green Paper: A European strategy for sustainable, competitive and secure energy

2006, March-June	Public consultation: Green Paper: A European strategy for sustainable, competitive and secure energy
2006, April 5	Directive 2006/32/EC of the European Parliament and of the Council on energy end-use efficiency and energy services
2006, October 19	COM(2006)545 final: Communication from the Commission, Action Plan for energy efficiency: Realising the potential
2007, January 10	COM(2007)1 final: Communication from the Commission to the European Council and the European Parliament: An energy policy for Europe
2007, December-2008, February	Public consultation: Revision of energy labelling framework directive 1992/75/EEC on domestic appliances
2008, April-June	Public consultation: Recasting of the energy performance of buildings directive
2008, November 13	COM(2008)778 final: Proposal for a Directive of the European Parliament and of the Council on the indication by labelling and standard product information of the consumption of energy and other resources by energy-related products
2008, November 13	COM(2008)780 final: Proposal for a Directive of the European Parliament and the Council on the energy performance of buildings
2008, November 13	COM(2008)781 final: Communication from the Commission to the European Parliament, the Council, the European Economic and Social Committee and the Committee of the Regions: Second strategic energy review: an EU energy security and solidarity action plan
2009, March 18	Commission Regulation (EC) No 244/2009 implementing Directive 2005/32/EC of the European Parliament and of the Council with regard to ecodesign requirements for non-directional household lamps
2009, June-August	Public consultation: Evaluation and revision of the action plan for energy efficiency (COM (2006) 545)
2010, May 19	Directive 2010/30/EU of the European Parliament and of the Council on the indication by labelling and standard product information of the consumption of energy and other resources by energy-related products
2010, May 19	Directive 2010/31/EU of the European Parliament and of the Council on the energy performance of buildings
2011, March 8	COM(2011)109 final: Communication from the Commission to the European Parliament, the Council, the European Economic and Social Committee and the Committee of the Regions: Energy efficiency plan 2011

2.4 The promotion of the use of renewable energy sources

During the European Council summit in March 2007, it was decided to increase the share of renewable energy in gross domestic consumption to 20 per cent. This is reflected in Directive 2009/28/EC, which additionally postulated an increase of the share of renewable energy specifically in the transport sector to ten per cent by 2020. When one focuses on the role of renewable sources and their advantages in comparison to fossil fuels, it is important to clarify exactly which sources are included in this category and to describe their specific attributes.

Fossil fuels like coal, oil, and natural gas are non-renewable because they originate from prehistoric plants and animals and require millions of years to form. They contain carbon or compounds of carbon which, when burnt, are released into the atmosphere in the form of carbon dioxide (CO_2). Despite the massive emissions caused by the combustion of fossil fuels, it is assumed that in particular oil will »remain the main source of supply of primary energy until at least the middle of this century« (European Commission, 2008a: 1), with global demand expected to rise by one per cent each year. Nevertheless, the European Commission, in a communication from October 2009, clearly stressed its aim to »reach a 80 per cent cut in greenhouse gas emissions by 2050 compared to 1990 levels« (COM(2009)519 final: 2). In order to both realize this goal and also to reduce the negative impacts of emissions on the environment, the European Commission promotes investments in the research and development of more innovative components, processes, and technologies such as carbon capture and storage which prevent carbon dioxide from being released into the atmosphere. This concept, however, is not entirely new: carbon capture and storage technologies have been used in some industries, such as the oil industry, for over 50 years (Praetorius and Schumacher, 2009: 5081).

As another strategy to decrease the atmospheric CO_2 concentrations in addition to reducing industrial emissions and energy consumption, the European Commission also focuses on the renewable energy sector, in particular on wind power, solar power, geothermal energy, hydro-electric power, ocean power and biomass. Among these, the use of wind power for electricity generation is considered to be the most promising in reaching the 20 per cent targets. Therefore, the European Commission has put great emphasis on the construction of offshore wind farms. In 2010 it presented a framework for further proceedings, which took into account the existing nature legislation in the member states (European Commission, 2010). Solar and geothermal power are often used for direct heating; either for water or for heating systems applied primarily in private households. To enhance the share of electricity generated from renewable sources, the European Commission also relies on photovoltaic technology. The main challenge here is improving efficiency, which means the ability to convert sunlight into electricity. According to the DG Energy, efficiency rates are at 15 per cent.[15] A more predictable form of generation is ocean energy, with wave and tidal energy currently being the most developed technologies in this field. Nevertheless, compared to the use of other renewable sources, this technology is still in its early stages and is not cost-effective due to, for example, the high fees and long procedures associated with receiving permission for construction.[16] Biomass can be used for electricity generation, heating, or the production of biofuels. It exists in three aggregate states: solid in the form of plants, as a gas derived from organic or landfill waste, and as a liquid, such as biofuels gained from crops.[17] Although the use of renewable sources seems to be promising for the environment, environmental associations such as the WWF have raised concerns regarding the efficiency of existing technology and the predictability of the generation of electricity. The WWF has also stressed the danger of unintended environmental consequences, such as the effects of hydroelectric power stations on the ecological system of rivers (WWF, 2007).

Which decisions constituted the most important steps promoting energy from renewable sources at the EU level? The present strategy concerning renewable energy can be traced back to a number of proposals issued since 1997. One of the first initiatives in this field was the European Commission's White Paper *Energy for the Future: Renewable Sources of Energy* issued in November 1997 (COM(97)599 final). At that time, the justification for this proposal was rooted in three different arguments. First, fossil energy sources should be partially replaced in order to reduce carbon dioxide emissions resulting from the use of oil, natural gas and coal, thus helping to mitigate climate change. The second important aspect concerns the security of energy supply (→ 2.5) as increasing the share of renewable energy reduces the Community's dependence on energy imports from other countries. Thirdly, by promoting renewable energy sources, existing technologies must be improved and this results in demand for innovation, which also strengthens the regional economy and provides new employment opportunities (Howes, 2010). Relying on these assumptions, the white paper addressed the future role of renewable energy while taking into account the challenges imposed by climate change, the rising dependence on energy imports, and the creation of the internal market. It was based on the perception that renewable energy sources were »unevenly and insufficiently exploited in the European Union« (COM(97)599 final: 4). The European Commission claimed that, despite it not being a question of the availability of these resources, they satisfied less than six per cent of the EU's

---

15 See: DG Energy: http://ec.europa.eu/energy/renewables/index_en.htm [Accessed 02 April 2011].
16 See: European Commission, Strategic Energy Technology Information System: http://setis.ec.europa.eu/technologies/Ocean-wave-power/info [Accessed 02 April 2011].
17 See: DG Energy: http://ec.europa.eu/energy/renewables/bioenergy/bioenergy_en.htm [Accessed 02 April 2011].

overall gross inland energy requirements. Thus, the white paper set the goal of doubling the share of energy provided by renewable sources to twelve per cent by 2010. In order to guarantee that this objective was attained, an action plan was included that suggested certain measures be adopted within a strict time frame. These measures were composed of advice on a variety of subjects, including: strategies to improve access of renewable energy sources to the electricity markets, regulatory and fiscal instruments, the promotion of co-operation between the member states, initiatives to facilitate investment and access to information in the field of renewable energy sources, and finally measures to reinforce the priority given to renewable energy in the Community policies (COM(97)599 final: 14ff.).

In Directive 2001/77/EC the Community recognized the need for further promotion of renewable sources in the electricity market. Member states were asked to regularly submit reports on their individual performance in reaching the target of increasing the share of energy consumption from renewable sources to twelve per cent by 2010. Since then, the European Commission has regularly assessed the degree to which the member states' indicative targets »are consistent with the global indicative target of twelve per cent of gross national energy consumption by 2010 and in particular with the 22.1 per cent indicative share of electricity produced from renewable energy sources in total Community electricity consumption by 2010« as well as the effectiveness of measures adopted by each member state in achieving these goals (Dir. 2001/77/EC). Similar efforts have been made in the biofuels sector. Directive 2003/30/EC *on the promotion of the use of biofuels or other renewable fuels for transport* was grounded on two basic assumptions. Firstly that the transport sector, which at the time of the release of the directive was responsible for 30 per cent of the Community's energy consumption, would expand and consume an even higher amount of energy in the future. Secondly, the Commission's White Paper *European transport policy for 2010: time to decide* soon followed (COM(2001)370 final), in which a 50 per cent increase in CO_2 emissions from transport was predicted for the period from 1990 to 2010. Thus, the directive called for a reduction in oil consumption in the transport sector in favor of alternative fuels (for example biofuels) (Dir. 2003/30/EC: 1). This would also support the Community in meeting its Kyoto targets and securing its energy supply in the long run. As one measure to achieve this goal, it was suggested that the member states ensure that a minimum proportion of two per cent of all fuels for transport should be placed on the market in the form of biofuels or other renewable fuels by the end of 2005. This proportion is to increase to 5.75 per cent by the end of 2011 (Dir. 2003/30/EC: Art.3.1). The *Renewable Electricity Directive* and the *Biofuels Directive,* issued in 2001 and 2003 respectively, did not include binding rules for national renewable energy targets but rather set benchmarks to be used for orientation. Closely related to the latter was the *Biomass Action Plan*, released in 2005 in order to foster the use of biomass in areas as heating, electricity, and transport. Furthermore, it proposed schemes for promoting the financing of biomass technologies and further research in this field (COM(2005)628 final).

In 2002 the Johannesburg Renewable Energy Coalition (JREC) was formed by 66 governments[18], all of which actively supported the view that increasing the share of renewable energy contributes a necessary step towards achieving sustainable development. Additionally, all governments committed themselves to enhanced co-operation in this area (Johannesburg Renewable Energy Coalition, 2002). Since then, the JREC Secretariat was hosted by the European Commission[19], which in 2006 called for private sector participation in the development of renewable energy technologies, especially in developing countries (COM(2006) 583 final).

Only a few months later, the *Renewable Energy Roadmap* (COM(2006)848 final) was released. This roadmap proposed to set binding rules for the members states and in this way suggested that the indicative targets formulated in the *Renewable Electricity Directive* and the *Biofuels Directive* be abandoned. Additionally, in order to simplify legislation, one target for the whole renewable energy sector should be fixed, instead of individual targets for the electricity, transport and heating and cooling sector (Howes, 2010). The benchmark of 20 per cent was suggested, which was later reflected in the *20-20-20 until 2020* goals (COM(2008)19 final; COM(2008)30 final).

These intentions were realized in the *Renewable Energy Directive*, which entered into force in June 2009 (Dir. 2009/28/EC). This includes concrete mandatory targets for the member states calculated so that an overall share of 20 per cent renewable energy use can be realized (Art. 3).

---

18 As of April 2011, 88 countries had joined the coalition.
19 See: http://ec.europa.eu/environment/archives/jrec/index_en.htm [Accessed 04 April 2011].

Table 5: National overall targets for the share of energy from renewable sources in gross final consumption of energy 2020 (Dir. 2009/28/EC, Annex I)

National overall targets for the share of energy from renewable sources in gross final consumption of energy in 2020		
Country	Share of energy from renewable sources in gross final consumption of energy, 2005 (in %)	Targets for share of energy from renewable sources in gross final consumption of energy, 2020 (in %)
Belgium	2.2	13
Bulgaria	9.4	16
Czech Republic	6.1	13
Denmark	17.0	30
Germany	5.8	18
Estonia	18.0	25
Ireland	3.1	16
Greece	6.9	18
Spain	8.7	20
France	10.3	23
Italy	5.2	17
Cyprus	2.9	13
Latvia	32.6	40
Lithuania	15.0	23
Luxembourg	0.9	11
Hungary	4,3	13
Malta	0.0	10
Netherlands	2.4	14
Austria	23.3	34
Poland	7.2	15
Portugal	20.5	31
Romania	18.8	24
Slovenia	16.0	25
Slovak Republic	6.7	14
Finland	28.5	38
Sweden	39.8	49
United Kingdom	1.3	15

European energy policy

Furthermore, it provides guidelines for the establishment of proportionate rules concerning the authorisation, certification and licensing of infrastructure needed for electricity production (Art. 13). Finally, it lists sustainability criteria for the use of biomass while taking into account the associated risks of biofuel production, in particular damage to land with »high biodiversity value« (Dir. 2009/28/EC, Art. 17.3). A report on the progress of the implementation of this directive in the member states is to be presented by the Commission by December 31, 2014. Table 5 (p. 59) shows the targets as calculated in the directive.

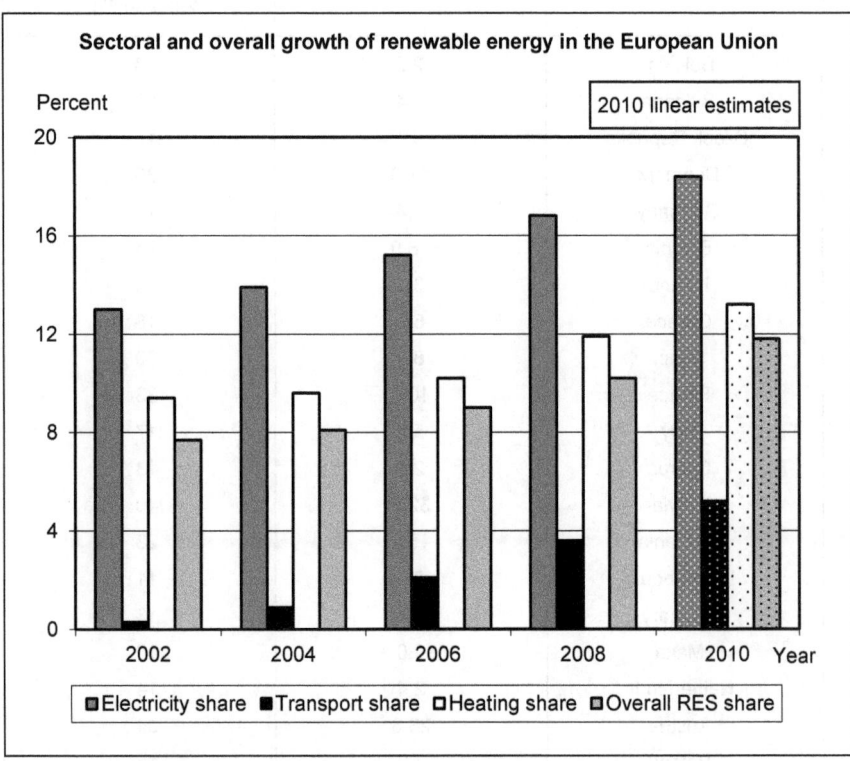

Figure 5: Sectoral and overall growth of renewable energy in the European Union (COM(2011)31 final: 3)

On the basis of this directive, in October 2009 the European Commission published a proposal for energy technology policy, known as the *Strategic Energy Technology (SET) Plan* (COM(2009)519 final), including concrete proposals on how to increase the share of renewable energy. Accordingly, knowledge transfer is to be accelerated, the leadership of EU industries in low-carbon technologies to be strengthened, and the mitigation of climate change to be achieved. In concrete

Renewable energy sources

terms, this means that by 2020 20 per cent of the electricity generated in the EU should result from wind power and at least 15 per cent from solar energy. Further, it would be ensured that carbon capture and storage technologies become cost-competitive. Nuclear energy was also intended to play a crucial role in the energy mix; the European Commission expected new generation-IV reactors to be commercially deployable by 2040 (COM(2009)519 final). In its report on the progress of the EU towards the 2020 targets, including increasing renewable energy to 20 per cent, the European Commission summarized to what extent the goals had been realized so far and where additional efforts were necessary to ensure better performance in the future. Figure 5 illustrates the performance of different sectors including estimated values for the year 2010. Table 6 finally summarizes the central initiatives concerning the goal of enhancing the share of renewable energy sources.

Table 6: Key events regarding the promotion of renewable energy sources (DG Energy)

Date	Key events regarding the promotion of renewable energy sources
1997, November 26	COM(97)599 final: White Paper for a Community strategy and action plan: Energy for the future: renewable sources for energy
2001, September 27	Directive 2001/77/EC of the European Parliament and of the Council on the promotion of electricity produced from renewable energy sources in the internal electricity market
2003, May 8	Directive 2003/30/EC of the European Parliament and of the Council on the promotion of the use of biofuels or other renewable fuels for transport
2005, December 7	COM(2005)628 final: Communication from the Commission, Biomass Action Plan
2006, March 8	COM(2006)105 final: Green Paper: A European strategy for sustainable, competitive and secure Energy
2006, March-June	Public consultation: Green Paper: A European strategy for sustainable, competitive and secure Energy
2006, August-October	Public consultation: EU Initiative on heating and cooling from renewable energy sources
2006, April-July	Public consultation: Review of EU biofuels directive
2006, October 6	COM(2006)583 final: Communication from the Commission to the Council and the European Parliament: Mobilising public and private finance towards global access to climate-friendly, affordable and secure energy services: The Global Energy Efficiency and Renewable Energy Fund
2007, January 10	COM(2006)848 final: Communication from the Commission to the Council and the European Parliament, Renewable Energy Road Map – Renewable energies in the 21st century: building a more sustainable future

European energy policy

2007, January 10	COM(2007)1 final: Communication from the Commission to the European Council and the European Parliament: An energy policy for Europe (First strategic European energy review)
2007, April-May	Public consultation: Biofuel issues in the new legislation on the promotion of renewable energy
2007, June 29	COM(2007)354 final: Green Paper: Adapting to climate change in Europe – options for EU action
2007, June-December	Public consultation: Green Paper: Adapting to climate change in Europe – options for EU action
2008, January 23	COM(2008)19 final: Proposal for a Directive of the European Parliament and of the Council on the promotion of the use of energy from renewable sources
2008, January 23	COM(2008)30 final: Communication from the Commission to the European Parliament, the Council, the European Economic and Social Committee and the Committee of the Regions, 20 20 by 2020: Europe's climate change opportunity
2008, November 13	COM(2008)781 final: Communication from the Commission to the European Parliament, the Council, the European Economic and Social Committee and the Committee of the Regions, Second strategic energy review
2009, April 23	Directive 2009/28/EC of the European Parliament and of the Council on the promotion of the use of energy from renewable sources and amending and subsequently repealing Directives 2001/77/EC and 2003/30/EC
2009, April 24	COM(2009)192 final: Communication from the Commission to the Council and the European Parliament, The renewable energy progress report
2009, October 7	COM(2009)519 final: Communication from the Commission to the European Parliament, the Council, the European Economic and Social Committee and the Committee of the Regions: investing in the development of low carbon technologies (SET-Plan)
2010, November 10	COM(2010)639 final: Communication from the Commission to the European Parliament, the Council, the European Economic and Social Committee and the Committee of the Regions, Energy 2020: A strategy for competitive, sustainable and secure energy
2011, January 31	COM(2011)31 final: Communication from the Commission to the European Parliament and the Council, Renewable Energy: Progressing towards the 2020 target

2.5 Additional measures to ensure energy supply security

The previous sections in this chapter have summarized a variety of key developments concerned with the liberalization of the energy market, the reduction of greenhouse gas emissions, energy efficiency improvements and the promotion of energy from renewable sources. All four topics are decisive components of an integrated European energy and climate change policy. The measures adopted so far contribute not only to the mitigation of environmental damage, but also to another important issue and subject of discussion worldwide – the question of how to ensure the security of energy supply in regions where resources are scarce and which consequently depend on imports from countries outside the EU. While the security of energy supplies has been one of the key issues on the European agenda since the 1970s, it has received further attention following the 2005 gas crises between Russia and the Ukraine that emerged due to disputes over the prices for gas and transit. Since then, comprehensive negotiations between both parties have taken place, however they have only resulted in short-term settlements of the issue. In January 2009 the dispute affected 18 European countries, all of which reported reductions or cut in their gas supplies from Russia transported through Ukraine.

The *20-20-20 until 2020*-targets therefore also attempted to make the European Union less dependent on energy imports. By enhancing the share of renewable energy used for electricity production, transport, heating and cooling, as well as by reducing overall energy consumption through efficiency measures, the security of energy supply can be noticeably improved.

Which additional efforts have been made by the European Commission to strengthen the security of energy supply in the EU? In the Green Paper *Towards a European strategy for the security of energy supply*, issued in 2000, the European Commission expressed its concerns regarding the growing dependence of Europe on energy imports. It assumes that by 2030, if appropriate action is not taken, the European Union will have to cover 70 per cent of its energy needs through oil and gas imports, mainly from the Middle East and Russia – an increase of 20 per cent compared to the amount imported in 2000 (COM(2000)769 final). This, on the one hand, would exacerbate the insecurity of energy supply, and, on the other hand, increase costs.

Important directives to safeguard the security of natural gas supply were released in 2004 (Council Dir. 2004/67/EC), which constituted the first legal framework in this field, and in 2005 (Dir. 2005/89/EC) to address the »security of electricity supply and infrastructure investment«. Both measures were also expected to have an impact on the proper functioning of the internal gas and electricity market. The former was repealed by Regulation 994/2010, which proposed establishing common standards which would guarantee numerous provisions, including that the gas demand in each member state is to be satisfied in the case of disruptions, that a risk assessment is to be developed by the end of 2011 as the basis for emergency plans, and that the exchange of information is to be improved, particularly for emergencies or bilateral agreements with non-EU countries. This regulation obviously reflects experience gained from the Russian-Ukrainian gas crisis and was adopted in order to create improved response mechanisms and thus to prevent such scenarios from occurring in the future.

European energy policy

Importantly, the European Union relies heavily not only on gas but also on oil imports. To reduce this dependence, member states are obliged to »maintain minimum stocks of crude oil and/or petroleum products« (Council Dir. 2006/67/EC). This directive takes into account the likeliness of an interruption of the supply of petroleum products and its potential impact on the European economy. This need was first acknowledged in the late 1960s and became apparent with the oil crisis and its far-reaching implications on the global economy in the 1970s. Since then, a variety of initiatives have been taken at the European level (Council Dir. 68/414/EEC; Council Dir. 72/425/EEC; Council Dir. 98/93/EC; Council Dir. 2006/67/EC; Directive 2009/119/EC).

The necessity to take action in the form of the directives summarized here as well as future efforts can be best understood by examining the extent to which the European Union will depend on gas and oil imports in the future.

Figure 6 illustrates that especially the European Union's dependence on gas imports will continue to increase over the next two decades, which indicates that the demand for gas will remain high while production in the EU member states will decline (European Commission, 2009a: 31).

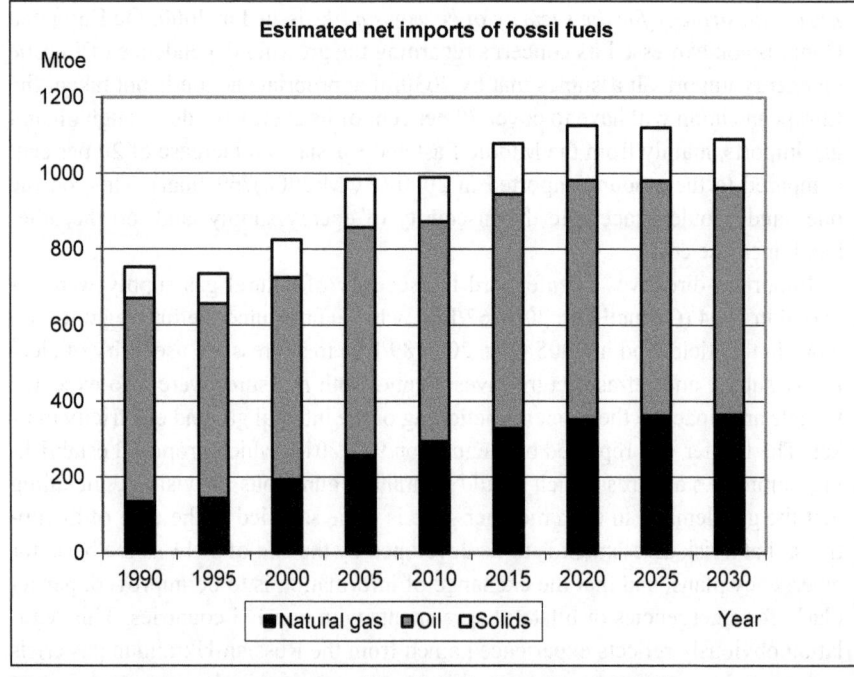

Figure 6: Estimated net imports of fossil fuels (baseline 2009) (European Commission, 2009a: 31)

Energy supply security

The Wuppertal Institute for Climate, Environment and Energy as well as the Government Institute for Economic Research (VATT) (2006) forecast similar developments. Accordingly, the production of fossil fuels will be reduced by 53 per cent, while demand will increase by 6 per cent. For the gas sector this implies that natural gas imports, compared to 2005 figures, will double by 2030. Concerning the origins of crude oil and natural gas imports, in 2008 Russia (33 per cent of all oil and 40 per cent of gas imports) and Norway (16 per cent of oil and 23 per cent of gas imports) were among the most important players[20]. Concluding, Table 7 summarizes the core initiatives adopted to improve the security of energy supply to the EU.

Table 7: Key events regarding the security of energy supply (DG Energy)

Date	Key events regarding the security of energy supply
1968, December 20	Council Directive 68/414/EEC imposing an obligation on Member States of the EEC to maintain minimum stocks of crude oil and/or petroleum products
1972, December 19	Council Directive 72/425/EEC amending the Council Directive of 20 December 1968 imposing an obligation on Member States of the EEC to maintain minimum stocks of crude oil and/or petroleum products
1998, December 14	Council Directive 98/93/EC amending Directive 68/414/EEC imposing an obligation on Member States of the EEC to maintain minimum stocks of crude oil and/or petroleum products
2000, November 29	COM(2000)769 final: Green Paper Towards a European strategy for the security of energy supply
2001, September 27	Directive 2001/77/EC of the European Parliament and of the Council on the promotion of electricity produced from renewable energy sources in the internal electricity market
2004, April 26	Council Directive 2004/67/EC concerning measures to safeguard security of natural gas supply
2005, June 22	COM(2005)265 final: Green Paper Energy efficiency or doing more with less
	Public consultation on the Green Paper until March 2006
2006, January 18	Directive 2005/89/EC of the European Parliament and of the Council concerning measures to safeguard security of electricity supply and infrastructure investment
2006, March 8	COM(2006)105 final: Green Paper: A European strategy for sustainable, competitive and secure energy
2006, July 24	Council Directive 2006/67/EC 2006 imposing an obligation on Member States to maintain minimum stocks of crude oil and/or petroleum products

---

20 See http://www.energy.eu/ [Accessed 01 April 2011].

2007, January 10	COM(2006)848 final: Communication from the Commission to the Council and the European Parliament, Renewable Energy Road Map – Renewable energies in the 21st century: building a more sustainable future
2007, January 10	COM(2007)1 final: Communication from the Commission to the European Council and the European Parliament: An energy policy for Europe (First strategic European energy review)
2008, January 23	COM(2008)19 final: Proposal for a Directive of the European Parliament and of the Council on the promotion of the use of energy from renewable sources
2008, November 13	COM(2008) 781 final: Communication from the Commission to the European Parliament, the Council, the European Economic and Social Committee and the Committee of the Regions, Second strategic energy review: an EU energy security and solidarity action plan
2009, April 23	Directive 2009/28/EC of the European Parliament and of the Council on the promotion of the use of energy from renewable sources and amending and subsequently repealing Directives 2001/77/EC and 2003/30/EC
2009, September 14	Council Directive 2009/119/EC imposing an obligation on Member States to maintain minimum stocks of crude oil and/or petroleum products
2010, October 20	Regulation (EU) No 994/2010 of the European Parliament and of the Council concerning measures to safeguard security of gas supply and repealing Council Directive 2004/67/EC
2010, November 10	COM(2010)639 final: Communication from the Commission to the European Parliament, the Council, the European Economic and Social Committee and the Committee of the Regions, Energy 2020: A strategy for competitive, sustainable and secure energy
2011, January 31	COM(2011)31 final: Communication from the Commission to the European Parliament and the Council, Renewable Energy: Progressing towards the 2020 target

2.6 Conclusions

The summary of the legislation in the five core sub-fields of European energy policy presented above served to answer the following empirical questions:

- Why has European energy policy been selected as a research field?
- Which interdependencies exist between energy policy and other EU policy areas?
- Which policy proposals have been issued by the European Commission (and other institutions) at what time?
- Which public and private actors have been affected by the policy proposals?

Conclusions

- During which stages of the policy process was it useful for the public and private actors concerned to submit position papers or meet decision-makers face-to-face? When were public and private actors given the opportunity to participate in stakeholder consultations on a particular issue?

The next section will focus on the theories that have been developed by various scholars to address research questions related to interest groups, their strategies, as well as their influence on political decisions. The approaches that have been selected to guide the hypotheses - the ACF, the actor-centered institutionalism, the literature on political opportunity structures, and approaches on interest groups' strategies - will be embedded in a wider discussion of scholarly works. In so doing, the achievements and shortcomings of each will be revealed.

Chapter 3. The current state of research on interest group politics and related fields

Interest group lobbying is not a new phenomenon. Representatives of public and private interests have long been acknowledged as legitimate and important actors in the political sphere. However, lobbyists currently influence the policy-making process to an extent that was not anticipated some decades ago. As a result of the large increase in the number of active lobbyists in Brussels as well as the diversification of their strategies, researchers are increasingly drawn to their lobbyist activities. In this chapter an overview is given of the research that has been conducted on interest groups and related fields. At the same time, the core theories that serve as the background of this work are summarized. To begin with an overview of the different periods of research on interest groups is provided (→ 3.1). The following chapters then deal with studies on multi-level governance and the approaches taken concerning the formation of networks (→ 3.2) and coalitions (→ 3.3) within the EU multi-level system. Chapter 3.4 then reviews research on collective action and social movements, before in Chapter 3.5 the focus is shifted to the function of institutions in the policy process, in particular the implications of the actor-centered institutionalism and the literature on political opportunity structures. The last two sub-chapters are concerned with research conducted on the factors which determine the strategies pursued by interest groups (→ 3.6) as well as their influence on the EU agenda and the policy outcome (→ 3.7).

3.1 Periods of research on the role of interest groups in the policy process

What is actually meant by the term *interest group*? Eising (Eising, 2008: 5; see also: Beyers, Eising and Maloney, 2008) introduces three decisive characteristics for defining interest groups: *organization, political interests* and *informality*. *Organization* refers to the »nature of the group« (Eising, 2008: 5), meaning that interest groups may be distinguished from other movements through their organizational character. According to March and Simon (1993: 2) organizations can be defined as »systems of coordinated action among individuals and groups«. This implies that some form of coordination is required between the members of the organization in order for it to pursue a common goal. The existence of *political interests* indicates that interest groups attempt to influence policy processes according to their own political ideas (Eising, 2008: 5). *Informality* describes the fact that »interest groups do not normally seek public office but pursue their goals through informal interactions with politicians and bureaucrats« (Eising, 2008: 5). Concerning the function of interest groups, Beyers, Eising and Maloney (2008) describe the term *interest group politics* as the »organisation, aggregation, articulation, and intermediation of societal interests that seek to shape public policies« (Beyers, Eising and Maloney, 2008: 1103; see also: Eising and Kohler-Koch, 2005a). One of the key components of these functions is the monitoring of the legislative procedure, generally starting with an initiative from the European Commission. Interest groups are expected to anticipate what is going to be discussed at the European level in order to be able to develop their own lobbying strategy as early as possible (Lahusen and Jauß, 2001: 109).

On a global level, the first wave of theoretical investigations into interest group activity occurred in the United States during the 1920s (Almond, 1983; Woll, 2006). At that time, the authors especially tried to analyze the nature of interests to be intermediated in Washington, DC. Herring (1929), for example, prepared a list of hundreds of interest groups that tried to influence the US government. He found that, although various interests were represented, business interests prevailed. Blaisdell (1941) came to a similar conclusion: he hinted at the consequences of the dominance of business interests for other sectors as well as the state. A second body of work shifted the focus to interest groups in countries outside the United States. Finer (1958) examined how the British lobbying system was organized and came to the conclusion that in Great Britain the administrative and the lobbying system are mutually dependent. Stewart (1958) was concerned with the impact of interest groups on the House of Commons. He argued that in Great Britain, in contrast to the US system, the parliamentary chamber was controlled by the parties rather than by interest groups.

In the following years more general theoretical studies appeared which were rooted in theories on international relations, especially neofunctionalism and intergovernmentalism (Eising, 2008: 6). Concerning the European Community, these analyzed the influence interest groups had on the European integration process. European integration is defined by Lindberg (1963: 6; see also: Haas, 1968; Eising, 2003) as:

> »(1) the process whereby nations forego the desire and ability to conduct foreign and key domestic policies independently of each other, seeking instead to make joint decisions or to delegate the decision-making process to new central organs; and (2) the process whereby political actors in several distinct settings are persuaded to shift there expectations and political activities to a new centre.«

Lindberg, as well as Haas, applied the concept of political integration to the European level. Whereas Haas expected the development of a political community to be superior to that of the nation state, Lindberg's expectations were less far-reaching and included the effects European integration had on national political structures, decision-making processes as well as the interests and strategies of politically relevant actors (Eising, 2003: 392).

Haas (1958) in particular published various major contributions from the neofunctionalist perspective on the European integration process and the actors that promoted it. He found that business associations and trade unions were the central actors which fostered the process of integration and considered their activities to be worthwhile, as they contributed to peace and economic welfare in Europe (Eising, 2008: 6). However, due to the slow-down of European integration in the 1960s and 1970s, doubts began to surface about the empirical suitability of Haas' assumptions. Haas (1975) himself questioned the spill-over of the integration process assumed in his own theory. Nevertheless the theory became increasingly relevant again with the creation of the single market in the 1980s and continues to be significant. McGowan (2007), after analyzing whether neofunctionalism is able to explain the EC competition policy, concludes that »Haas' interpretation still holds analytical purchase as a mid range theory that is applicable to the dynamics and development of individual sectors« (McGowan, 2007: 13).

In the meantime researchers like Hoffmann (1966) shifted their focus to approaches derived from an intergovernmental perspective that better served to explain the member states' resistance to further European integration (Eising, 2008: 6). Intergovernmentalism then replaced former neofunctionalist assumptions and shed new light on the structures and processes at the EU level. The impact of interest groups was widely neglected in these studies.

In the 1980s the question of the function of business interests gained renewed importance due to progress in European integration. Transnational companies in particular had contributed decisively to the removal of barriers for the free movement of capital, goods, services and persons as ensured by the Single European Act of 1986. However, transnational companies would not have been able to profit from these transformations without the initiative of the European Commission. In its White Paper *Completing the internal market* (COM(85)310 final), the European Commission strongly argued for the implementation of all measures required to fulfil this goal. As supranational institutionalists such as Sandholtz and Zysman (1989) claim, the interplay between the European institutions and business elites constituted the trigger for establishing the envisaged reforms. These scholars were confronted by the liberal intergovernmentalists, who assigned less influence to interest groups at the EU level in general and described national governments as the dominant actors (Moravcsik, 1998). Following intergovernmentalist tradition from the 1960s, Moravcsik stresses the leading role of national governments in interstate bargaining. However, his theory does not regard states as *black boxes* whose governments have fixed preferences (Moravcsik, 1993: 481). Instead, it is

State of research

assumed that governments filter domestic interests and form their preferences on the basis of what is prioritised by domestic actors:

»There is little doubt that the EU's policy-making process is closest to the pluralist model found in the United States, in which governments formulate policies in conjunction with societal interests but implement them alone. But although the EU's policymaking resembles the pluralist much more than the statist or the corporatist [...], it is less »pluralistic« in interest group access, given that business is the interest mainly represented [...]« (Schmidt, 1997: 166).

Schäfer and Streeck (2008) describe the emergence of a so-called *euro-corporatism* that is quite distinct from the corporatist structures well-known at the national level. Accordingly, the European integration process and the development of a modern capitalist system have countervailed the idea of a tripartism of business, labor and the state. European integration has resulted in the disintegration of corporatist relations at the national level, especially due to the weakening of labor unions. At the European level, the authors claim that the lack of commitment among the employer organizations and the heterogeneity of labor unions' interests would undermine previously established corporatist structures (Schäfer and Streeck, 2008: 204).

In the meantime, new concepts have been developed in order to capture these findings theoretically. With the help of terms like *multi-level* or *network governance* (Jachtenfuchs and Kohler-Koch, 1996a; Eising and Kohler-Koch, 1999; Hooghe and Marks, 2003) scholars have tried to emphasize the complexity of state-society relations. It has often been hypothesized that these new modes of steering would lead to a loss of state sovereignty (Brunnengräber and Walk, 2007). Closely related are studies concerned with the legitimacy of European policy-making. In this context, the democratic deficit of the EU has often been criticised: while some scholars are convinced that the EU is as democratic as it could or should be (Moravcsik, 1998), others accuse the EU institutions of not being in line with even minimalistic democratic principles (Follesdal and Hix, 2005).

This summary of the research results focusing on interest groups has shown that the issue has been analyzed from various perspectives over the last decades. In turn, these results have been used to develop different models of the European decision-making process. The following sections will critically assess the models that are most decisive for answering the main research questions.

3.2 Literature on multi-level and network governance

Since the late 1990s, discussions concerning governance have increasingly entered policy-making literature. According to the European Commission's White Paper, *European governance* refers to the »rules, processes and behavior that affect the

Multi-level and network governance

way in which powers are exercised at European level, particularly as regards openness, participation, accountability, effectiveness and coherence« (COM(2001)428 final: 8).

But what are the basic concepts that lie at the heart of the governance debate? One of the most often cited sources is from Rosenau and Czempiel (1992): »Governance without government« became a commonly used phrase to describe the characteristics of modern policy-making. Similarly, Jachtenfuchs and Kohler-Koch (1996a) ask under what circumstances governance can succeed if jurisdiction is dispersed over multiple levels rather than centralized. Various interpretations have emerged of what exactly *governance* refers to, a question that becomes particularly obvious when scholars attempt to translate *governance* into other languages. In Germany, for example, based on the translation of governance as *Steuerung*, it has been discussed whether the term is little more than an advancement of *Steuerungstheorie* initially developed in the 1970s (Mayntz, 2004). In 1995 Mayntz and Scharpf preferred to interpret it as *Regelung* (Mayntz and Scharpf, 1995: 16), a definition which provides more room for interpretation. Benz and his collaborators (Benz, Lütz, Schimank, and Simonis, 2007; see also Benz, 2006) point at the various dimensions of the governance concept, thereby highlighting the participation of private actors as central element. A similar interpretation is presented by Héritier (2002) who emphasizes that »governance implies that private actors are involved in decision-making in order to provide common goods and that non-hierarchical means of guidance are employed« (Héritier, 2002a: 3). Rhodes (1997) also stresses the non-hierarchical character of governance emphasizing the involvement of private corporate actors in the formulation and implementation of policies.

Governance does not only refer to different dimensions within the nation state. *Multi-level governance* (MLG) emerged in the early 1990s as a concept »to capture developments in EU structural policy following its major reform in 1988« (Bache and Flinders, 2004: 2; see also Jachtenfuchs and Kohler-Koch, 1996a). The phrase was first used by Marks (1992) who developed an approach that, in contrast to earlier attempts, combined insights from international relations theories with those gained in the study of domestic politics. Closely related to multi-level governance is Putnam's *two-level game*, which is based on the assumption that national political leaders act simultaneously at two different levels (Putnam, 1988: 434):

> »Across the international table sit his foreign counterparts, and at his elbow sit diplomats and other international advisors. Around the domestic table behind him sit party and parliamentary figures, spokespersons for domestic agencies, representatives of key interest groups, and the leader's own political advisors«.

State of research

What is crucial to multi-level governance is the dispersion of authority across a variety of levels. In their definition, Kohler-Koch and Rittberger (2006) especially emphasize the vertical dimension:

>»MLG posits that decision-making authority is not monopolized by the governments of the Member States but is diffused to different levels of decision-making – the sub-national, national and supranational levels« (Kohler Koch and Rittberger, 2006: 34).

According to Benz (see for example 2007; 2010), the causes for this dispersion of authority lie in the increasing interdependencies between local, regional, national, and international policies that require the coordination across multiple levels. This issue was first explored during the 1960s when researchers seeking to explain European integration – meaning the transfer of competencies to the EU – considered why national governments had given up some of their powers in favor of supranational institutions. Kohler-Koch and Rittberger (2006), however, identified a *governance turn* in EU studies. More recent works regard the EU institutional setting as a given and analyze its impact on policies and politics at the EU and the national level. With the accession of the new member countries in 2004, scholars have increasingly concentrated on the role of regions (Kohler Koch and Rittberger, 2006: 31ff.). According to the authors, existing research on EU governance mainly consists of two different strands: the first focuses on the EU as a regulatory state while the second analyzes new modes of governance (Kohler-Koch and Rittberger, 2006: 27). Whereas the first approach presupposes that »the EU polity has achieved a considerable degree of maturity as a political system that has come to exercise 'classical' functions of political systems«, the second is concerned with the impact of new forms of policy-making which rely on *soft law*, such as the open method of co-ordination (OMC), as have been introduced by the Maastricht Treaty (Kohler-Koch and Rittberger, 2006: 35-36).

Concerning the dispersion of power in different policy fields, Brunnengräber (2007), in his study of multi-level climate governance, tries to identify new relations between actors and strategies. He draws on the assumption that the conventional categories in terms of institutions and territories no longer serve to reflect current constellations. Fairbrass and Jordan (2004) analyze to which degree national political and societal actors in the UK have been involved in the implementation of EU directives on biodiversity protection. They conclude that the selected cases serve well as examples for multi-level governance because:

>»They are both characterized by subnational mobilization, complex, uncertain, and contested decision-making, entrepreneurial action on the part of the Commission and Parliament, unintended policy outcomes and learning on the part of the member states« (Fairbrass and Jordan, 2004: 162).

Regarding the European energy market, Eberlein (2007) inquires if a shadow of hierarchy is required to produce the desired policy results in sectoral governance.

He concludes that »governance and government have complementary contributions to make to policy efficacy« (Eberlein, 2007: 89). He considers non-state actors as vital for the policy process, as only they are able to provide specific sectoral knowledge. In addition, their involvement constitutes a source of the EU's legitimacy.

The concept of multi-level governance has also often been applied to global policy-making (Behrens, 2010). In the context of *global governance*, a term derived from the literature in international relations, scholars often hint at the new demands national governments are confronted with in the age of globalization. They call for a new *global governance* in order to be able to handle challenges that cannot be dealt with within the limited scope of the nation state (Zürn, 2006; for an overview see also Messner and Nuscheler, 2003). The rising importance of *global governance* has also been widely acknowledged among practitioners, especially in policy fields such as economic, environment or energy policy. The United Nations Environment Programme (UNEP) is but one example of the efforts at the global level to bring together a wide range of actors, ranging from governments and industry to environmental organizations and research institutions. However, as Hooghe and Marks (2003) criticize, although consensus regarding the general need for global governance may exist, disagreement on how to establish effective governance structures often prevails.

In the context of the discussion on multi-level governance another approach has emerged: the concept of *network governance*. Research on networks is, in principle, not a new phenomenon. Since the 1940s and 1950s scholars have increasingly directed their attention to the analysis of social networks, particularly in the disciplines of sociology and social psychology (see for example Bavelas, 1950; Festinger 1954; Festinger, Schachter and Back, 1963; for an overview see Lazer, 2011). Prominent works have been published by Freeman (1979), who discusses the concept of centrality and related measurement problems, and Granovetter (1973: 1360) who argues that »the degree of overlap of two individuals' friendship networks varies directly with the strength of their tie to one another«. Additionally, he explores the impact of this assumption on the »diffusion of influence and information, mobility opportunity, and community organization« (Granovetter, 1973: 1360). Since the 1970s the literature on networks remained fairly stable before gaining new relevance in the 1990s (Lazer, 2011). On the one hand, it is rooted in the context of the interorganizational theory (Benson, 1978; Scharpf, 1978), while on the other hand it has increasingly been used with regard to interest group politics and their function in the policy process (Dowding, 1995; Thatcher, 1998).

Particularly problematic for the concept of network governance is the sheer variety of approaches that have been developed to analyze networks and similar concepts. These are based on different definitions and implications for actor constellations and their roles in the policy process. In some studies the *policy network* is compared to the concepts of the *issue network*, the *policy community*, or the *iron triangle*. According to Richardson (2006a), the term *policy community* describes »very close and stable relationships between policy actors« and is closely related to the definition of a community as a group of people who jointly own a common good, who are similar in character and who pursue common interests. While the *policy community* is an expression which was originally derived from research in the UK, the *issue network* and the *iron triangle* are terms commonly used in American literature (Adam and Kriesi, 2007; for the concepts *policy community* and *issue network* see especially Heclo and Wildavsky, 1975). The *iron triangle* serves to describe the relationship between government agencies, legislative bodies and interest groups in the United States, which can be characterized as stable and operating routinely. Contrastingly, the *issue network* is regarded as an ad-hoc coalition that is »more open to innovative policies« (Bogason, 2006; Adam and Kriesi, 2007: 144).

In order to clarify the existing research, Börzel (2011) categorized the various network concepts. Firstly, networks may serve as a »tool to analyse interactions and relations between actors engaged in public policy-making« either by applying quantitative or qualitative methods (Börzel, 2011: 49). Secondly, from an ontological point of view, »networks connote specific types of interest intermediation entailing different forms of institutionalized exchange relations between the state, business and civil society« (Börzel, 2011: 49). Following a third strand, networks may be understood as a form of governance.

The concept of networks as types of interest intermediation can be traced back to Marsh and Rhodes (1992; see especially Rhodes and Marsh, 1992) who rejected the dichotomy of corporatism and pluralism often postulated in the 1960s and 1970s as being inconsistent and of little relevance for empirical studies. They criticized the fact that the existing variety of state-society-relations could not be captured by corporatist or pluralist models. Therefore, Marsh and Rhodes developed a typology allowing »for a more 'fine grain' analysis« (in Börzel, 2011: 50). Three features are central to their approach (Marsh, 1998): First, networks are understood as »structures of resource dependency«. Second, networks are assumed to influence policy through the way they constrain the policy agenda and by doing so, induce continuity. Thirdly, change in the network as well as in the policy outcome is mostly caused by exogenous factors: »As such, the implication is that, to understand and explain policy change, we need to understand and explain network change« (Marsh, 1998a: 11).

According to Kohler-Koch (1999), the mode of *network governance* stresses the interdependence of actors in pursuing a certain aim and can be traced back to the intention of the European Commission to integrate private actors into the problem-solving process. This was done in order to enhance the democratic legitimacy of the Union and increase the probability of policy ratification in the member

Multi-level and network governance

states. Similar to Rhodes and Marsh (1992), Eising and Kohler-Koch (1999) also tried to find a concept that reached beyond the established typology of statism, pluralism, and corporatism, which would be able to capture modern forms of policy-making. Under pluralist and corporatist systems the state functions as a referee or mediator, while under networks it assumes the role of an activator who coordinates the interests related to a certain policy issue. Table 8 provides a complete overview on the different modes.

Table 8: Core elements of ideal types of governance (Eising and Kohler-Koch, 1999: 6)

	Core elements of ideal types of governance			
	Statism	**Pluralism**	**Corporatism**	**Network**
Role of the state	Authority	Referee	Mediator	Activator
Dominant orientation	Pursuit of common 'national' interest	Pursuit of individual interest	Integrating conflicting group interest	Co-ordinating related interest
Patterns of interaction	Command and control based on majority rule	Competition and bargaining to build minimum winning coalitions	Concerted negotiations to reach consensus	Multilateral negotiations to approximate positions
Dominant actors	State actors	State actors and multitude of interest groups and parties	State actors and functional peak associations	State actors and multitude of stakeholders
Level and scope of political allocation	Central level covering all issue areas	Overall and issue specific at respective government level	National or sub-national level covering specific issue areas	Functionally specific agreements cutting across different levels

The central idea of the mode of network governance is that policy-making takes place in »highly organised social sub-systems« (Eising and Kohler-Koch, 1999: 5) in which both state and societal actors participate in the problem-solving process:

> »Thus, in these patterns of interaction, state actors and a multitude of interest organizations are involved in multilateral negotiations about the allocation of functionally specific 'values'« (Eising and Kohler-Koch, 1999: 5).

State of research

While this definition implies that governance is exercised *by* networks, in which »the authoritative allocation of values is negotiated between state and societal actors« (Börzel and Heard-Lauréate, 2009: 135), Börzel and Heard-Lauréate postulate that the forms of informal politics that occur in the European multi-level system can better be described as governance *in* networks (Börzel and Heard-Lauréate, 2009: 140). This latter understanding takes into account the importance of supranational institutions casting a *shadow of hierarchy* that ultimately determines the outcome of policy-making. In particular, hierarchical structures prevail between the European Commission and the stakeholders concerned with a policy issue:

> »While it takes advantage of private actor resources to increase its action capacity, the Commission seeks to preserve its autonomy and has little interest in extending the involvement of private actors beyond consultations« (Börzel and Heard-Lauréate, 2009: 140).

The network approach is also a central theme in Bache's (2008) work on multi-level governance. He postulates that the network concept functions as a conceptual bridge between multi-level governance and Europeanization. He argues that »Europeanization that promotes a shift toward multi-level governance within states would require a redistribution of domestic power resources in favour of subnational and nonstate actors« (Bache, 2008: 36).

Adam and Kriesi (2007) developed a typology of policy networks to measure their potential to initiate policies. They stress the autonomous and self-organizing nature of networks, where negotiation and problem-solving take place without government steering (Adam and Kriesi, 2007: 130). The only superior function governments can play in this context is to manage the interactions between the members of a network and, in this way, to promote the importance of finding a solution to the negotiated problem. In addition, Adam and Kriesi emphasize that networks cannot be described as *one* new governing structure, as differential patterns of networks exist which in turn lead to multiple categories (Adam and Kriesi, 2007: 130). Their typology is based on two dimensions: the *distribution of power* (concentration or fragmentation) and the *type of interaction* (conflict, bargaining or cooperation) (ibid: 134). With regard to the first dimension, concentration can be understood as power being concentrated in one dominant actor or coalition of the network, whereas fragmentation means that it is shared between different actors or coalitions. Here the authors refer to Sabatier's and Jenkins-Smith's (1999) *Advocacy Coalition Framework* which assumes that the actors in a political subsystem build coalitions and that these coalitions are not equally powerful. The second dimension focuses on the degree of cooperation. The resulting combinations of these two dimensions are listed in Table 9.

Table 9: Typology of network structures (Adam and Kriesi, 2007: 135)

Typology of network structures			
Distribution of power	Type of interaction		
	Conflict	Bargaining	Cooperation
Concentration	Dominance	Asymmetric bargaining	Hierarchical cooperation
Fragmentation	Competition	Symmetric bargaining	Horizontal cooperation

According to Adam and Kriesi (2007: 145), the typology of policy networks described above can also be used to measure the potential and form of policy change. Table 10 presents an overview of the potential and type of policy changes of different kinds of networks.

Table 10: Potential and type of policy change (Adam and Kriesi, 2007: 145)

Potential and type of policy change			
Distribution of power	Type of interaction		
	Conflict	Bargaining	Cooperation
Concentration	Moderate potential for rapid (serial) shift	Low to moderate potential for incremental change	Low potential for change – maintenance of status quo
Fragmentation	High potential for rapid (serial) shift	Moderate to high potential for incremental change	Low to moderate potential for change-maintenance of status quo

The first dimension - *distribution of power* - is expected to be an indicator for the potential for change: the higher the fragmentation of power, the greater the potential for change. The second dimension focuses on the degree of cooperation, which is expected to determine the form of policy change.

A different perspective is adopted by Coen and Thatcher (2008) who do not attempt to analyze the impact of networks on policy outcome but instead seek to discover why the European Commission, national governments and regulatory agencies accept or even foster the emergence of networks in the field of European energy policy. The question of why networks form can however also be approached from a different and more individual perspective; »the idea that individuals who are similar to one another are more likely to form ties« (Lazer, 2011: 62; see also: McPherson, Smith-Lovin and Cook, 2001). Beyers and Kerremans (2004) analyze which factors determine the way policy networks are organized among various actors. They demonstrate how a) the institutional organization of government and b) political cleavages affect network formation (Beyers and Kerremans, 2004: 1120). In their definition of networks they refer to Scharpf (1997) and regard them as »constellations of interdependent actors with different capabilities and policy positions that provide solutions to policy problems« (Beyers and Kerremans, 2004: 119).

The question of why and how networks form is of great importance here. The analysis takes a closer look at what determines the emergence of coalitions of energy actors which then attempt to influence the decision-making process. Therefore, the studies referred to above provide valuable insight into these dynamics.

This sub-chapter concludes with some critical comments from authors who question the value of many applications of the network concept found in the literature. Börzel (1997), for instance, claims that it is often only used as a descriptive tool to depict existing structures and relations. Moreover, a variety of definitions and applications in different disciplines exist which only share the minimal common denominator that networks are understood as:

> »[...] a set of relatively stable relationships, which are of non-hierarchical and interdependent nature linking a variety of actors, who share common interests with regard to a policy and who exchange resources to pursue these shared interests acknowledging that co-operation is the best way to achieve common goals« (Börzel, 1997: 1).

Peters (1998) criticizes the generalizability of the network approach and views it as largely inapplicable to the USA as, compared to Europe, American politics is far less structured. Instead of engaging in cooperation, US interest groups prefer to act individually. Therefore, generalizable hypotheses should not be based on the network approach (Peters, 1998: 31-32).

3.3 Theories on coalition-formation

Another strand of literature focuses on what determines the formation of groups and coalitions. Different authors have tried to define what is actually meant by the term *coalition* as it can generally include any kind of collective action. Berry

(1989: 166) uses the term *ad hoc coalitions* to describe alliances that »exist for the specific purpose of working on a single issue and dissolve when that issue reaches some resolution or when the coalition partners no longer feel the effort is worthwhile«. Mahoney (Mahoney, C., 2008) distinguishes *ad hoc issue coalitions* from *networks*: while networking describes more informal coalition activity, an ad hoc issue coalition is »a very specific type of coalition of groups – one that forms for a single discrete issue fight« (Mahoney, C., 2008: 168). In her definition, she refers to Pijnenburg (1998) who analyzed the formation of ad hoc coalitions of companies. According to his concept, ad hoc coalitions are characterized by a low degree of formalization and a high degree of autonomy of the coalition partners.

The scientific discussion on the emergence of groups was initiated by Truman (1951) after World War II who assumed that groups are formed spontaneously as soon as their potential members sense a common interest. This interest can be provoked, for example, by discontent with the status quo. The formation of one group can also in turn mobilize other competitive actors to form associations and pursue opposite interests. Olson (1965) then contradicted this theory by stating that individuals cannot be expected to engage in cooperation as long as they can expect to reap benefits as a result of the provision of a collective good, regardless of whether they become active or not.

An important contribution was made by Riker (1962) who attempted to explain the dynamics of coalition-formation in politics. Drawing on game theoretic analyses, he describes coalitions as partnerships of three or more individuals analogous to »n-person games« (Riker, 1962: 35). Three propositions are crucial for his analysis of what determines the formation of coalitions: First, according to the *size principle,* winning coalitions with complete and perfect information tend to include no more than the minimal number of persons necessary to attain the envisaged goals. This hypothesis contradicts the findings by Downs (1957), who assumes that political parties as specific types of coalitions attempt to maximize their votes by integrating as many potential members as possible. Second, the *strategic principle* states that in those systems to which the *size principle* can be attributed, »participants in the final stages of coalition-formation should and do move toward a minimum winning coalition« (Riker, 1962: 211).

At this point, some of Riker's central terms should be clarified: In order to describe this and other potential results of the coalition-formation process, he differentiates between *winning, losing, blocking,* and *grand coalitions* (Riker, 1962: 103). The best *winning coalition* is able to gain »the sum of the maximum that each of the players outside the winning coalition can lose« (Riker, 1962: 40), an assumption that is in accordance with the zero-sum condition, which states that the sum of what the winners of the game collect is equal to what the losers have to abandon. A *minimal winning coalition* is defined by the fact that it is no longer successful as soon as one of its members decides to leave the group. Additionally,

State of research

it should not include more members as are necessary in order to become a winning coalition (→ *size principle*). This proposition becomes clear when applied to the daily business of political parties: it is assumed that a coalition of the two leading parties, meaning of two coalitions that are close to minimal winning coalitions, is improper because the new coalition arising from cooperation would be too large to provide its members with any benefits:

> »When a coalition includes everybody, the winners gain nothing simply because there are no losers. [...] If they have no such control, all losers could invariably join the winners and hereby both produce a valueless coalition of the whole and nullify the winners' victory« (Riker, 1962: 39).

This is what Riker calls a *grand coalition*. The opposite of a winning coalition is called either a *losing* or a *blocking* coalition. While a losing coalition is defined as the complement of a winning coalition, blocking coalitions are those that consist exactly of n/2 members with n being an even number describing the sum of all potential coalition members. If two blocking coalitions exist, they complement each other and no further development can be expected (Riker, 1962: 40; 104).

Finally, the third principle is labelled the *disequilibrium principle* and asserts that systems which meet the conditions of the first two principles lack sufficient stability because »they contain forces leading toward decision regardless of stakes and hence toward the elimination of participants« (Riker, 1962: 211). Here Riker contradicts the »theory of the balance of power« according to which rational politics is characterized by a certain degree of stability:

> »While the theory does not deny the occurrence of decisions, it does assert that the decisions are so bounded by the internal logic of the decision-making process that no member of the system is eliminated or destroyed« (Riker, 1962: 160).

However, the question remains as to why individuals or organizations should become a member of a coalition if the costs and gains connected with the decision cannot be estimated. As coalition-formation is a dynamic process, in the course of which each new participant might change the coalition's internal structure and consequently the strategic decisions made by the whole body, the potential members cannot possess any concrete knowledge about the exact type of coalition they are about to join. Riker also provides an answer to this question: for him, the role of the leader and the so-called side payments offered constitute the decisive factors through which coalition members are integrated:

> »The means by which leaders do so is the offer of what is called in the (perhaps unnecessarily) vivid language of the theory 'side payments'. While in common usage this phrase refers to payments of money, it should be emphasized that it is intended to cover all artifacts and sentences (such as promises on policy) that can conceivably have value for the members of the body« (Riker, 1962: 105).

Riker refers to five groups of side payments (Riker, 1962: 109 ff.). With the first, *threat of reprisal*, the leader has the power to threaten individuals with reprisals if they do not join the coalition. In this case, the side payment exists in the guarantee not to realize the threat. However, this kind of argument can only exist in dictatorships, where no independent decision-making is possible. The second group is defined as »payments of objects, the value of which can be reckoned in money«. While direct monetary payments would be considered inappropriate in public institutions, the grant of other goods, such as job positions, embodies a side payment which can be easily valued by estimating the annual income or the prestige of the office-holder. The third group, *promises on policy*, describes a quasi-pecuniary side payment typical for political negotiations. One can imagine the following scenario: a political government issues a proposal on a law to be passed. The leader of a coalition, either in favor or against the proposed law, may easily unite all those who intend to influence the political decision-making process according to their common interests. If the government adopts these interests, the leader has no incentive to attract his followers any longer, unless a new proposal arises with which similar strategies can be pursued. This leads to the fourth group, *promises about subsequent decisions*, which argues that the leader will maintain a similar role in the future: »The institutional leader (for example the majority leader), who is expected to lead in the future, can believably offer promises about anticipated decisions, while the occasional leader usually cannot« (Riker, 1962: 113). The last group, *payments of emotional satisfaction*, describes what Weber labelled as a leader's *charisma*, which gives followers the feeling that every proposal is correct and thus should be adopted.

A different approach to the question of why individuals join political organizations is pursued by Morales (2009). The central goal of her research is to identify why some people actively participate in politics while others prefer not to get involved. She focuses on political membership and its variations in different western democracies. Relying on the results reported in literature on new social movements, she analyzes the effects of two potential determinants, namely, on the one hand, the »institutional configurations related to political opportunity structures«, and, on the other hand, the »patterns of political mobilisation« (Morales, 2009: 1). By introducing these two variables, she also contradicts studies which rely solely on individual attributes as the driving force for political activity. In her results, Morales admits that although personal characteristics indeed do play a role in a citizen's decision for political membership, one especially has to take into account the social and political context in which the citizens operate in order to achieve a comprehensive understanding of their actions. These structural forces also serve to explain the varying forms of political membership that can be identified across different nations. C. Mahoney (2008) analyzes the impact of institutions, issues, and interests on actors' decisions to join a coalition. Her empirical findings reveal that »institutional explanations are only part of the story« (Mahoney, C., 2008: 182). In addition, issue characteristics, such as the degree of conflict, the salience of an issue and its scope, and the type of interests represented by the organization that joins a coalition are decisive.

Another prominent work with regard to coalition-formation which serves as a major theoretical component of this work is the literature of Sabatier and Jenkins-Smith (1988; 1993; 1999; further developed by Sabatier and Weible, 2007). According to their Advocacy Coalition Framework (ACF), actors form coalitions within existing policy subsystems in order to pursue a common aim based on a collectively shared belief system. Participants of an advocacy coalition can, for example, be members of political parties, interest groups, elected political representatives, experts, researchers or journalists. This means that membership is not restricted to any political or societal level and also goes beyond the dimensions of the so called *iron triangle* of legislators, agency officials and interest group representatives (Sabatier and Weible, 2007: 192). On the basis of its common belief system, an advocacy coalition attempts to influence the policy process and to translate the joint beliefs of its members into a specific policy outcome.

The ACF was revised in 1993 and 1999. As a result of various case studies made by the authors themselves as well as other researchers, in the succeeding years additional important modifications have been conducted. The following remarks summarize the main assumptions of the ACF as formulated in 1999, taking into account the most important revisions made since then.
The basic assumptions are (Sabatier and Weible, 2007: 191-192):

> (1) »a macro-level assumption that most policy-making occurs among specialists within a policy subsystem but that their behavior is affected by factors in the broader political and socio-economic system«;
> (2) »a micro-level 'model of the individual' that is drawn heavily from social psychology«;
> (3) »a meso-level conviction that the best way to deal with the multiplicity of actors in a subsystem is to aggregate them into 'advocacy coalitions'«.

These propositions deserve further attention. With regard to the first assumption, a *subsystem*, on the one hand, is determined by a *functional* or *substantive* dimension, which refers to the content of a specific policy. On the other hand, it is defined by a *territorial* dimension, which specifies the region in which the negotiated policy will be applied (Sabatier and Weible, 2007: 192). An important distinction is made between *mature* and *nascent* subsystems, with the former being defined by its existence over an extended period. This means that institutions with well established specialized subunits exist within theses subsystems and experienced actors such as interest groups have emerged after several years of seeking to influence the policy process (Sabatier and Weible, 2007: 192). Examples of mature subsystems can be found within the Organization for Economic Cooperation and Development (OECD) where most policy fields fulfil these criteria. Nascent subsystems, in contrast, can be described as still being in the process of forming. These are common in developing countries, where »the instability of the broader political system« and »the lack of trained personnel« hamper the establishment of institutions and the long-term organization of public actors (Sabatier and Weible, 2007: 193).

The second assumption formulates a specific model of the individual derived from social psychology (Sabatier and Weible, 2007: 192). In contrast to rational choice frameworks, which explain actors' decisions as the result of rational cost-benefit-calculations (Ostrom, 2007), the ACF assumes that although individuals are rationally motivated, their rationality is bounded by their cognitive constraints. Consequently, individuals »filter perceptions through their belief system« (Weible and Sabatier, 2007: 127). This theoretical conflict is reflected in the distinction between *logic of appropriateness*, according to which people do what they consider to be appropriate in the context of existing norms, and *logic of consequences*, which emphasizes that people rationally consider the expected consequences of their actions (March and Olsen, 1996).

With regard to actors' perceptions, the ACF differentiates between three hierarchical levels of beliefs (Sabatier and Weible, 2007: 194-196): At a broad level are *deep core beliefs* which consist of general opinions about normative questions, for example democratic and economic principles. At the second level are *policy core beliefs* which define how to translate the deep core beliefs into practice. Examples include the evaluation of the importance of different policy-related values or policy problems in the subsystem, attitudes towards the allocation of authority between government and market, and the function of the public in the policy process. It is assumed that advocacy coalitions can be identified by as little as two or three joint policy core beliefs, as these represent fundamental choices and are not changed voluntarily (Sabatier and Weible, 2007: 195). However, as the authors admit, one should be aware that advocacy coalitions are not always easy to identify due to the fact that a clear division between one coalition and another one may not always be obvious and policy core beliefs might not always correspond to deep core beliefs. Related to the policy core beliefs, Sabatier and Weible specified the category of *policy core policy preferences* as »the stickiest glue that binds coalitions together« (Sabatier and Weible, 2007: 195). Policy core policy preferences are beliefs that are »subsystemwide in scope«, »highly salient«, and that have been »major sources of cleavages for some time« (Sabatier and Jenkins-Smith, 1999: 134). Thus, policy core policy preferences create a vision of how the subsystem ought to be, and, consequently, determine a coalition's strategic direction as opposed to those of its antagonists. Finally, the last level of the belief system consists of *secondary beliefs*, which include detailed rules and guidelines. As they are »narrower in scope than policy core beliefs, changing them requires less evidence and fewer agreements among subsystem actors and thus should be less difficult« (Sabatier and Weible, 2007: 196).

State of research

The third basic assumption of the ACF was formulated to recognize the growing »importance of interpersonal relations« for explaining human behavior (Sabatier and Weible, 2007: 196). It assumes that policy-making is largely determined by networks of various policy participants that are concerned with a specific issue. In order to be able to successfully influence the policy outcome, these policy participants have to seek allies with similar goals, additional resources, and complementary strategies. Thus, the aggregation of multiple actors within a subsystem into advocacy coalitions is the most reasonable approach (Sabatier and Weible, 2007: 196).

Despite its value for social science analyses, the authors are also aware of the shortcomings of their approach. These exist, for example, in its inability to explain why some actors decide to actively participate within a coalition while others prefer to benefit as *free-riders* from the coalition's achievement of collective goods (Sabatier and Weible, 2007: 197). Related to the free-rider problem is the conflict that exists between scholars with regard to the impact of material self-interest in contrast to the impact of norms and beliefs on social behavior as reflected in the discussion between theorists of liberal intergovernmentalism and constructivist approaches (see for example Fearon and Wendt, 2001; Moravcsik, 1993; 1997; Wendt, 1999; Risse, 2004). Though Jenkins-Smith and St. Clair (1993), based on their previous research, assume that material self-interest constitutes a factor that is much more relevant for *material* groups than for *purposive* groups, the question nevertheless remains if the two types of groups and their motivations can be so clearly distinguished from one another.

Several authors have adopted the ACF for their own case studies. Kriesi and Jegen (2000) analyzed the choices made by political elites in the field of the Swiss energy policy. They conclude that these choices are based on either *value-rational* or *instrumentally rational* considerations. This indicates that different types of rationality are not exclusive, but rather complement each other (Kriesi and Jegen, 2000: 21). This work contributes to the discussion above with respect to the dominant model of the individual assumed in the different approaches to the topic.

Sewell (2005) used the ACF to analyze the development of negotiations surrounding the United Nations Framework Convention on Climate Change (UNFCCC) and the implementation process of international agreements in the United States, the Netherlands, and Japan. He analyzed the determinants of an advocacy coalition's power in international negotiations and thereby focused on actors' resource dependency. In order to find out to what extent resources influence the power of an advocacy coalition within a subsystem, referring to Kelman (1987), he defines a set of five resource types, which consist of *decision-making authority, ability to offer inducements, persuasiveness, deference,* and *strategic skill* (Sewell, 2005: 13). These are tested for their potential as sources of political power, as in »the context of the ACF, a coalition's possession of the various sources of power ultimately defines the range and effectiveness of the various strategies, approaches and tools (guidance instruments) that it can employ in the pursuit of its objectives« (Sewell, 2005: 13). However, as he stresses, the fact that an advocacy coalition has the power to initiate policy change within a subsystem at the international level does not necessarily imply that policy change can also be induced at the national level:

> »If the effective implementation of an international treaty requires the convergence of beliefs among all of the coalitions dominating each of the overlapping international, national, and sub-national subsystems, one can understand why treaty implementation is so difficult, and why »involuntary defection« poses a significant problem« (Sewell, 2005: 208).

Princen (2007) analyzed the impact the governance structures within a multi-level system have on the relations between the state and its society. He argues that the division between state actors and societal actors does not mirror the existing constellations in the policy process. Rather he prefers to differentiate between different kinds of advocacy coalitions in which various actors - state as well as societal representatives - cooperate in order to communicate their ideas and interests. His central question focuses on the factors that determine the shift in the power relations between the coalitions involved, which he illustrates through two case studies concerned with the anti-smoking and the alcoholism policies pursued by the European Union and the World Health Organization. According to his results, international governance structures in the form of *political opportunity structures* and the *types of policy outputs* indeed have a considerable impact on the power relations between the advocacy coalitions within a subsystem. Furthermore, the *organizational capacities* of the members of an advocacy coalition largely determine its success (Princen, 2007: 29).

3.4 Approaches to collective action and social movements

One of the predecessors of present approaches to advocacy coalitions and social movements (for the latter see below) is Olson's theory of collective action (Olson, 1965) in which he attempts to explain why rational actors decide to act jointly in order to achieve a common goal. Collective action can be defined as »the investment of resources by individuals or organisations and the bringing together of these individuals or organisations in the collective pursuit of a common interest, which may result in selective or collective benefits« (Aspinwall and Greenwood, 1998a: 11). Four elements of this definition must be emphasized: first, the resources invested by the actors involved, either time or money; second, the actors' willingness to join a formal or informal movement or organization indicates their commitment to a common goal; third, the common interest of the members of this movement or organization, which must be determined such that it does not contradict the individual interests of each member; and finally fourth, the selective or collective benefits which are expected to be provided as a result of collective action.

Olson (1965) initially elaborates on the function of organizations and assumes that they serve to further the common interests of its members. The phrase common interest is crucial to his theory, as one can expect that the members of an organization also have individual self-interests that influence their actions. However, these self-interests, according to Olson, are why it is generally unlikely that rational actors decide to act jointly in order to pursue a common goal:

> »Indeed, unless the number of individuals in a group is quite small, or unless there is coercion or some other special device to make individuals act in their common interest, rational, self-interested individuals will not act to achieve their common or group interests« (Olson, 1965: 2).

This hypothesis can be illustrated by an example which relates to the behavior of the citizens of a nation state: one can assume that all citizens have a common interest in the effectiveness of state institutions – they call for democratic government, an efficient administrative body, an encompassing social security system and a fair judicial system. However, if a government would leave it to the people to decide how much they were personally willing to invest for the provision of these collective goods, the costs would be distributed quite unfairly:

> »The basic and most elementary goods or services provided by government, like defense and policy protection, and the system of law and order generally, are such that they go to everyone or practically everyone in the nation« and it would »obviously not be feasible, if indeed it were possible, to deny the protection provided by the military services, the police, and the courts to those who did not voluntarily pay their share of the costs of government« (Olson, 1965: 14).

Clearly, as each individual can benefit from collective goods regardless of whether he invests his own resources or not, it does not make sense, at least from a rational point of view, to pay for their provision. The result would be that those people who feel morally obliged would make their contribution, while others would simply enjoy the benefits of state institutions (→ for further discussion on the *free-rider problem* see Sabatier and Weible, 2007: 197).

In a group as large as a nation state, the voluntary contribution of an individual citizen is almost invisible. In contrast, in a small group one can easily reconstruct who has invested resources, who benefits from the provided goods and to what extent. As a consequence, in small groups mechanisms exist that allow free-riders to be automatically excluded from the group by the other members. To avoid the free-rider problem, large groups have two possibilities: either they must force citizens to make contributions (for example through the introduction of taxes in the nation state) or they must provide additional incentives which are only available

Collective action and social movements

to those who act collectively. Under these conditions, according to Olson, collective action can also be ensured in large groups.

Olson's logic of collective action is based on Samuelson's theory of government expenditure on collective consumption goods. Samuelson (1954) argued that even if public goods are made available to one person, they can be utilized by others at no additional cost. This is what the author calls the *jointness of demand* (Samuelson, 1954: 389), implying that the consumption of a public good by one person does not affect another persons' ability to consume the good to the same extent.

Collective action is also a central theme in the work of Marx and McAdams (1994). In their book they attempted to shed light on central elements which are related to this concept. Accordingly, *collective behavior* is described as a general term which includes any group behavior that can be observed within a society (Marx and McAdams, 1994: 2). Closely related is the question of what constitutes a group. Marx and McAdams define collective or general group behavior by comparing it to (mature) social movements and identify three aspects that distinguish both categories from one another: The first is that while collective behavior can be characterized by its noninstitutionalized structures, social movements rely heavily on »established cultural guidelines« (Marx and McAdams, 1994: 72). This goes hand in hand with the second element, the spontaneous nature of collective behavior in contrast to the well-planned nature of social movements. The third element concerns the duration of collective behavior and social movements:

> »While the vast majority of social movements die aborning, the successful ones can last for years or even decades. Even then, many of the social movements do not so much disappear as become incorporated into the institutional life of society« (Marx and McAdams, 1994: 72).

Following this understanding, social movements are often regarded as the origin of formal organizations. One of the often referred to definitions of social movements is quoted from Tilly (1984). He describes a social movement as:

> »[...] a sustained series of interactions between power-holders and persons successfully claiming to speak on behalf of a constituency lacking formal representation, in the course of which those persons make publicly visible demands for change in the distribution or exercise of power, and back those demands with public demonstrations of support« (Tilly, 1984: 306).

What is striking in this definition is the lack of formal representation as a central characteristic, which coincides with the proposition that social movements can be the origin of formal organizations but cannot be initially identified with one organization.

Concerning the question of what leads to the emergence of a social movement, various perspectives exist, some of which are summarized here (Marx and McAdams, 1994: 78 ff.). The first are the so-called *strain theories*, which assume that social movements arise out of strain in society. As such, social movements are the result of people's attempts to manage the challenges of their daily lives which they can no longer cope with on an individual basis. A second related perspective emphasizes the impact of resource-mobilization as a determinant of the emergence of social movements (McCarthy and Zald, 1977). The authors argue that there is always strain in society and, thus, this cannot serve as an explanation for people taking action. Instead, the emergence of social movements depends on whether individuals are able to mobilize resources that are required to launch the movement. They consider the following aspects to be relevant: a) societal support and constraint, b) the variety of resources to be mobilized, c) linkage between social movements and other groups, d) external support as condition for the movement's success, and e) the strategies applied by authorities to control the movement (McCarthy and Zald, 1977: 1213). By emphasizing these conditions, the authors depart from the assumptions of other theories, which rely mainly on psychological motivations for collective behavior. A third perspective to be mentioned here is political-process theory, which focuses on the power relations within a social system which provide access to some actors while excluding others (Marx and McAdams, 1994: 83). This branch is closely related to the literature on political opportunity structures, which describes the impact of so-called *windows of opportunity* on the assertiveness of political groups (Kitschelt, 1986). An analysis of the interrelations between a movement and its environment was conducted by Jenkins and Perrow (1977) exploring the case of the U.S. farm workers' movement in the late 1960s. They conclude that the farm workers at that time were successful in pushing the government towards reform of the status quo because an »altered political environment« existed »in which the challenge operated«. This change in the environment originated »in economic trends and political realignments that took place quite independent of any 'push' from insurgents« (Jenkins and Perrow, 1997: 263-266).

How do these remarks on collective action and social movements relate to the issue of the formation of networks and coalitions? Della Porta and Caiani (2009) define social movements as »dense informal networks of collective actors involved in conflictual relations with clearly identified opponents, which share a distinct collective identity, using mainly protests as their modus operandi« (della Porta and Caiani, 2009: 6). This understanding is close to how Diani and Bison define social movements: for them social movements are »networks of informal interactions between a plurality of individuals, groups, or associations, engaged in political or cultural conflict, on the basis of a shared collective identity« (Diani and Bison, 2004: 282; see also: Diani, 1992: 13). In order to clarify the central theme of their analysis, Diani and Bison present a very useful overview of how to differentiate between social movements and other collective action processes. The analysis of collective action processes along three dimensions leads to the categories presented in Table 11.

Table 11: Collective action processes (based on Diani and Bison, 2004)

Collective action processes		
Social movements	Adversarial coalitions	Organizational action
- Often conflictual orientations; identified social and political opponents	- Often conflictual orientations; opponents explicitly identified	- Often conflict between different organizations
- Dense informal inter-organizational networks, but unstable membership criteria	- Collective actors densely connected; actors share resources to achieve goals as long as it is necessary	- Low density of networks; exchange largely within organization; some established membership criteria
- Actors linked by solidarities and shared identities	- Actors not backed by strong identity links; purely instrumental	- Weak identity links between actors

The three dimensions are the following:

- »presence or absence of conflictual orientations to clearly identified opponents«;
- »dense or sparse informal exchanges between individuals or organizations engaged in collective projects«;
- »strong or weak collective identity between members of those networks« (Diani and Bison, 2004: 282-283).

According to Diani and Bison, all of these collective action processes can be considered as types of networks. In this work the term network is too broad to describe the forms of collective action that are central to the investigation, namely the formation of coalitions in the field of European energy policy. Importantly, coalitions can also be established among members of a larger network. What additionally distinguishes them from mere networks is that they can be formed on an ad hoc-basis (see especially Pijnenburg, 1998) with regard to a single issue for a limited period, while networks are generally perceived as being concerned with more than just one specific topic and often persistent over time.

3.5 The role of institutions in the policy process

The role of institutions in the policy process has been widely discussed in the literature. However, to be able to fully understand the impact of institutions on actors, interactions, and policy outcomes, it must be clarified what exactly is implied

State of research

by this term and how it is understood in this work. Hall and Taylor (1996) categorized different institutionalist approaches that all fall under *new institutionalism*. However, as the authors stress, this new institutionalism actually includes at least three different theoretical approaches, namely *historical institutionalism, rational choice institutionalism*, and *sociological institutionalism*.

Beginning with the first case, historical institutionalism, institutions, often associated with organizations, are defined as »formal or informal procedures, routines, norms and conventions embedded in the organizational structure of the polity or political economy« (Hall and Taylor, 1996: 6). Four characteristics are described as essential for historical institutionalism: First, the relationship between the institutions and the behavior of the individual is »conceptualized in broad terms«. This implies that two perspectives on individual behavior exist. Following a calculus approach, individuals act strategically in order to maximize their benefit. Institutions affect individuals' behavior by providing a degree of certainty about how other actors will behave. In contrast, a cultural approach assumes that actors' strategic behavior is limited by subjective interpretations and established patterns. Institutions in this context provide a template for action (Hall and Taylor, 1996: 8). Second, historical institutionalists are »especially attentive to the way in which institutions distribute power unevenly across social groups« (Hall and Taylor, 1996: 9). Institutions affect the power relations between social groups by, for example, granting specific actors disproportionate access to the decision-making process while excluding others. As a third characteristic, historical institutionalism is concerned with the role of a certain degree of path dependence. This does not necessarily mean that the same forces always lead to the same outcome, but rather that »the effect of such forces will be mediated by the contextual features of a given situation often inherited from the past« (Hall and Taylor, 1996: 9). Finally, though historical institutionalists describe institutions as being highly important for structuring political life, they do not neglect the role of other factors, such as socioeconomic developments, ideas, or beliefs (Hall and Taylor, 1996: 10).

Rational choice institutionalism (see for example North, 1990) developed almost concurrently with historical institutionalism. The first of its main assumptions is concerned with actors' motivation for action. It is assumed that they have fixed preferences and behave entirely strategically in order to maximize their personal gains (Hall and Taylor, 1996: 12). The role of institutions in this context is to »structure such interactions, by affecting the range and sequence of alternatives on the choice-agenda or by providing information and enforcement mechanisms that reduce uncertainty about the corresponding behavior of others« (Hall and Taylor, 1996: 12). The second characteristic refers to the image of politics: rational choice institutionalists »tend to see politics as a series of collective action dilemmas« (Hall and Taylor, 1996: 12). These occur due to the fact that actors' efforts to realize their own preferences lead to collectively suboptimal outcomes: »Typically, what prevents the actors from taking a collectively-superior course of action is the absence of institutional arrangements that would guarantee complementary behavior by others« (Hall and Taylor, 1996: 12). These explanations for coordination problems have become widely known as the *prisoner's dilemma* and the *tragedy of the commons* in Game Theory (Scharpf, 1997). As an additional attribute, rational choice institutionalists have distinctive explanations for the origin of institutions. Accordingly, actors voluntarily create institutions for their own purposes (Hall and Taylor, 1996: 13).

The third category, known as sociological institutionalism, developed towards the end of the 1970s within the subfield of the organizational theory. Following this perspective, institutions do not only include formal rules and norms, but also »symbol systems, cognitive scripts, and moral templates that provide the 'frames of meaning' guiding human action« (Hall and Taylor, 1996: 14). As a second characteristic, sociological institutionalism follows the cultural approach referred to above concerning the relationship between institutions and individual action: »Institutions influence behavior not simply by specifying what one should do but also by specifying what one can imagine oneself doing in a given context« (Hall and Taylor, 1996: 15). This understanding of institutions reflects elements of social constructivism. Concerning the question of how institutions originate and change, sociological institutionalists argue that an institution »enhances the social legitimacy of the organization or its participants« (Hall and Taylor, 1996: 16). This is in clear contrast to what rational institutionalists claim when emphasizing the efficiency resulting from institutional arrangements.

Despite the differences between the three branches, overlaps do exist. Garrett and Weingast (1993; in: Hall and Taylor, 1996), for example, acknowledge that institutional norms may serve as a *focal point* for rational actors. What all forms of institutionalism have in common is the assumption that »rules and systems of rules in any historically given society not only organize and regulate social behavior but make it understandable and, in a limited conditional sense, predictable for those sharing in rule knowledge« (Burns, Baumgartner and Deville, 1985: 256; in: Scharpf, 1997: 40). This is also applicable to the work of Mayntz and Scharpf referred to below.

Mayntz and Scharpf (1995a; Scharpf, 1997) combine actor-centered and institution-centered theories in their attempt contribute to the central concern of political science and political sociology: the »understanding and the improvement of the conditions under which politics is able to produce effective and legitimate solutions to policy problems« (Scharpf, 1997: 1). They state:

> »The approach proceeds from the assumption that social phenomena are to be explained as the outcome of interactions among intentional actors – individual, collective, or corporate actors, that is – but that these interactions are structured, and the outcomes shaped, by the characteristics of the institutional settings within which they occur« (Scharpf, 1997: 1).

State of research

Some elements underlying this assumption require clarification: First, the *intentional actors* whose interactions lead to a specific outcome. *Intentional* in this context implies that actors are not driven by mere natural impulses but that they follow certain intentions. What further characterizes actors are their *capabilities*, including personal properties, physical resources, technological capabilities, and those that are created by the institutional setting and reflected in the competencies or the participatory rights (Scharpf, 1997: 43). *Orientation*, as the third characteristic of actors, covers perceptions and preferences that are either changeable through persuasion and learning processes or stable over time (Scharpf, 1997: 43). The emphasis on perceptions indicates that actors' intentions do not only emerge form pure objective knowledge. Rather, individuals also act according to how they perceive reality and which consequences they expect from their intended action: »Intentional action, in other words, cannot be described and explained without reference to the subjective 'meaning' that this action has for the actor in question« (Scharpf, 1997: 19). Scharpf argues that it can neither be assumed - as done in neoclassical economics or in the neorealist theory – that actors derive their goals from mere cost-benefit calculations, nor that actors only follow cultural norms – as done by some sub-forms of sociological theory. This proposition reflects Scharpf's understanding of *institutions* as the second decisive element of the approach: the definition of institutions does not only include »formal legal rules that are sanctioned by the course system«, but also »social norms that actors will generally respect and whose violation will be sanctioned by loss of reputation, social disapproval, withdrawal of cooperation and rewards, or even ostracism« (Scharpf, 1997: 38).

Actors rarely act alone, choosing instead to interact with others in order to find solutions to policy problems. This means that they are not able to predict an outcome on the basis of their own perceptions and preferences. This dilemma is captured by the term *actor constellations*, which describes »the players involved, their strategy option, the outcomes associated with the strategy combinations, and the preferences of the players over these outcomes« (Scharpf, 1997: 44). Depending on a policy problem, the actors that are concerned with it, their preferences, expectations and strategies, an actor can be engaged in varying actor constellations, which then have a different effect on the actor's ability to realize his intentions in the final outcome. Important in this context are also the *modes of interaction*, ranging from *unilateral action* to *negotiated agreements, majority votes* and finally *hierarchical direction* (Scharpf, 1997: 46). These modes are primarily determined by institutional rules.

According to Scharpf, by combining the analysis of actor constellations with information about the dominant modes of interaction, scholars are able to create a

Institutions

highly useful analytical tool for explaining policy outcomes. In addition, conclusions can be drawn on the ability of different institutional structures to effectively solve different kinds of policy problems (Scharpf, 1997: 49).

Figure 7 illustrates how the central elements of the actor-centered institutionalism are interconnected.

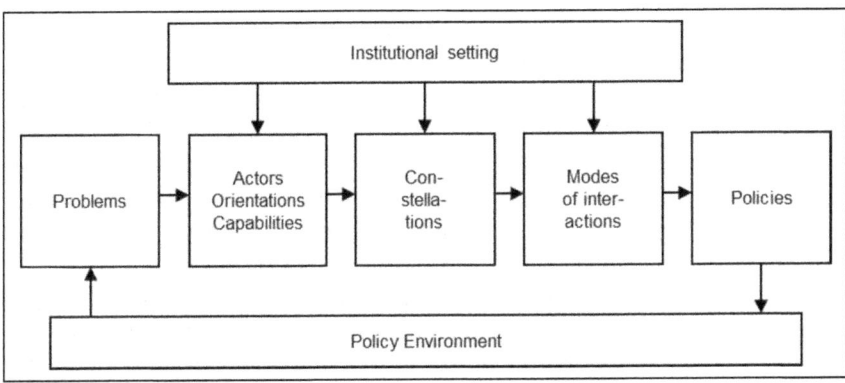

Figure 7: The domain of interaction-oriented policy research (Scharpf, 1997: 44)

Scharpf uses game-theoretic models as analytical tools for his analyses. In doing so, he is able to bridge the gap between game theorists and empirical policy researchers. This work adopts some of the basic assumptions made by Scharpf, however without using game theory in the empirical section.

Closely related to institutionalist approaches is the concept of *political opportunity structures* (POS). The concept of political opportunity structures was developed in the 1960s and 1970s as a part of the literature on collective action and social movements (see for example Lipsky, 1968 and Eisinger, 1973). Kitschelt (1986) defines POS as »specific configurations of resources, institutional arrangements and historical precedents for social mobilisation, which facilitate the development of protest movements in some instances and constrain them in others« (Kitschelt, 1986: 58). In his study on the anti-nuclear movements in France, Sweden, the United States and West Germany, he illustrates that the political opportunity structures in each country determined the movements' strategies and their impact on the national energy policy. He distinguishes between three characteristics of political opportunity structures: First, the mobilization of a movement depends on the »coercive, normative, remunerative and informal resources« (Kitschelt, 1986: 61) that a movement can make use of. Second, the institutional setting, such as »reinforcing patterns of interaction between government and interest groups, and electoral law« (Kitschelt, 1986: 61) determines the access of

95

State of research

movements to the public and political sphere. These are also described as the *institutional* opportunity structure or *political regimes*. Third, a movement is influenced by »opportunities to mobilize protest that change over time« (Kitschelt, 1986: 62). This last category implies what Kitschelt calls a *demonstration effect*: the formation or disintegration of a movement can encourage other movements to behave similarly.

Tarrow (1991) considers the degree to which a political system grants access to groups that intend to participate in the decision-making process as most important. Furthermore, the stability or instability of political constellations is taken into account. Third, the existence of influential allies and, fourth, political conflicts within and among elites are decisive. While the first three aspects are concerned with the institutional setting, the last one refers to the power relations. All of these political opportunity structures are assumed to particularly encourage groups that lack proper representation to engage in protest:

> »Political opportunities cannot make the poor conscious of grievances of which they were formerly unaware, but it can help them to detect where and how the system is most vulnerable, enabling them to overcome their habitual disunity and lack of information« (Tarrow, 1991: 36).

Kriesi narrows these four elements of a political system down to three that he regards as useful for the analysis of the impact of political opportunity structures on social movements: the »formal institutional structure«, the »informal procedures and prevailing strategies with regard to challengers«, and the »configuration of power relevant for the confrontation with challengers« (Kriesi, 1995: 168). The formal institutional structure refers to the openness of a political system to input and its ability to successfully cope with existing problems (output). The informal procedures include shared understandings of the policy process that guide decision-making. Authorities can pursue either exclusive or integrative strategies, with the choice of strategy being largely dependent on a country's tradition of how to deal with so-called challengers of the system. The configuration of power especially refers to the distribution of power among political parties and intervenes between the formal structure and the informal procedures: »It modifies the openness of access channels and the system's capacity to act and it modulates the general strategic legacy« (Kriesi, 1995: 180).

Sabatier and Weible also contributed to the literature on political opportunity structures. They responded to the various criticisms that the early version of the ACF had to face - especially in regard to its pluralist assumptions - and revised the typology in order to also include the characteristics of European corporatist regimes. Originally, the ACF assumed that interest groups are well organized while political parties are weak and that a variety of access possibilities exist to influence the policy-process (Sabatier and Jenkins-Smith, 1988; Sabatier and Weible, 2007). Later, a new variable was introduced labelled *coalition opportunity structures*,

Institutions

which - in accordance with Lijphart (1999) -describes »the degree of consensus needed for major policy change« and »the openness of political systems« (Sabatier and Weible, 2007: 200). The first aspect implies that if a high degree of consensus is required, a coalition should include as many actors as possible. In so doing, conflict can be minimized and compromise more easily achieved. The second aspect addresses the variety of decision-making venues and their accessibility.

Princen and Kerremans (2008) analyzed the degree to which political opportunity structures and the strategies pursued by interest groups in the EU multi-level system are perceived as mutually dependent in the social sciences. The authors themselves define political opportunity structures as a »set of characteristics of a given institution that determines the relative ability of (outside) groups to influence decision-making within that institution« (Princen and Kerremans, 2008: 1130). In their approach, Princen and Kerremans review how different strands in the literature conceptualize political opportunity structures. They identify two perspectives: one that describes opportunity structures as objective conditions that are taken for granted and another one that, vice versa, views opportunity structures as not just a given but also as a result of the political process (Princen and Kerremans, 2008: 1142-1143).

As demonstrated above, the literature on political opportunity structures contributes to a better understanding of a) why some groups are granted access to the political decision-makers while others are not, b) what kinds of strategies different actors can pursue to influence the decision-making process, c) which policy outcomes are likely to result from the interaction with groups, and d) under what conditions interest group activity and opportunity structures are mutually constitutive. Thus, the literature on political and especially the institutional opportunity structures provides many valuable insights. Chapter 3.7 describes further approaches to the impact of political opportunity structures on actors' access to and influence on the policy process.

3.6 Literature on actors' strategies to influence political decision-making

Different studies have explored the strategies of interest groups in the European multi-level system in great detail. What can be described as basic concern from an organization's point of view can be summarized under the key word *organizational maintenance*. This can be considered a central goal that the leaders of an organization must keep in mind while considering which strategies might be useful to influence the policy process. The question that arises in this context is what determines the continued existence or decline of groups and which strategies can be pursued in order to ensure a group's maintenance. Salisbury (1969) emphasizes the need for a sufficient balance between the benefits group members receive from their membership and the return or profit group leaders gain as outcome of their investment:

> »Briefly, the argument is that interest group origins, growth, death, and associated lobbying activity may all be better explained if we regard them as exchange relationships between entrepreneurs/organizers, who invest capital in a set of benefits, which they offer to prospective members at a price-membership« (Salisbury, 1992: 4).

In contrast, Walker (1983) argues that »the maintenance of groups depends even more upon the success of group leaders in securing funds from outside their membership which are needed to keep the groups in operation« (Walker, 1983: 390).

To answer the question of why certain coalition partners are selected, considerations about organizational maintenance must also be taken into account. Coalition partners have to be chosen by the association leaders with the consent of their members to ensure their ongoing financial support.

At this point, the question arises of which additional characteristics potentially successful lobbying strategies must fulfil and how these are categorized in the literature. Interest groups that try to influence the European decision-making process usually engage in comprehensive lobbying strategies. Lobbyists and the European institutions, above all the European Commission, have a mutual interest in establishing stable relations in order to exchange information. According to Lahusen and Jauß (2001), to be successful interest groups should lobby at different levels (*multi-level strategy*) and include various potential addressees (*multi-voice strategy*). Closely related are analyses that characterize the strategies interests groups pursue as *multi-level venue-shopping*. This term describes an attempt to make use of multiple access points which are expected to maximize an interest group's chance to assert its interests (Mazey and Richardson, 1996). The concept of venue-shopping was developed by Baumgartner and Jones (1991) who studied civilian nuclear policy in the USA. They define venue-shopping as a strategy that »relies less on mass mobilization and more on the dual strategy of the presentation of image and the search for a more receptive political venue« (Baumgartner and Jones, 1991: 1050). This argument is reflected in Beyers' *compensation hypothesis*. He assumes that if interest groups lack access to the domestic level, they try to compensate for this disadvantage by addressing the European level: »In other words, European network strategies can compensate for the lack of domestic access and may be pursued by societal interests that are domestically weak« (Beyers, 2002: 592).

The impact of the institutional setting on interest group strategies has also been addressed by Beyers (2004). In his work he focuses on the political practices of European interest associations. He analyzes the determinants of interest groups' strategies including two different points of view. On the one hand he refers to the impact resources have on actors' choices of strategies, on the other hand he questions the effect of the institutional setting on the way actors try to communicate

Strategies to influence political decision-making

their interests. Resources are taken into account as the survival of interest groups in the European multi-level governance system at least partly depends on their financial endowment. Thus, »costly and inefficient strategies are avoided« (Beyers, 2004: 212). However, in contrast to resource-based explanations, Beyers prefers to adopt the institutionalist perspective. From this point of view, »institutional variability leads to incentives and constraints that influence the emergence of particular political practices« (Beyers, 2004: 212; see also: Aspinwall and Schneider, 2000). Consequently, the author differentiates between two different influence strategies, namely *voice* and *access*, which are assumed to result from the institutional incentives. The first type refers to »public political strategies, such as media campaigns or protests« and is further subdivided into *information politics* and *protest politics*. The second category implies direct access to the »venues where political bargaining takes place«, a system of »advisory bodies, technical committees, agencies and, to some extent, parliamentary committees« which the public is largely excluded from (Beyers, 2004: 213). The latter can also be equated with *inside lobbying* (Broscheid and Coen, 2003). Comparing these strategies, Beyers concludes that both – voice and access strategies – are not only used separately, but also in combination with each other (Beyers, 2004: 234). He stresses that the »claim that interest associations avoid public activism because this does not fit with the presumed technocratic nature of the European regulatory polity« could be definitively rejected in his study. How and why voice and access strategies were linked was mainly determined by institutional factors. For example, the data showed that diffuse interests were more successful in gaining access to the European Parliament than to the European Commission, while specific interests gained access to the European Commission. In addition, the hypothesis »gaining access to the EP has a strong positive effect on voice« among diffuse interests was supported by the findings. However, when it came to voice strategies, primarily information politics instead of protest politics were used (for a description of protest politics see also: Imig and Tarrow, 2001). Furthermore, Beyers distinguishes between strategies aiming at influencing the European Commission cabinets, which are mainly responsible for political advice, and the Directorates General, which, above all, are concerned with questions of technical realization. Especially diffuse interests tended to combine access and voice strategies when addressing the European Commission cabinets (as well as the EP and the Council) (Beyers, 2004:232). When addressing the Directorates-General, actors combined access with voice strategies more infrequently; specific interests tended to avoid voice strategies completely (Beyers, 2004:235).

The differentiation between access and voice strategies also resembles the categories used by C. Mahoney (2008). She distinguishes between *inside* and *outside lobbying* tactics. While the first term summarizes all strategies which include »participating in hearings, consultations, and stakeholder meetings; drafting legislation and amendments; sending position papers, letters and faxes; meeting with policy-makers one-on-one and with their staff; organizing cocktail parties, seminars, and conferences« (Mahoney, 2008: 127), the second captures those activities that are used to increase public attention in order to influence policy-makers indirectly, such as the use of different communication media (Mahoney, 2008: 147). Beyers, Eising and Maloney (2008) attempt to attribute insider and outsider strategies to different stages. In nascent stages of development, interest groups pursue outsider strategies. As soon as groups have obtained more experience and acquired sufficient resources, they are more likely to seek and also gain direct access to the policy process. However, »established groups specialised in insider strategies may turn to outsider strategies when their insider position and the related policy monopoly comes under pressure as a result of successful mobilisation by outsiders' developments within a policy area« (Beyers, Eising and Maloney, 2008: 1121).

In the context of multi-level venue-shopping, different ways of issue-framing are also analyzed in the literature. As Mazey and Richardson (1997) emphasize, when addressing political institutions interest groups tend to frame their positions in a way that is consistent with their own preferences. One example is that business groups often stress the impact of a certain policy initiative on the competitiveness of their own industry and, in so doing, imply that the realization of this policy initiative may affect the overall sector in terms of revenues and the potential to preserve jobs. During the policy process, some groups then tend to reformulate their position in order to enhance their chance of achieving their goals.

3.7 Studies on the determinants of the access and influence of interest groups

In various studies scholars have tried to develop models to answer the question of why particular interest groups indeed have influence on the European policy process and are able to initiate policy change. As the ACF is one of the core theoretical approaches guiding this work, this subsection begins by considering how the authors approach the question of interest group influence.

When Sabatier and Jenkins-Smith and later Sabatier and Weible discuss the determinants of major policy change, the questions arise of what is actually meant by the term policy change and how policy change can be achieved on the basis of the assumptions made in the ACF. Sabatier and Weible (2007: 198) point to »a degree of belief change among some of the policy participants or a replacement of a dominant coalition by a minor coalition« as the precondition for policy change. Similarly, Sabatier and Jenkins-Smith (1999) distinguish between minor and major policy change. While the former is regarded as the consequence of changes solely to secondary beliefs, the latter refers to a change in long-established and deeply rooted policy core beliefs.

The ACF originally assumed (Sabatier and Jenkins-Smith: 1988) that it is unlikely to initiate changes from within the system, as deep core beliefs and policy core beliefs are relatively stable and constant over time. In the early version of the ACF, only two possibilities are described which could potentially lead to policy change: *policy-oriented learning* and *external perturbations* or *shocks* (Sabatier and Jenkins-Smith, 1999; Sabatier and Weible, 2007). In the later version of the ACF (Sabatier and Weible, 2007) the authors added two new factors as potential causes for policy change: *internal shocks* and *negotiated agreements*. In the following section these four variables and the underlying mechanisms that might initiate policy change will be briefly discussed.

Policy-oriented learning is defined as »relatively enduring alternations of thought or behavioral intentions that result from experience and/or new information and that are concerned with the attainment or revision of policy objectives« (Sabatier and Jenkins-Smith, 1999: 123; Sabatier and Weible, 2007: 198). However, whether policy-learning indeed occurs is assumed to vary according to the level of the dominant beliefs. It is hypothesized that policy-oriented learning can rarely be achieved when more normative *deep core beliefs* and *policy core beliefs* prevail as they are »very resistant to change in response to new information« (Sabatier and Weible, 2007: 198). However, policy-learning can alter secondary beliefs because the »relatively narrow scope requires less evidence and belief change among fewer individuals« (Sabatier and Weible, 2007: 198). The next factor, *external perturbations* or *shocks*, is described as a necessary but insufficient condition for policy change (Sabatier and Weible, 2007: 198). External perturbations include, for example, events such as changes in the socio-economic conditions, shifting power proportions within a government, or environmental catastrophes. These can have an impact on the *policy core beliefs* of a dominant advocacy coalition and force the members of the coalition to reconsider their original targets and strategies. In this way, they may »shift agendas, focus public attention, and attract the attention of key decision-making sovereigns« (Sabatier and Weible, 2007: 199). However, as Sabatier and Weible describe, the »most important effect of external shocks is the redistribution of resources or opening and closing venues within a policy subsystem, which can lead to the replacement of the previously dominant coalition by a minority coalition« (Sabatier and Weible, 2007: 199). In the context of the European Union, the »redistribution of resources« might refer to the financial support that is offered by the European Commission to NGOs in order to support their activities. In the case of decisive perturbations, the attention of the European institutions might shift from one group to another, which can have an effect on a group's power in the policy-making process.

Several researchers have considered the impact *external perturbations* may have on policy change and have used the ACF for various case studies. Nohrstedt (2005) examined the outcome of the Swedish government decision to conduct a referendum on the future role of nuclear energy in the aftermath of the accident at the Three Miles Island Nuclear Generating Station in Dauphin County, Pennsylvania, in March 1979. The consequence of the negative referendum was the parliament's decision that nuclear power was to be abolished by 2010 at the latest. From a theoretical point of view, the study was based on the ongoing need »to identify more precisely the causal mechanisms driving policy change« (Nohrstedt, 2005: 1041). Nohrstedt concludes that major policy change cannot only be initiated by the factors suggested by Sabatier and Jenkins-Smith (1988) or Sabatier and Weible (2007), but that in addition short-term interests can result in major policy change (Nohrstedt, 2005: 1041). This argument is supported by his findings that the Swedish Social Democrats discarded their long-established policy core beliefs – to continuously rely on nuclear energy – in favor of the decision to abolish nuclear energy as it was demanded by the public. This indicates that the short-term interests in the form of vote maximization, party cohesion, and representation indeed determined the decision for the policy outcome. According to Nohrstedt, his results »point to the importance of strategic interests and, therefore, to the necessity for the ACF to recognize the role played by broader political developments leading up to policy change initiatives« (Nohrstedt, 2005: 1055).

In recent years, Sabatier and Jenkins-Smith as well as Sabatier and Weible have revised the model of the ACF as developed in the 1990s. For example, due to several empirical applications of the ACF, they came to the conclusion that not only *external* but also *internal* shocks, meaning crucial developments inside the policy subsystem, could result in major policy change (Sabatier and Weible, 2007: 204). In reference to Birkland (2004) they argue that internal - as well as external - shocks function as *focusing events* that »attract public attention; highlight policy vulnerabilities, failures, or neglect; and bring new information into the policy process« (Sabatier and Weible, 2007: 204). It is assumed that internal shocks affect policy core beliefs in the way that they reaffirm the policy core beliefs of the less influential advocacy coalitions while challenging those of the dominant advocacy coalition (Sabatier and Weible, 2007: 205). Consequently, the balance of power between the actors within a subfield may be altered and thus the probability for policy change enhanced. The final factor mentioned by the authors as influencing policy change is labeled *negotiated agreements*. This was introduced in order to »identify the conditions under which – in the absence of major external or internal perturbation – agreements involving policy core changes are crafted among previously warring coalitions« (Sabatier and Weible, 2007: 205). In accordance with research on alternative dispute resolution, nine provisions are identified as necessary for successful negotiations and policy implementations (Sabatier and Weible, 2007). Among them are 1) the agreement between all actors that the existing status quo cannot longer be accepted (*a hurting stalemate*), 2) the necessity to include all relevant actors into the policy making process (*composition*), 3) the existence of a neutral mediator (*leadership*), 4) the establishment of the right to veto (*consensus decision rule*), 5) the rule that funding should result from sources that belong to different coalitions (*funding*), 6) the commitment of the participants to regularly attend meetings in order to enhance effectiveness (*duration and commitment*), 7) the concentration on an empirical instead of a normative issue, as an agreement on the former is easier to achieve (*importance of empirical issues*), 8) the establishment of trustful relationships between all participants (*the importance of building trust*), and finally 9) the importance of ongoing negotiation as one of only a few alternative venues for achieving compromise (*alternative venues*).

The main propositions made by the authors of the ACF emphasize the assumption that actors alone face severe difficulties when attempting to influence the policy process as the beliefs of opponents and decision-makers can be very resistant to change – unless extraordinary events occur or certain conditions are fulfilled. Numerous other researchers have approached the question of interest group power in initiating policy change by taking different variables into account. Of these, the most important are briefly summarized below.

In the literature, access to the decision making process is often considered a precondition for influence. Subsequently, some studies explicitly focus on what determines the mobilization and participation of interest groups. Mahoney (2004) analyzes the role of institutions and their incentives to shape political participation. She investigates the ways in which government activity (*demand-side forces*) influences the mobilization of interests (*supply-side*) and their integration in the policy-making process (Mahoney, 2004: 441). Based on the analysis of a data set, which includes almost 700 interest groups which attempt to communicate their interests at the European level, she concludes that three paths prevail through which institutional demand side forces mobilize interest groups. The first exists in the direct subsidy of these actors through political institutions. Second, interests groups are included in »formal arenas of policy debate« through the establishment of consultative committees in some areas (Mahoney, 2004: 462). Finally, the European institutions' direct interest group activity through the »expansion of competencies via successive treaties« and the »selective development of chosen policy areas« (Mahoney, 2004: 441, 462). Another valuable study dealing with the question of interest group access is from Bouwen (2002), who explains the degree of interest group access to the European institutions by taking into account the function of so-called access goods. These access goods, especially in the form of information, are demanded by European institutions and have to be provided by groups seeking access to the decision-makers. From the perspective of the organizational theory, Eising (2007) aims at a more comprehensive explanation of what determines the access patterns of business associations. His study is based on the observation that thus far no coherent picture has been developed of the factors which determine to which institutions interest groups gain access to. Access is defined as the »frequency of contacts between interest organizations and EU institutions« (Eising, 2007: 331). What he excludes from this definition are the indirect contacts and media strategies. Eising identifies four dimensions as responsible for interest group access: 1) *institutional context*, 2) *resource dependencies*, 3) *interest group organization*, and 4) *strategic choices* (Eising, 2007: 329). He concludes that all these dimensions are relevant and that similar studies should be careful not to overestimate the importance of a single factor.

Instead of analyzing the factors which determine the extent of interest group access, other scholars attempt to verify that interest groups indeed have been able to successfully influence policy. This, however, leads to another important question: the definition of influence and power. Following the Weberian concept, power is the »the opportunity to impose one's will in a social relationship, even against resistance, without consideration to what this opportunity rests on« (Weber, 1922, in Woll, 2007:75). Dahl (1957) reformulated this as: »A has power over B to the extent that he can get B to do something that B would not otherwise do« (Dahl, 1957: 203, in Chalmers, 2011: 474). In a more recent study, Dür and de Bièvre (2007: 3) define actors as powerful »if they manage to influence outcomes in a way that brings them closer to their ideal points«.

Some scholars focus on the impact different actors possess in the agenda-setting phase (Princen, 2009; Baumgartner and Jones, 1993; 2009). Princen is concerned with the development of EU agendas in the fields of environmental and health policies and compares these to agendas in the United States. He defines an agenda as a »set of issues that receive serious consideration in a political system« (Princen, 2009: 19), where issues are understood as »a conflict between two or more identifiable groups over procedural or substantive matters relating to the distribution of positions or resources« (Cobb and Elder, 1972: 82, in Princen, 2009: 22). Issues can be placed high or low on an agenda, or even excluded completely. Princen identifies three steps through which an issue has to proceed in order to become an EU agenda item (Princen, 2009: 151): 1) policy networks must create a transnational policy debate on an issue, 2) EU policy-makers, above all the European Commission, have to be receptive to this particular issue and develop a debate within the EU institutions, and 3) the issue has to be supported by at least some EU policy-makers who are willing to overcome resistance from opponents. The receptiveness of EU policy-makers who push the issue forward is regarded as a central element here. The attention institutions direct towards issues can also be described by the *institutional receptiveness*. Such receptiveness, however, is limited to a certain number of issues as institutions do not have the time capacity or human resources to adopt them all. Non-governmental actors are aware of this and consequently place a great deal of emphasis on finding venues (Baumgartner and Jones, 1991) that are potentially receptive to their concerns:

> »In terms of explaining the success of venue shopping (by effecting a venue 'shift'), the key concept is the 'receptiveness' of a venue to a given interest. In explaining the receptiveness of venues, Baumgartner and Jones emphasise the link between institutions and policy images (e.g. 1993: 31). They point out that venues tend to focus on certain aspects of an issue because of their institutional remit and the type of persons that participate in the venue« (Princen and Kerremans, 2008: 1137).

Compared to the researchers cited above, Michalowitz (2005; 2007) is not concerned with the power interest groups possess in the agenda-setting phase, but rather with their impact on the policy outcome. She analyzed how and to what degree interest groups in the IT and transport sector contributed to EU policy-making - thereby acknowledging that policy outcomes cannot always be linked to lobbying activities (Michalowitz, 2007: 133). Michalowitz concludes that two factors have turned out to be especially decisive for interest group influence, namely »the congruence of the interests pursued with the interests of public actors and structural conditions« (Michalowitz, 2007: 149). Furthermore, interest groups are assumed to be more powerful when exerting technical rather than directional influence. While Michalowitz does not consider the resources an interest group is endowed with as relevant for its influence, other scholars pay special attention to the relationship between resources and a successful lobbying strategy. Indeed, contradictory findings exist. While, for example, Klüver (2010, in Klüver, 2011) emphasizes a »positive effect« of resource endowment, Mahoney (Mahoney, C., 2007, 2008) and Baumgartner, Berry, Hojnacki, Kimball and Leech (2009) do not support this assumption.

In recent years, scholars have started to shift their focus to lobbying coalitions. One convincing example is provided by Klüver (2011) who develops a model for measuring coalition influence. She identifies *information supply*, *citizen support* and *market power* of lobbying coalitions as key factors for determining their influence. However, comprehensive research on lobbying coalitions is scarce, particularly with regard to the question of whether coalition-formation increases coalition members' influence on decision-makers. The study of the influence of interest groups must however be viewed critically. As Eising and other scholars emphasize concerning to interest group activity that »having access does not imply that their contacts have an effect on EU policies« (Eising, 2007: 331; see also: Beyers, 2002; Dür, 2008). Indeed, it is a challenging endeavour to measure whether interest groups have been able to exert influence on a policy outcome. Decision-making is an ongoing process and, thus, even for decision-makers it can be difficult to say at which point in time and for what reason they have taken into account certain concerns or even changed their minds. Dür (2008) identifies three obstacles that complicate the study of influence. The first is to find a suitable definition of what is actually understood by the term influence. The second is concerned with the different roads that lead to influence while the third obstacle, and probably the most challenging, is how to measure influence: »In sum, measuring interest group influence is difficult, and most methods that have been tried are problematic in one way or the other« (Dür, 2008: 1225). To overcome these obstacles, Chalmers (2011) suggests a different approach. Instead of interpreting influence in the Weberian notion – as influencing *foes* – he draws on studies that rather understand lobbying as the exchange of information between interest groups and like-minded *friends*: »Given their limited resources, interest groups therefore transmit information to those who are already most likely to support their cause« (Chalmers, 2011: 474). Coming from this starting point, he formulates his main hypothesis: »The more efficient interest groups are at information processing, the more influence they will have« (ibid: 473). Information processing, composed of information gathering and information transmission, serves as a central indicator to measure influence. Drawing on empirical results from elite interviews and an online survey, Chalmers concludes that »interest group influence in the EU is, on balance, fair and impartial. No single type of group or groups dominates the process and no groups are excluded« (ibid).

The previous subsections summarized what has already been achieved by other scholars, which aspects contradict each other, and what research gaps still exist. The ACF, actor-centered institutionalism, the literature on institutional opportunity structures, and selected approaches on interest groups' strategies and influence are crucial for this work. Building on their assumptions, the following chapter presents a description of the independent and dependent variables and the theoretical hypotheses (→ 4.1.3). However, first some general remarks on the research design will be made (→ 4.1).

Chapter 4. Research design and case studies

This section presents the research design before outlining the case studies drawn from the field of European energy policy.

4.1 Research design

As indicated in Chapter 1, the central research questions guiding this analysis are:

Firstly, what are the factors leading to the formation of interest group coalitions in European energy policy? And secondly, what determines the strategies pursued by the coalition members to influence the EU policy process?

At a secondary level the impact of coalitions and of the strategies adopted by the coalition members on the receptiveness of the European Commission, the European Parliament, and the Council of the European Union is assessed. As already indicated, this work presents the hypothesis that coalitions of European associations and/or NGOs exist that can shape policy outcome. Taking this aspect into account contributes to resolving the question of the circumstances under which actors have an impact on the European decision-making process.

In order to answer the research questions four cases have been selected (→ 4.1.2). For the case studies theoretical hypotheses have been formulated based on the background of the central theories outlined in Chapter 3 (→ 4.1.3). Finally, the analytical tools used for the empirical research are described (→ 4.1.4).

4.1.1 The benefits of process-tracing case studies

Qualitative case studies in the social sciences have often been criticized for not producing objective and generalizable results. According to their critics, scholars engaged in qualitative research mostly analyze only a few cases (*small-N studies*). While this technique can provide insights into the mechanism between causes and effects of a particular incident, such analyses do not allow for more general explanations. Moreover, they do not meet the criterion of replicability as others could face difficulties while replicating research that is based on qualitative data gathering and evaluation (for overviews on the debate between researchers doing quantitative and qualitative studies see for example: Adcock and Collier, 2001; Ebbinghaus, 2006; Gerring, 2004; 2007; Mahoney and Goertz, 2006). Gerring (2007) regards the case study method only as suitable as long as it satisfies the criteria applied to experiments as done, for example, by physicists: »To the extent that a single case, or a small number of cases, exemplify a quasi experimental design, the case study method is vindicated« (Gerring, 2007: 172). Riker (1962) also describes this aspect very adequately:

> »What social scientists have so greatly admired about the physical sciences is the fact that these latter actually measure up to our notion of what science should be. That is, they consist of a body of related and verified generalizations which describe occurrences accurately enough to be used for prediction. […] Generalizations are verified because, drawn as they are from a carefully constructed and precise theory, they have themselves been stated in a way that admits of verification by experiment, observation, and prediction« (Riker, 1962: 3-4).

However, case studies have contributed greatly to social science research. According to Bennett and Elman (2007) they have been just as important as quantitative approaches (Bennett and Elman, 2007: 170). Qualitative analyses are especially valuable when it comes to the study of a unique case or when the possibility exists that more than one causal mechanism leads to the expected outcome (Hancké, 2009). Hypothesizing that coalitions of European associations and/or NGOs exist that can shape policy outcome raises the question of what determines the formation of these coalitions in the first place. The factors influencing the formation of coalitions in general can be manifold and different theories stress, for example, either the role of societal norms, rational self-interests or the effect of institutions on actors' behaviors. Thus, it is likely that varying causal pathways lead to the formation of a coalition rather than a single causal chain. This argument in favor of qualitative methods is also supported by Achen and Snidal (1989) who emphasize that case studies serve to identify causal factors that have previously been unnoticed:

> »In international relations, only case studies provide the intensive empirical analysis that can find previously unnoticed causal factors of historical patterns. […] Because they are simultaneously sensitive to data and theory, case studies are more useful for these purposes than any other methodological tool« (Achen and Snidal, 1989: 167-168).

Regarding the generalizability of case studies, predictions about the outcome of other cases not included in the original study must be treated with great care. As Hancké (2009) argues, case studies are always constructed by the researcher and not randomly chosen. Such cases »in a statistical sense, will never be representative, even if you think it is a typical case« (Hancké, 2009: 43). What, however, can be done quite well using the case study method is the generation or testing of an established theory, which can then lead to new or complementary arguments or even the falsification of a previously acknowledged theory:

»This explicit selection bias means that they can be quite powerful tools to test and/or unpack an existing theory and come up with new, better arguments about causal mechanisms, especially when paired with one or more other cases in the right way« (Hancké, 2009: 55).

If a researcher intends to address more comprehensive questions rather than a unique case, the use of *process-tracing* is a promising tool (George and Bennett, 2005: 206). Process-tracing serves to identify a causal mechanism between (an) independent variable(s) and the outcome, the dependent variable (George and Bennett, 2005: 206). The method has increasingly been used in the social sciences over the last two decades, especially with regard to the analysis of outcomes whose occurrence could not be explained in terms of only two or three independent variables (Hall, 2003).

As the identification of *causal mechanisms* is regarded as the central element of the method, these terms should be clarified. A mechanism can be defined as

»[...] a set of hypotheses that could be the explanation for some social phenomenon, the explanation being in terms of interactions between individuals and other individuals, or between individuals and some social aggregate« (Hedstroem and Swedberg, 1998: 25, 32-33).

Concerning the causality of this mechanism, George and Bennett (2005: 212ff.) differentiate between *linear* and more *complex* causality. While the former exists in the form of a »direct chain of events« and reflects a rather simple picture, the latter is more typical for the phenomena identified in social science. Here again a distinction can be made between three types: the *convergence* of several conditions not directly related to each other, *interacting* causal variables, which are mutually dependent, and *path-dependent* sequences of events, according to which an outcome is regarded as the almost inevitable consequence of a set of causes. Although process-tracing can be applied to all these types, the researcher will of course be confronted with different degrees of complexity.

If the method is applied in an analytical way, hypotheses can be formulated for parts of the causal mechanism. In order to gain a complete picture, the researcher has to formulate a single hypothesis for all intervening variables in the causal chain and thus can ensure that no influencing factor is neglected. These hypotheses can adopt an anticipatory or a retrospective manner so that they either predict future developments or analyze past mechanisms that lead to a present outcome. Referring to the latter, process-tracing almost resembles the work of police officers who try to clarify the causes and effects of individual actions.

A further benefit of the method is that it serves to identify the determinants of deviant cases, which are not covered by existing theories and which often cannot be explained in large-N studies relying on quantitative analyses (George and Bennett, 2005: 215). In contrast with other methods, process-tracing cannot only identify if two variables A and B are related, but also how and why they are linked to each other. That means that one receives information on the intermediate steps between A and B which can be tested one after the other. The relation between A and B can be described as resulting from a causal mechanism (rather than a correlation) as soon as the causality for each intermediate step can be revealed (Hancké, 2009: 59). Following this logic, insights gained from process-tracing can be generalizable to similar cases despite the concerns on the generalizability of qualitatively gathered data referred to above:

> »Once you have then concluded which one of the theories works best by confronting the available data with the different arguments, you can then use that insight as a way to generalise to other cases. When that works, the single case has produced an explanation that ought to be helpful in understanding many other, similarly structured, situations« (Hancké, 2009: 60).

4.1.2 Case selection

For this study, *crucial* cases have been selected. Here, cases are defined as the processes surrounding the formation of coalitions between European associations and/or NGOs and the strategy choices made by the coalition members with regard to four crucial legislative acts of European energy policy. The cases are - using Gerring's terminology - *crucial* in the sense that they have been »chosen for reasons of analytic utility« (Gerring 2001: 219). Each case has to provide information on the dependent and independent variables in order to ensure that the hypotheses guiding the analysis can be tested. One core hypothesis of this study is, for example, that coalitions are formed between European associations and/or NGOs representing at first glance contradictory interests (environment vs. industry vs. finance). Another one that - in contrast to the assumptions of the ACF - coalitions are not only formed on the basis of long-term belief or norm systems, but also as a result of short- and long-term interests. Furthermore, the legislative acts selected from the field of European energy policy have affected a wide range of industry branches, environmental NGOs, and different political and societal levels, and thus facilitate the analysis of the reasons for cross-sector interest group coalitions within the EU multi-level system. In this way, the analysis of crucial cases can serve to »confirm or disconfirm an existing theory, or to suggest modifications in that theory« (Gerring, 2001: 220).

The case selection also requires that the cases can be compared to each other. Therefore, all cases occurred between 2002 and 2010. Figure 8 illustrates the main EU initiatives (action plans, green papers, etc.), stakeholder consultations and subsequent regulations and directives in the field of European energy policy during this time. What can be observed is the increasing density of initiatives at the EU level. It can be assumed that the lobbying activities by various actors increased during the same period.

Research design

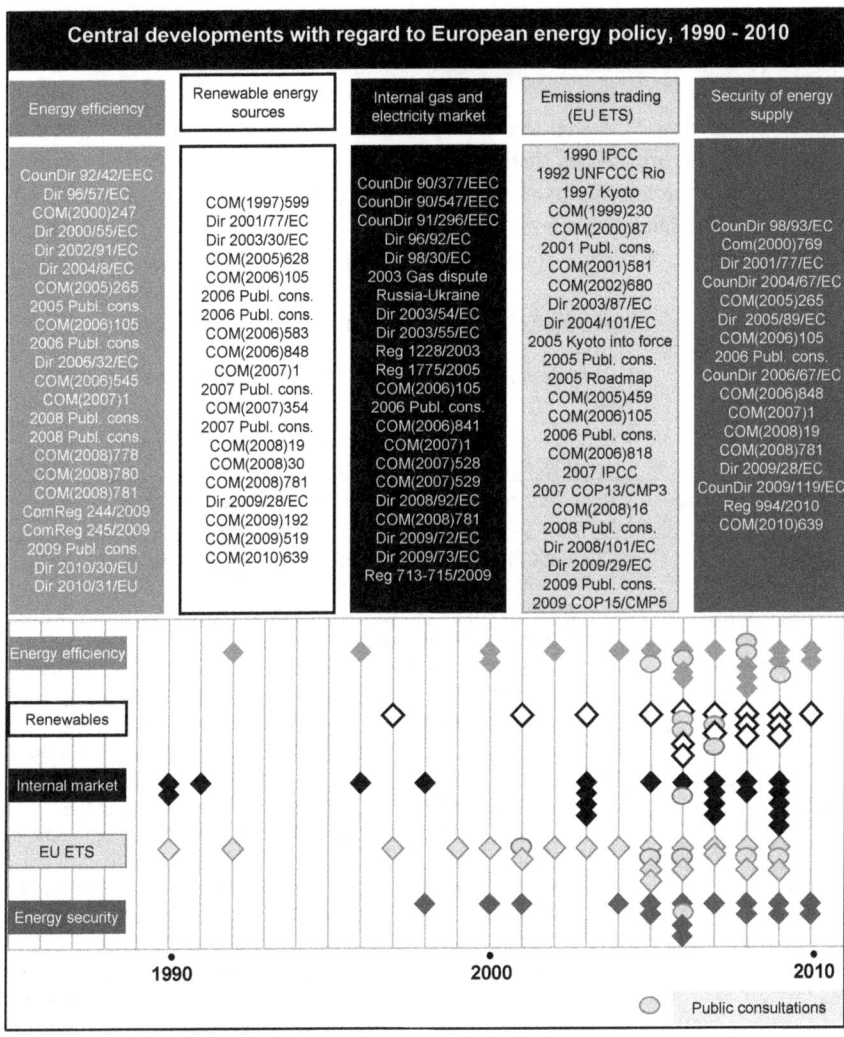

Figure 8: Central developments with regard to European energy policy, 1990 - 2010

The cases have been derived from four core subfields of European energy policy, in which the number of initiatives and thus the mobilization of public and private interests has increased considerably over recent years:

a) the creation of the internal market for gas and electricity (third liberalization package);
b) the extension of the EU ETS (inclusion of aviation);

Research design and case studies

c) the question of energy efficiency (energy performance of buildings); and
d) the promotion of renewable energy sources (biofuels).

An additional case study on the issue of energy security was not conducted as related questions are already dealt with in three of the four other cases. Regarding the creation of the internal market for gas and electricity, the policy process leading to the third liberalization package has been selected as the first case study. Table 12 lists the core developments related to the third liberalization package.

Table 12: Core developments related to the third liberalization package

Date	Core developments related to the third liberalization package
2006, March 8	COM(2006)105 final: Green Paper: A European strategy for sustainable, competitive and secure energy
2006, March-September	Public consultation: Green paper: A European strategy for sustainable, competitive and secure energy
2007, September 19	COM(2007)528 final: Proposal for a Directive of the European Parliament and of the Council amending Directive 2003/54/EC concerning common rules for the internal market in electricity
2007, September 19	COM(2007)529 final: Proposal for a Directive of the European Parliament and the Council amending Directive 2003/55/EC concerning rules for the internal market in natural gas
2009, July 13	Directive 2009/72/EC of the European Parliament and of the Council concerning common rules for the internal market in electricity
2009, July 13	Directive 2009/73/EC of the European Parliament and of the Council concerning common rules for the internal market in natural gas
2009, July 13	Regulation (EC) No 713/2009 of the European Parliament and of the Council establishing an Agency for the Cooperation of Energy Regulators
2009, July 13	Regulation (EC) No 714/2009 of the European Parliament and of the Council on conditions for access to the network for cross-border exchanges in electricity
2009, July 13	Regulation (EC) No 715/2009 of the European Parliament and of the Council on conditions for access to the natural gas transmission networks

In March 2006 the European Commission initiated public consultation on the Green Paper *A European strategy for sustainable, competitive and secure energy*, which, among other topics, raised questions concerning the internal energy market. In September 2007 the European Commission subsequently proposed two directives including the rules for the internal markets in electricity and natural gas (COM(2007)528 final and COM(2007)529 final). The directives (Dir.

2009/72/EC and Dir. 2009/73/EC) repealing the second liberalization package were adopted in July 2009, together with three regulations.

As the second case the inclusion of aviation in the EU ETS is analyzed. Although the first steps towards the establishment of the EU ETS date back to the 1990s, the directive establishing a scheme for greenhouse gas emission allowance trading was not adopted until 2003. It was then obvious to energy actors that the DG Environment was going to propose including additional industry sectors such as aviation in the EU ETS in the near future (Environmental News and Data Services, 2003). Public consultation on measures of how to reduce the impact of aviation on climate change was initiated in 2005. In 2006 a proposal for a directive aiming to include aviation activities in the scheme for greenhouse gas emission allowance trading was published, which subsequently resulted in Directive 2008/101/EC. Table 13 lists the core developments related to the inclusion of aviation in the EU ETS.

Table 13: Core developments related to the inclusion of aviation in the EU ETS

Date	Core developments related to the inclusion of aviation in the EU ETS
2003, October 13	Directive 2003/87/EC establishing a scheme for greenhouse gas emission allowance trading within the Community
2005, March-May	Public consultation: Reducing the climate change impact of aviation (DG Environment)
2005, September 27	COM(2005)459 final: Communication from the Commission: Reducing the climate change impact of aviation
2006, December 20	COM(2006)818 final: Proposal for a Directive of the European Parliament and of the Council amending Directive 2003/87/EC so as to include aviation activities in the scheme for greenhouse gas emission allowance trading
2008, January 23	COM(2008)16 final: Proposal for a Directive of the European Parliament and the Council amending Directive 2003/87/EC so as to improve and extend the greenhouse gas emission allowance trading system of the Community
2008, November 19	Directive 2008/101/EC amending Directive 2003/87/EC so as to include aviation activities in the scheme for greenhouse gas emission allowance trading within the Community (entered into force February 2, 2009)

Developments surrounding the energy performance of buildings as part of the EU's strategy to increase energy efficiency serve as the background for the third case study. The first directive concerning the energy performance of buildings was adopted in 2002. In 2005, the Green Paper *Energy efficiency or doing more with less* was issued on general questions related to energy efficiency. Public consultations on the green paper as well as on measures to improve the energy performance of buildings were initiated in 2006 and 2008 and resulted in the proposal for a

Research design and case studies

directive (COM(2008)780 final). The respective legislative act, Directive 2010/31/EU, was adopted in May 2010.

Table 14: Core developments related to the directive on the energy performance of buildings

Date	Core developments related to the directive on the energy performance of buildings
2002, December 16	Directive 2002/91/EC of the European Parliament and of the Council on the energy performance of buildings and its amendments
2005, June 22	COM(2005)265 final: Green Paper Energy efficiency or doing more with less
2005, June - 2006, March	Public consultation: Green Paper Energy efficiency or doing more with less
2006, October 19	COM(2006)545 final: Communication from the Commission, Action Plan for energy efficiency: Realising the potential
2008, April-June	Public consultation: Recasting of the energy performance of buildings Directive
2008, November 13	COM(2008)780 final: Proposal for a Directive of the European Parliament and the Council on the energy performance of buildings
2010, May 19	Directive 2010/31/EU of the European Parliament and of the Council on the energy performance of buildings

Finally, as the fourth case the promotion of biofuels in the context of EU legislation on the future role of energy from renewable sources in the transport sector has been selected. Table 15 summarizes the key developments:

Research design

Table 15: Core developments related to the promotion of biofuels for transport

Date	Core developments related to the promotion of biofuels for transport
2001, September 12	COM(2001)370 final: White Paper: European transport policy for 2010: time to decide
2003, May 8	Directive 2003/30/EC of the European Parliament and of the Council on the promotion of the use of biofuels or other renewable fuels for transport
2005, December 7	COM(2005)628 final: Communication from the Commission: Biomass action plan
2006, February 8	COM(2006)34 final: Communication from the Commission: An EU strategy for biofuels
2006, April-July	Public consultation: Review of EU biofuels directive (DG Energy and Transport)
2007, January 10	COM(2006)848 final: Communication from the Commission to the Council and the European Parliament: Renewable Energy Road Map – Renewable energies in the 21st century: building a more sustainable future
2007, April-May	Public consultation: Biofuel issues in the new legislation on the promotion of renewable energy
2008, January 23	COM(2008)19 final: Proposal for a Directive of the European Parliament and of the Council on the promotion of the use of energy from renewable sources
2009, April 23	Directive 2009/28/EC of the European Parliament and of the Council on the promotion of the use of energy from renewable sources and amending and subsequently repealing Directives 2001/77/EC and 2003/30/EC

Three important steps have to be emphasized here: the public consultation periods between April and July 2006 and May and June 2007 for biofuel issues in the new legislation on the promotion of renewable energy and the proposal for a directive on the promotion of the use of energy from renewable sources (COM (2008)19 final), which then resulted in the directive on the promotion of the use of energy from renewable sources (Dir. 2009/28/EC) adopted in April 2009.

4.1.3   Variables and hypotheses derived from the theoretical background

As a theory should best be »composed of propositions formulated in terms of variables observed either within social systems or at the level of systems« (Przeworski and Teune, 1970: 31), this chapter specifies the dependent and independent variables and hypotheses that have guided this work. The hypotheses are embedded in several theoretical approaches, namely the Advocacy Coalition Framework (Sabatier and Jenkins-Smith, 1988; 1993; 1999; Sabatier and Weible, 2007), actor-

Research design and case studies

centered institutionalism (Mayntz and Scharpf, 1995a; Scharpf, 1997), the concept of political or institutional opportunity structures (Kitschelt, 1986; Tarrow, 1991), and different approaches on interest groups' strategies (Baumgartner and Jones, 1991; Beyers, 2004; Mazey and Richardson, 1996), the achievements and shortcomings of which have already been revealed in previous sections (→ 3).

The central dependent variables are:

a) the formation of coalitions between European associations and/or NGOs in the field of European energy policy; and
b) the strategy choices made by the coalition members.

These variables need further explanation. According to the ACF, advocacy coalitions are »composed of people from various organizations who share a set of normative and causal beliefs and who often act in concert«. To further its objectives »at any point in time each coalition adopts a strategy(s) envisaging one or more institutional innovations« (Sabatier, 1988: 133). Borrowing from this definition, this work assumes that coalitions can contain actors with different backgrounds - for example societal interests and industry - and that they adopt measures to influence the policy process. What, however, distinguishes the understanding of coalitions used here from the quotation above is that a) the focus clearly lies on coalitions between European associations and/or NGOs, and that b) coalition members do not necessarily share a set of beliefs, but can also decide to cooperate on the basis of shared, sometimes short-term, interest. In reference to Baumgartner, Berry, Hojnacki, Kimball, and Leech (2009), Klüver (2011: 2) simply states: »Lobbying coalitions are defined as sets of actors who share the same policy goal«. This definition does not specify whether a policy goal is derived from interests or norms.

Concerning the duration of a coalition, this work adopts the perspective that coalitions can be short or long term or even recurring, which means that they may exist for only a couple of months or for several years, or are even formed several times on different occasions. The variables that are assumed to determine the persistence of coalitions are specified below. It should be stressed that the focus does not lie on formal coalitions that resemble organizations with an administrative body or are based on a signed contract, but rather on - sometimes ad-hoc - forms of informal cooperation that may lack organizational structures, a letterhead or a spokesperson.

What distinguishes a coalition from a network is that the network concept is much broader than that of a coalition. In their typology of networks, Adam and Kriesi (2007: 146) describe the *relationships* between actors as the fundamental element of a network: »actors are no longer regarded as atomized and isolated, but

Research design

as mutually interlinked«. These linkages, however, can be manifold. Mahoney emphasizes that »networking ranges on a continuum from very informal and loose, composed of information-sharing, to highly coordinated enterprises with logos, letterhead and secretariat« (Mahoney, C., 2008: 167). Here mere information-sharing is excluded from the definition of a coalition. Consequently, coalitions are identified by the joint action of their members in the form of regular meetings in order to coordinate the actors' positions and strategies, the joint formulation of a declaration on a specific goal to be attained or on a code of conduct to be observed, and/or the actors' joint submission of a position paper or report to policy-makers. In contrast, networks are assumed to exist between people that share an interest in a topic, but do not necessarily take joint action. Members of a network also do not have to have the same interests in every respect. A representative of wind energy can, for example, belong to a network promoting the enhanced use of renewable energy sources and regularly exchange information with other members while not necessarily being involved in a coalition that aims to strengthen the biomass sector.

Members of informal coalitions can be further characterized by their high degree of autonomy (Mahoney, C., 2008; Pijnenburg, 1998; Mulford and Rogers, 1982), meaning that they can decide independently of other coalition members whether to act as part of the group or pursue their individual lobbying strategy.

In the field of European energy policy, the following groups of actors may be regarded as potential coalition members:

a) European associations representing
   - intensive energy consumers/emission producers;
   - energy producers/providers;
   - technologies/materials/services related to energy consumption/emission output;
   - technologies/materials/services related to energy production/provision.
b) European NGOs concerned with the consequences of energy production and consumption.

After the variables determining the formation of coalitions have been identified, a closer look is taken at the strategies adopted by the coalition members. It is assumed that organizations are generally concerned about what is captured by the term *organizational maintenance*. The survival of the organization can be regarded as a central goal the organizational leaders have to keep in mind while considering which strategies might be useful to influence the policy process. Concerning the strategies, Beyers (2004) distinguishes between *voice* and *access* strategies. The first type includes either *information* or *protest politics* and aims to increase public attention. The second is characterized by the direct exchange of information with the decision-makers, either through personal contacts or participation in official stakeholder consultations. These categories are adopted here. Access strategies aim to establish personal contact with political decision-makers either through formal or informal meetings. Furthermore, the submission of position papers is also considered to be part of an access strategy. Position papers can be submitted in the course of official stakeholder consultations or they can be sent to the decision-makers and policy officers on an ongoing basis during the decision-making process. In contrast, typical voice strategies include press releases or media campaigns. These have the potential to increase public awareness of the coalition members' goals and in this way may increase also the attention of political decision-makers. Thus this work considers whether both access and voice strategies are pursued by coalitions and whether they are pursued only at the European or also at the national level, in the latter case through the national members of the European associations and/or NGOs that belong to a coalition. This would then be categorized as *multi-level venue-shopping* (Baumgartner and Jones, 1991). What is described by this term is the attempt to strategically contact political institutions at different levels, especially when lobbying at one level appears to be unsuccessful or if additional benefits can be expected from lobbying at several levels. According to Eising, national interest groups are unlikely to extend their lobbying to the EU level because »they are tied to their national members and to the national context in which they emerged« (Eising, 2009: 90). Therefore, Eurogroups (or coalitions of Eurogroups) usually direct their attention to the EU institutions, while national associations focus on the national level (ibid: 91).

Over the course of venue-shopping at different levels (through different organizations) the image of an issue which is presented to one institution may be subject to changes when presented to another institution. This assumption is reflected in the approaches of Mazey and Richardson (1997) and Baumgartner and Mahoney (2008), according to which interest groups formulate different position papers depending on the political institution addressed (→ *issue-framing*). This does not imply that the general idea of a position is changed but that, for example, some arguments are framed differently.

Once the determinants of the formation of coalitions and the strategies adopted by the coalition members have been identified, an assessment is made of how different actor constellations and their strategy choices affect the receptiveness of the European Commission, the European Parliament, and the Council and in this way increase the probability that an issue is adopted on the institutional agenda. Receptiveness, however, is naturally limited to a certain number of topics because institutions do not have the resources to deal with all of them. Non-governmental actors are aware of this and consequently put a great deal of emphasis on trying to find access venues.

Research design

The question now arises of which variables have an impact on the formation of a coalition and the strategies adopted by the coalition members. Here the following independent variables are considered to be relevant:

1) institutional opportunity structures:
   a. institutional agendas, b. institutional rules, c. office-holders;
2) motivation: a. short-/long-term interests, b. long-established norms;
3) information and expertise: a. relevant information and expertise, b. no relevant information and expertise;
4) reputation: a. good reputation, b. bad reputation;
5) resources: a. many human/financial resources, b. few human/financial resources.

These variables also need further consideration: The first variable is labelled *institutional opportunity structures*. Regarding to the role of institutions, Eising (2005: 7) assumes that the institutional setting defines »opportunities of interest organizations to get in touch with the EU decision makers«. These *institutional opportunity structures* can best be described in terms of the EU's »segmentation into three pillars, the distinct allocation of powers to its legislative and executive institutions, and the vertical and functional differentiation of these institutions« (Eising, 2005: 7). Eising draws on literature on political opportunity structures which also serves as a theoretical background here. What Sabatier and Weible (2007) consider as *coalition opportunity structures* is described as the *openness of the political system* and the *degree of consensus* needed to achieve policy change (Sabatier and Weible, 2007: 199). According to Kitschelt (1986) political opportunity structures are defined as »specific configurations of resources, institutional arrangements and historical precedents for social mobilisation, which facilitate the development of protest movements in some instances and constrain them in others« (Kitschelt, 1986: 58). The definition adopted here is narrower, including *institutional agendas*, *institutional rules*, and *office-holders*, but not the configurations of resources mentioned by Kitschelt. In contrast, resources were selected as an additional variable. *Institutional agendas* are included because they reflect the intentions of the European institutions and therefore constitute an important landmark for interest groups. *Institutional rules* refer to the legislative competences and procedures applied to the decision-making process. The variable *office-holders* captures all persons that either work for the European associations and NGOs or represent the European Commission, the European Parliament, and the Council and that are directly involved in the daily business of policy-making.

Regarding *institutional agendas* it is assumed that European associations and/or NGOs usually form coalitions after the European Commission has included an issue on its agenda. If they intend to influence the policy process at a very early stage, they do so only on behalf of their own association or organization as seeking allies can be very time-consuming.

H 1.1 If European associations and/or NGOs decide to form a coalition, they only do so **after** the European Commission has included an issue on its agenda. If no EC initiative exists they do not usually seek allies.

The interactions between European associations and/or NGOs were analyzed because compared to national associations they are more likely to be consulted by the European institutions as they aggregate the EU-wide interests of a particular sector. Coalitions of European associations and/or NGOs are even better able to communicate »European encompassing interests« (Eising, 2009) because they can unite different perspectives on a particular issue and translate them into a concrete policy position. Moreover, members of European institutions are excluded from the definition of a coalition and are instead viewed as members of wider networks, for example forums that serve to exchange information on a specific topic. Here, coalitions are identified by the joint action of their members in the form of regular meetings in order to coordinate the actors' positions and strategies, the joint formulation of a declaration on a specific goal to be attained or on a code of conduct to be observed, and/or the actors' joint submission of a position paper or report to policy-makers.

After common goals have been identified, coalition members develop a strategy of how to influence the decision-making process at the coalition level. With reference to the concept of *multi-level venue-shopping* developed by Baumgartner and Jones (1991), Hypothesis 1.2 addresses the strategies pursued by coalitions of European associations and/or NGOs in response to the institutional agenda at the level of the EU member states.

H 1.2 If an issue currently debated at the EU level has also been placed high on the agenda of some member states, a coalition of European associations and/or NGOs will also advise the national members to seek access to the respective national-level decision-makers.

Since the co-decision procedure in accordance with the Lisbon Treaty has become the *ordinary legislative procedure*, meaning that co-decision has become the norm for policy-making, MEPs play a more significant role as potential addressees of lobbying strategies: »After the institutional position of the EP had been upgraded with the introduction of new legislative procedures - the co-operation and the co-decision procedures - pressure groups much intensified their action with the EP as a new channel of influence« (Lehmann, 2007: 14). Hypothesis 1.3 deals with the impact of *institutional rules* on the strategies pursued at the coalition level. It was formulated based on the assumption that MEPs have become increasingly open to the lobbying efforts of interests groups. On the other hand, the Council is more responsive to particular national interests that cannot be included in a position published by the coalition as a whole.

H 1.3 If co-decision procedure is applied, coalitions seek access to the MEPs rather than to members of the Council.

Finally, the influence of the variable *office-holders* on coalition-formation and the strategy choices of the coalition members are described by Hypotheses 1.4 and 1.5.

H 1.4 If useful personal contacts exist between individuals belonging to a European association and/or NGOs, the formation of a coalition is likely. In contrast, if personal animosities prevail, a coalition is unlikely to be formed.

H 1.5 If office-holders alternate, coalition members will reconsider their strategies in order to increase the receptiveness of the new person in office.

Motivation serves as the second variable, denoting that actors intending to form a coalition are either primarily driven by (sometimes short-term) interests or by long-established norms. This does not imply that those driven by interests do not act in accordance with a normative framework, nor that those following normative beliefs do not also have short-term, at times perhaps quite material, interests. However, it is important to identify which characteristics prevail in a given situation. Following Sabatier and his collaborators, one would have to assume that the central characteristic of a coalition is that its members share a belief system. According to the ACF (Sabatier and Weible, 2007: 192), the actors' rationality is bounded by cognitive constraints. As a consequence, individuals »filter perceptions through their belief system« (Weible and Sabatier, 2007: 127). The theoretical duality of norms and interests is also reflected in the distinction between the *logic of appropriateness*, according to which people do what they consider to be appropriate in the context of existing norms, and the *logic of consequences*, which emphasizes that people rationally consider the expected consequences of their actions (March and Olsen, 1996). Sabatier and his collaborators regard the joint *policy core beliefs* as most decisive for identifying a coalition as these represent fundamental choices and are not changed voluntarily (Sabatier and Weible, 2007: 195). Examples include the evaluation of the importance of different policy-related values or policy problems in the subsystem, attitudes towards the allocation of authority between government and market, and the function of the public in the policy process.

In contrast, Scharpf (1997; see also Mayntz and Scharpf, 1995a) argues that it can neither be assumed, as done in neoclassical economics or in the neorealist theory, that actors derive their goals from mere cost-benefit calculations, nor that actors only follow cultural norms - as claimed by some sub-forms of the sociological theory. Instead, what influences individual decisions are institutions consisting of social norms that are generally shared and therefore respected *and* formal rules that actors observe on the basis of more rational considerations.

Including insights from actor-centered institutionalism in addition to those from the ACF, this work assumes that both interests and norms (collectively labelled as *motivation*) are frequently at the core of coalitions in EU policy-making. It is subsequently suggested that the persistence of a coalition depends on whether it has been formed on the basis of common (short- and long-term) interests or on the basis of shared (long-established) norms.

In order to assess if a coalition is rooted in interests or norms, the content of the position papers submitted by the coalition members to the decision-makers is analyzed. In doing so, one has to be aware that actors sometimes justify their intentions by referring to specific norms - such as environmental standards -, although they actually pursue quite rational interests (an increase in sales). To ensure that the underlying intention is evaluated correctly, the overall goals of the associations or NGOs as outlined on their websites or in their statutes are also taken into account.

> **H 2.1** If actors share common (short- and long-term) interests, they are more likely to form an informal ad-hoc coalition in order to influence the policy process. Although the coalition is likely to exist only as long as it serves a specific goal, it may be reactivated in the future.

> **H 2.2** If actors share long-established norms, they tend to form a coalition that is more persistent over time. As a result of this ongoing cooperation, it is likely that the informal coalition will be formalized.

Furthermore, if a coalition based on long-established norms has been formalized, meaning for example that it has established an administrative body to coordinate the action of the coalition members, it is more likely to pursue both access *and* voices strategies in the form of information (in contrast to protest) politics (Beyers, 2004).

> **H 2.3** If coalition members who share long-established norms decide to establish a formal coalition, it is more likely that this coalition will, in addition

Research design

to access strategies, also pursue voice strategies in the form of information politics.

The third variable has been labelled *information and expertise*. Information refers to the knowledge interest associations have about the consequences a policy initiative will have for a certain sector and about the policy positions of other actors in the field. In their definition of *coalition resources*, Sabatier and Weible (2007: 203) also include information as one variable referring to the information a coalition has on the severity of the problem, as well as the costs and benefits of alternative policy choices. Beyers and Kerremans (2004: 1123) define information as the »knowledge about the consequences of or the need for certain policies«. Expertise is understood as the »the ability to assess information«. Policy-makers often have »incomplete information about the consequences of specific policies for specific constituencies« and are, furthermore, dependent on the expertise interest associations can provide on a subject currently negotiated at the EU level. Consequently, it is essential that a coalition has information and expertise in order to receive attention. To measure whether an association or NGO possesses information, the indicators used by Chalmers (2011) are considered: »Information gathering refers to how interest groups manage to keep up-to-date on EU policy initiatives by monitoring decision-maker activities [...]« (Chalmers, 2011: 477). One result of his online survey with various interest groups was that efficient monitoring can best be realized with the help of informal sources at the EU level. Here it is assumed that access to informal sources can almost only be realized if an association or NGO has a representation in Brussels. Furthermore, it must engage in networking activities, such as the participation in forums or the attendance of conferences. In second place, EU sources (for example EU press releases, green and white papers) and formal sources (for example newspaper articles, TV news and books) are considered to be important. Through modern media, all actors have similar chances to access these resources; therefore informal sources are described as more relevant.

Expertise is measured by taking into account whether an association or NGO conducts scientific research, either in-house or by commissioning research, and publishes scientific articles or reports in order to strengthen its policy position. Hypothesis 3.1 deals with the impact of information and expertise on the formation of coalitions:

H 3.1 If European associations or NGOs possess information and can provide expertise concerning a specific policy issue, they are more likely to be included in a coalition.

Information is further assumed to influence the strategies pursued by the coalition members.

H 3.2 If coalition members possess comprehensive information on the policy process as well as on the decision-makers concerned, the coalition is more likely to reformulate a position paper when submitting it to different institutions.

This does not mean that the general position is changed, but that case-by-case different arguments are stressed in order to enhance the chance of being heard.

As the fourth variable, *reputation* has been selected. *Reputation* is defined as the *representativity* and *credibility* of a coalition, respectively its members. The credibility of a coalition is assessed by political decision-makers in terms of how credible they consider the statements made by a coalition to be. Representativity can be measured by taking into account the number of members a coalition of European associations and/or NGOs has. As Beyers and Kerremans (2004) conclude, »not only does the exchange of useful expertise and information matter, but public officials also take into account the public support mobilized interests enjoy« (Beyers and Kerremans, 2004: 1121). Here it is argued that the reputation of an organization impacts greatly on its choice of potential coalition partners. If the decision to form a coalition with another actor threatens its credibility, it risks losing members and the financial contributions its work depends on and thus may no longer be able to ensure its survival (Beyers, 2004) (→ *organizational maintenance*). It might also experience difficulties in gaining access to the European institutions as it will no longer be considered as a reliable discussion partner.

H 4.1 If a European association or NGO can improve its reputation by cooperating with other actors, a coalition is more likely to be formed. If, in contrast, its good reputation is likely to be damaged by forming a coalition with another actor, it will decide against cooperation.

H 4.2 If coalition members have a bad reputation, the coalition will have difficulties in gaining access to the European institutions.

The last variable considered as relevant here, *resources*, was adopted with reference to Eising (2005) and Sabatier and Weible (2007). Eising considers organizational resource dependencies (as well as institutional (political) opportunity structures and organizational characteristics) as highly relevant for gaining access to the European institutions:

Research design

»Access is the outcome of either the successful attempt of an interest group to approach the EU institutions or of its incorporation into EU policy-making by the EU institutions. It results from resource dependencies of interest groups and political institutions, from the political opportunities that are enshrined in the EU institutional structure, and from the interest groups' capacities to access the EU institutions that are conditioned by their organizational characteristics as well as their embeddedness in national-sectoral structures« (Eising, 2005: 5).

Sabatier and Weible describe resources as one of two decisive characteristics of coalitions. They define coalition resources as formal legal authority to make policy decisions, public opinion, information, mobilizable troops, financial resources, and skilful leadership (Sabatier and Weible, 2007: 202-203). Though the assumption made by Eising that resources are crucial for explaining the access of interest groups is reasonable, here resources - defined here as human and financial resources – are considered as less influential when it comes to the decision for or against coalition-formation. On the one hand, acting as a coalition can save resources as the amount of work and the financial means required for a specific lobbying strategy can be shared among the coalition members. On the other hand, the process of negotiating with potential coalition partners can be time-consuming and cost-intensive. Therefore, in terms of resources, there are good reasons for as well as against coalition-formation.

H 5.1 The amount of resources a European association or NGO possesses has no crucial impact on whether it becomes a member of a coalition.

Despite this, coalitions whose members are well equipped with financial and human resources are able to pursue more comprehensive lobbying strategies. For example, they have the manpower to write more than only one position paper in order to target different decision-makers, and the financial resources to benefit from the services offered by consultancies (see for example Lahusen, 2002) or to commission private research studies.

H 5.2 If coalition members have ample financial and human resources, the coalition can pursue more comprehensive lobbying strategies. These can include venue-shopping at multiple levels as well as different framings of a position, responding to the individual concerns of the addressee.

4.1.4 Data gathering tools: interviews and document analysis

After the relevant cases had been selected and the hypotheses formulated, the research question was considered by conducting interviews as well as an extensive analysis of the legal documents (directives, regulations, etc.) and position papers submitted by European associations and NGOs to EU decision-makers. The interviews with various European associations and NGOs as well as the European Commission, the European Parliament and the Council served to answer the following questions:

1) In which way have different energy actors been affected by the central initiatives of European energy policy?
2) What kinds of strategies have they pursued in order to influence the policy process?
3) Have coalitions been formed with other energy actors? If 'yes': During which stages of the policy process have they been formed? Which factors determined the decision to form a coalition with other actors? How long have the coalitions been active? Have they been periodically dissolved and reactivated?
4) What kinds of strategies have been pursued by the coalition?
5) How have the different energy actors perceived their impact on the receptiveness of European institutions towards their positions? How effective have European institutions considered the strategies pursued by the (coalitions of) energy actors to be?

A total of 52 interviews were conducted between August 2009 and May 2011. These included 27 with European industry associations, eight with European NGOs, and 17 with policy advisors from the European Commission (DG Energy, DG Climate Action, DG Mobility and Transport), MEPs or, if the MEP contacted was not available for an interview, his/her direct assistant, and persons from the General Secretariat of the Council. All interviews were done by telephone and lasted between 30 and 60 minutes, depending on the availability of the person contacted. The interview partners were guaranteed that their names and positions within the association or institutions would not be mentioned in this work or any publication resulting from it. Therefore, the case studies use abbreviations, such as *EP1* for MEPs, *EC1* for members of the European Commission, *Council1* for members of the Council, *EUNGO1* for policy advisor working for European NGOs, and *EUAssoc1* for those working for European associations being interviewed, the figure indicating the number of the interview in chronological order.

As qualitative case studies have often been criticized for not producing replicable results (see for example King, Keohane and Verba, 1994, Chapter 1; Bennet and Elman, 2007), the following section provides a detailed description of how the interview partners were selected and why. The selection of interview partners from the variety of people working for the European institutions was guided by the question of who had had the most contact with the policies relevant to this work. Among the European Commission, these were first and foremost the DG Energy,

Research design

the DG Climate Action, and the DG Mobility and Transport and thus policy advisors from these DGs were contacted. In former times, the DG Environment and the DG Enterprise and Industry had been concerned with the selected policies but had since shifted responsibilities. Among the European Parliament, those MEPs (or their direct assistants) being a member of or a substitute for the EP committees on *Environment, Public Health and Food Safety* and on *Industry, Research and Energy* were addressed. Regarding the Council, people were contacted who worked either for the DG C of the General Secretariat, responsible for questions of competitiveness, innovation and research, industry, the internal market, competition, transport and energy, or for the DG I, among others responsible for environment and climate change issues.

Table 16: Types of interest representatives (European Commission) [21]

Types of interest representatives
☐ Professional consultancies / law firms involved in lobbying EU institutions
☐ law firm
☐ public affairs consultancy
☐ independent public affairs consultant
☐ other (similar) organisation
☐ «In-house» lobbyists and trade associations active in lobbying
☐ company
☐ professional association
☐ trade union
☐ other (similar) organisation
☐ NGO / think-tank
☐ non-governmental organisation / association of NGOs
☐ think-tank
☐ other (similar) organisation
☐ Other organisations
☐ academic organisation / association of academic organisations
☐ representative of religions, churches and communities of conviction
☐ association of public authorities
☐ other (similar) organisation

---

21   Search options as of July 16, 2010. The register has been revised in June 2011. Therefore, the search options have changed in the meantime. The register from now on can be accessed at: http://ec.europa.eu/transparencyregister/info/homePage.do?locale=en#en.

Research design and case studies

Information on interest associations being active at the European level was gathered from the register of interest representatives available on the website of the European Commission. By July 2010, 2870 interest groups had registered on a voluntary basis.

The database on interest representatives was a result of the European Transparency Initiative (ETI), which was launched on November 9, 2005 in the context of »a review of its [the European Commission's] overall approach to transparency« (COM(2006)194 final). Interest groups were asked to register and in this way to indicate their commitment to a code of conduct consisting of seven basic rules about the expected behavior of actors involved in lobbying activities.

Among these were the obligations to clearly name the organization the interests were articulated by as well as its general purposes and goals, to provide complete and trustworthy information, and not to induce members of the European institutions to break the rules. This database was published in June 2008.

Table 17: Fields of interest (European Commission) [22]

Fields of interest		
☐ All fields of interest		
☐ Agriculture	☐ Audiovisual and media	☐ Budget
☐ Competition	☐ Consumer affairs	☐ Culture
☐ Customs	☐ Development	☐ Economic affairs
☐ Education	☐ Employment and social affairs	☐ Energy
☐ Enlargement	☐ Enterprise	☐ Environment
☐ Equal opportunities	☐ External relations	☐ External trade
☐ Fisheries and aquaculture	☐ Food safety	☐ Foreign and security policy
☐ General and insititutional affairs	☐ Humanitarian aid	☐ Information society
☐ Internal market	☐ Justice and home affairs	☐ Public health
☐ Regional policy	☐ Research and technology	☐ Sport
☐ Taxation	☐ Trans-European networks	☐ Transport
☐ Youth		

---

[22] Search options as of July 16, 2010. The register was subsequently revised in June 2011 and thus search options may have changed. The register can now be accessed at: http://ec.europa.eu/transparencyregister/info/homepage.do.

Research design

In order to select potential interview partners, the register was first examined with regard to the types of actors. The various choices are outlined in Table 16. As shown in Table 17, the fields of interests as stated by the organization could also be queried.

First, among the *in-house-lobbyists and trade associations active in lobbying* which are concerned with *energy,* representatives of a *professional association* or a *trade union* were selected. As a result[23], 356 interest representatives were identified, of which 159 could be considered as European associations, whereas the others fell into the category of global, national or subnational associations. Some of these described themselves as being active at different levels, for example subnational, national, and European. In these cases, the associations were categorized according to their primary concerns and/or the origin of the majority of their members.

Second, among the *in-house-lobbyists and trade associations active in lobbying* concerned with *energy*, an additional query was made to locate those which indicated belonging to *other (similar) organization*s. A total of 75 were found, of which 29 could be characterized as European associations. Thus in total 188 European associations were identified within the field of the in-house-lobbyists and trade associations that were somehow concerned with energy-related questions.

However, taking a closer look at the European associations, it became obvious that not all were directly or extensively affected by the EU legislation in the field of European energy policy, even though they had indicated interest in it. Thus, an additional filter was applied in order to select those associations that were most relevant for this work. As the register did not offer more detailed selection criteria, the websites of each association were examined for more information. Based on this, a categorization for associations considered to be relevant was formulated, consisting of:

- intensive energy consumers/emission producers;
- energy producers/providers;
- technologies/materials/services related to energy consumption/emission output;
- technologies/materials/services related to energy production/provision.

Consequently, a total of 89 associations that fell into one of these four categories were considered to be relevant. This list was later complemented by organizations

---

23 Results of analysis conducted in July 2010.

found to be decisive during the empirical research despite not appearing in the register.

Third, 195 *NGOs/think tanks* concerned with *energy* which represented a *nongovernmental organisation/association of NGO* or *other (similar) associations* were selected[24]. Among these, 73 could be considered as European NGOs, whereas the others fell into the category of global, national or subnational NGOs. The 73 European NGOs were further filtered according to whether they were concerned with the consequences of energy use. 23 organizations met this criterion.

A semi-structured interview outline (see for example Corbetta, 2003; Seale, 1998; Weiss, 1994) was created in order to make sure that all relevant topics were addressed while maintaining sufficient flexibility to react to unexpected information provided by the interview partner, for example on potential additional variables. Before each interview was conducted, information on the corresponding association/NGO or individual was gathered from the internet, for example regarding the association's statutes, its members, partnerships, and its policy positions, or the individual's professional experience. The interview outline for the European associations and NGOs was divided into four sections. The first one asked for the coalitions the association had been a member of; the second and the third dealt with the interests and strategies pursued by the coalitions compared to the interests and strategies pursued by the associations on their own behalf. The fourth section included questions about how the association perceived the influence it had on the EU institutions and on the policy process when acting as a coalition member compared to when acting alone. The interview outline for the European institutions focussed on how the policy-makers assessed the strategies pursued by European associations and NGOs and coalitions of these.

The interviews were accompanied by the document analysis. As relevant documents, especially the EU legal documents and the position papers submitted by the European associations and NGOs or coalitions of European associations and/or NGOs to the decision-makers were considered. These documents were accessible either via the European Commission's or the stakeholder websites. The document analysis served to identify:

1) the central issues debated within the field of European energy policy;
2) the actors concerned with these issues, especially those that had not registered in the database of interest groups;
3) the coalitions that had been formed by different actors and that had made their cooperation public by formulating a joint position paper, report or similar document; and

---

24 Results of analysis conducted in July 2010.

4) the positions a European association and/or NGO had submitted on behalf of its own organization compared to the positions submitted by the coalition.

4.2 Case studies

The following sections describe the case studies that were conducted in order to test the hypotheses outlined in Chapter 4.1. Here, cases are defined as the processes surrounding the formation of coalitions between European associations and/or NGOs and the strategy choices made by the coalition members with regard to four crucial legislative acts of European energy policy. The cases were derived from four core subfields of European energy policy in which the number of initiatives has increased considerably over recent years. As a consequence, various public and private interests have mobilized in order to influence the policy process:

a) the creation of the internal market for gas and electricity (third liberalization package);
b) the extension of the EU ETS (inclusion of aviation);
c) the question of energy efficiency (energy performance of buildings); and
d) the promotion of renewable energy sources (biofuels for transport).

4.2.1 The policy process leading to the third liberalization package

In March 2006 the European Commission initiated public consultation on the Green Paper *A European strategy for sustainable, competitive and secure energy* (COM(2006)105 final). Comments were invited on six aspects:

- the completion of the internal electricity and gas markets;
- the energy supply security;
- the sustainability of the energy mix;
- climate change;
- an energy technology plan; and
- the external energy policy (European Commission, 2006).

In total, 1680 comments were received. With reference to the completion of the internal electricity and gas markets, general concern was expressed about the proper functioning of the market. Although existing legislation was considered to be sufficient by many respondents, as a result of incomplete implementation in some member states, the progress achieved so far was described as unsatisfactory (ibid: 22). In particular, the European Commission was asked to ensure that legal unbundling, meaning the legal separation of production and transmission, was achieved. Furthermore, regulators considered the option of ownership unbundling as the most effective method for promoting investment, fair access, and transparency. The adoption of further legislative measures on unbundling was however rejected by energy producers, who preferred to first concentrate on completing the implementation of the existing directives (ibid: 25).

As another measure to achieve the goal of a single energy market, some respondents emphasized the harmonization of grid access conditions. The Green Paper *A European strategy for sustainable, competitive and secure energy* stated that consumers »need a single European grid for a real European electricity and gas market to develop. This can be done by ensuring common rules and standards on issues that affect cross-border trade. Progress is being made on these issues, but it is too slow« (COM(2006)105 final: 6). Associations of industrial companies were in favor of new common rules at the European level. They considered »the European grid codes as the way to harmonised or equivalent and non-discriminatory grid access conditions, to a transparent environment for investments« (European Commission, 2006: 23). The necessity of establishing a European grid code was, however, questioned especially by federations of energy and gas companies, who criticized it »as unnecessary in view of the existing national grid codes« (ibid).

Figure 9 illustrates which additional measures respondents supported in order to achieve the goal of a single energy market. 41 per cent were in favor of harmonization of grid access conditions, 39.7 per cent supported reinforced separation of network operation from production and supply (unbundling) and 38.2 per cent stressed the need to create a European energy regulator. 22.2 per cent emphasized that the powers and the independence of national regulators should be reinforced and 15.6 per cent suggested creating a body of transmission system operators (TSO) at EU level. Six per cent of respondents also suggested other measures.

It should be noted that in contrast to the areas of European energy policy described in the following sub-chapters, liberalization efforts have hardly been influenced by the general public or by environmental groups. This was the result of, on the one hand, a lack of resources on the part of the respective interest organizations, especially in the early days of the liberalization efforts, and on the other hand of the minor level of involvement of the DG Environment in the political negotiations (Eising, 2000: 204).

Two directives, which together with three regulations constitute the third liberalization package, were proposed in September 2007 to remove remaining barriers (COM(2007)528 final and COM(2007)529 final). Ownership unbundling was considered by the European Commission as the preferred option:

»The concrete proposal in this respect makes it clear that the preferred option of the Commission remains ownership unbundling. In practice this means that Member States must ensure that the same person or persons cannot exercise control over a supply undertaking

Case studies

and, at the same time, hold any interest in or exercise any right over a transmission system operator or transmission system« (COM(2007)528 final: 5; COM(2007)529 final:5). By including the proposal of ownership unbundling, the European Commission »responded to reports of continued misuse of network ownership to hinder fair access for competing suppliers and energy consumers« (Eikeland, 2011:244).

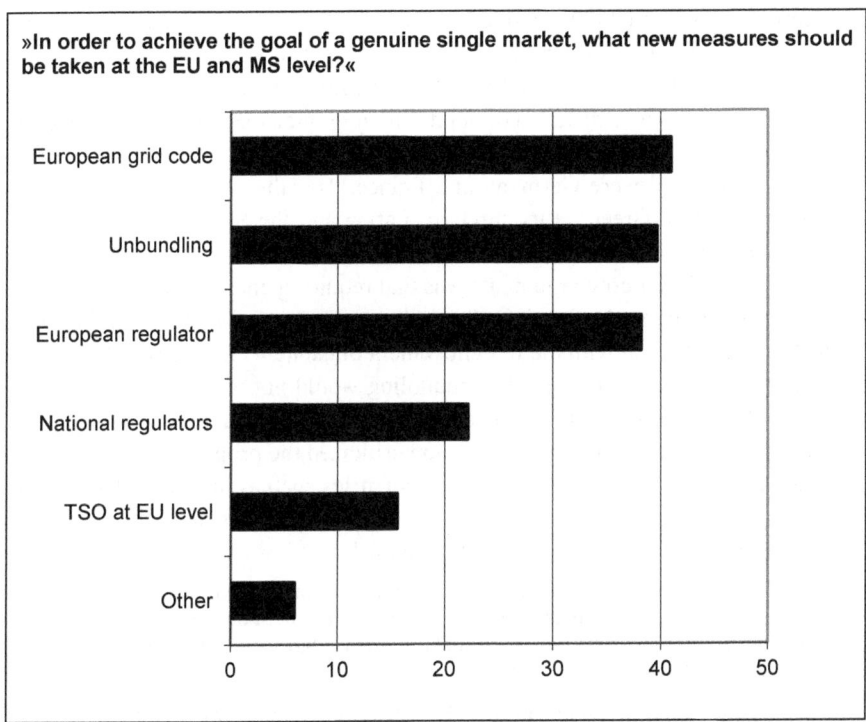

Figure 9: Measures to achieve a genuine single market (European Commission, 2006: 48)

In addition, the establishment of the *Agency for the Cooperation of Energy Regulators* (ACER, founded in 2010), an institution that was expected to assist the national regulatory authorities and coordinate the work between them, was suggested as a means of addressing the lack of coherence between national energy regulators, a factor that was identified as a core reason for the unsatisfactory functioning of the energy market. The main tasks and competences of this agency were summarized as follows:

- »Providing a framework for national regulators to cooperate«;
- »regulatory oversight of the cooperation between transmission system operators«;

133

Research design and case studies

- »individual decision powers«;
- »general advisory role« (ibid: 11-12).

The European Commission emphasized that the agency was not intended to be a substitute for national regulatory authorities, but to provide a framework for improved cross-border cooperation.

Between 2007 and 2009, negotiations between the member states especially focussed on the topic of unbundling. As the EU Commissioner for Energy at that time, Andris Piebalgs, confirmed in February 2008: »At this stage, we know that member countries have different opinions - their opinion on ownership unbundling hasn't converged« (EurActiv, 2008). Among the opponents of the European Commission's proposal were Germany and France. Together with six other states - Austria, Bulgaria, Greece, Luxembourg, Latvia and the Slovak Republic - they presented their own proposal on how to achieve the benefits of a liberalized energy market. One of their core arguments was that requiring energy-producing companies to give up control of their transmission systems was »not compatible with constitutional law and with the free movement of capital« (EurActiv, 2008a). Furthermore, they argued, ownership unbundling would not result in the effects desired by the European Commission, such as larger investment in grids and reduced energy prices. The European Commission criticized the proposal as not going far enough (EurActiv, 2008b). In particular, countries such as the Netherlands, Denmark, Spain, Portugal and Poland, however, exerted pressure on the coalition lead by Germany and France, arguing that the new deal

> »will forbid energy producers from buying up the transmission businesses of energy companies in European countries where full unbundling has been introduced. This effectively means, for example, that EDF would not be allowed to buy up high-tension electricity lines in the Netherlands« (EurActiv, 2008c).

In the Council, an agreement on the third energy package was officially reached in January 2009. The compromise negotiated between the Council and the European Parliament, which was finally adopted in July 2009, offered three options for the companies in the member states. The first was ownership unbundling as proposed by the European Commission in 2007. The second and the third included the possibilities to set up either an independent system operator (ISO) or an independent transmission operator (ITO). The third option was included in response to the proposal made by Germany and France: »They obtained the right for former state monopolies - such as EDF and GDF in France and E.ON and RWE in Germany - to retain ownership of their gas and electricity grids, provided that they are subjected to outside supervision« (EurActiv, 2009b).

The analysis of the position papers submitted to the European decision-makers between 2006 and 2009 in response to either the public consultation on the green paper or the proposals for directives led to the identification of several European associations which tried to influence the policy process. The energy actors who

Case studies

were especially concerned with the 3rd liberalization package were: a) European associations representing intensive energy consumers, b) energy producers/providers, c) technologies/materials/services related to energy consumption, and d) technologies/materials/services related to energy production/provision. The following summary highlights the most important of these. First of all, EURELECTRIC, the European sector association representing the interests of the electricity industry, and Eurogas, the European association representing natural gas companies and federations of natural gas companies, articulated their positions on an individual basis. In reaction to the European Commission's preference for ownership unbundling, EURELECTRIC raised its concerns about the introduction of further legal rules. The association argued that the current legal framework was sufficient for creating a healthy internal energy market and that the European Commission should thus ensure that Directive 2003/54/EC was implemented correctly in the member states: »The Directive has found the correct balance, allowing companies to retain ownership of their networks while putting in place strict rules to ensure the independence of network operators in relation to the networks they operate, maintain or develop« (EURELECTRIC, 2007: 19). Eurogas shared the perspective that further unbundling would overburden the industry and therefore supported the argument raised by EURELECTRIC that the implementation of existing legislation should be the top priority (Eurogas, 2006: 2). Furthermore, commenting on the proposed powers of the European regulator, Eurogas emphasized that national regulatory authorities »have to enjoy full and equal independence and also need to have sufficient powers and resources to carry out their duties effectively and in a timely manner« (Eurogas, 2006a: 2). In this regard, EURELECTRIC (2006a: 8) believed that, first of all, the focus should remain on developing the regulatory process at the regional level and adapting national regulations in cases where they contradict each other.

Sector-specific interests were also articulated by European associations representing the coal and petroleum industry, namely the European Association for Coal and Lignite (EURACOAL) and the European Petroleum Industry Association (EUROPIA). In their individual position papers, they emphasized the importance of fossil fuels for a competitive and secure energy market. EURACOAL stressed that due to its price stability, especially coal could »contribute to the competitiveness of industry in Europe and to the availability of energy resources for everybody« (EURACOAL, 2006).

Position papers were also submitted by associations representing the interests of transmission system operators, such as ETSO, the European Transmission System Operators, and UCTE, the Union for the Coordination of the Transmission of Electricity. These associations together with four others (ATSOI, BALTSO, NORDEL, and UKTSOA) were the predecessors of the newly founded European

Network of Transmission System Operators for Electricity (ENTSO-E). They argued that a European grid code should not be developed at the European level, because »the synchronized electricity regions in Europe have already developed their regional grid codes via the sister organizations of ETSO [...]« (ETSO, 2006: 2). Regarding the issue of unbundling, ETSO criticized that »TSO ownership unbundling is not itself sufficient to create a truly single market« and that options other »than the specific ISO-model proposed by the EC« were available (ETSO, 2007: 2). In contrast, the Council of European Energy Regulators (CEER) considered the option of ownership unbundling as suitable and preferred the method to other measures (CEER, 2006: 4). Furthermore, CEER provided recommendations on what kinds of obligations a European grid code should include and how regulatory functions should be allocated to different levels.

From the perspective of energy consumers, the inefficiencies of the energy market constituted a clear disadvantage, especially for energy intensive industries, such as the metal and the pulp and paper industries. In particular, stakeholders from these industries criticized the lack of predictability of electricity prices: »In power intensive industries investment horizons are long, and therefore long-term power price security at a level that allows operations to be viable is a key requirement« (EUROMETAUX, 2006: 2; see also CEPI, 2007). Therefore, they called for a comprehensive legislative package including »the ownership unbundling of grid-operators from the integrated power companies« (EUROMETAUX, 2006: 3), arguing that only through these measures could the European Commission realize a truly competitive market. Cefic, the European Chemical Industry Council, concurred with the energy intensive industries and called for new legislation on unbundling. In addition, the association considered the creation of a European energy regulator to be essential in order to improve the functioning of the internal energy market (Cefic, 2006).

Some of the individual European associations referred to above, however, did not only formulate papers on behalf of their own associations but in addition also acted in the context of coalitions. In September 2006 the Alliance of Energy Intensive Industries published a paper (Alliance of Energy Intensive Industries, 2006) expressing its members' views on the development of the electricity and gas markets. The alliance has been increasingly active since 2004, especially with regard to EU legislation on emissions trading but also extending other topics. The paper on the internal market was signed by nine European associations representing highly intensive industrial energy consumers, among them EUROMETAUX and CEPI. In this paper, the members of the alliance directly referred to the related green paper. Similar to the position of EUROMETAUX from July 2006, they also emphasized the need for long-term energy price security and improved market efficiency, for example by introducing ownership unbundling. What is striking

Case studies

when comparing the papers issued by EUROMETAUX and the Alliance of Energy Intensive Industries is that the wording partly coincides, which indicates that segments from the EUROMETAUX-paper were utilised in the publication by the alliance (see for example EUROMETAUX, 2006: 2 and Alliance of Energy Intensive Industries, 2006: 2-3).

The position papers published by the alliance since 2004 have not always been signed by the same associations. While some signatories are identical, others vary depending on the topic at hand (see for example Alliance of Energy Intensive Industries, 2006; 2007). Due to diverging interests between the petroleum industry and the highly-intensive energy consumers, EUROPIA, for example, which participated in the alliance with regard to the EU ETS (see for example Alliance of Energy Intensive Industries, 2010), did not sign the statement on the internal market.

The name - Alliance of Energy Intensive Industries - implies a certain degree of formality. Nevertheless, this coalition of industry associations has not set up a website or designed a specific letterhead. Nor does an administrative body to coordinate the work between the coalition members or a spokesperson, who is allowed to speak on behalf of all of them, exist.[25] Furthermore, the Alliance of Energy Intensive Industries could not be found in the transparency register run by the European Commission and the European Parliament.[26] Concerning the length of time this coalition has been in existence, one can say that the duration has neither been short- nor long-term, but that the coalition has been formed on different occasions, such as the political negotiations about the EU ETS or the creation of an internal energy market, and that it has appeared in various constellations. All aspects considered, this form of cooperation can be categorized as a semi-formal coalition.

It is striking that while renewable energy associations issued a common position responding to the Green Paper *A European strategy for sustainable, competitive and secure energy* through the European Renewable Energy Council (EREC) (EREC, 2006) (the umbrella organization of the leading European renewable energy industry, trade and research associations) the European associations representing different fossil fuel energy sources did not join forces - neither within the sector nor with other industries. In an interview with a representative of a fossil energy industry sector[27], two reasons were given for not having formed coalitions: The first was simply that interests between different associations diverged to such an extent that no common position on the topic could be agreed upon. The second and from a theoretical perspective probably more interesting reason provided was

---

25   Confirmed in telephone interview with *EUAssoc2*, conducted 20 August 2009, 03.00 pm.
26   As of 26 October 2011.
27   Telephone interview with *EUAssoc7*, conducted 5 March 2010, 10.00 am.

that due to the »dirty image« of the fossil energy sources, it is difficult to find potential coalition partners. In particular, the bad reputation of fossil fuels with regard to environmental pollution prevent many actors from cooperating. Therefore, the sector typically submits position papers to the decision-makers only on behalf of its own industry, despite the fact that overlapping interests with other associations exist. In some cases where common interests can indeed be identified between the fossil fuel energy industry and other »cleaner« industries, cooperation takes place in a way that is not obvious to outsiders. For example, the associations may meet behind closed doors to coordinate their arguments and strategies of how to influence the policy process and then go ahead on their own. In doing so, they can ensure that they present the same arguments in favor or against a policy initiative and, at the same, time do not emphasize certain aspects that could disadvantage other cooperating parties. This is here categorized as an invisible coalition.

In the following, the hypotheses developed in the previous section are applied to the case of the 3rd energy market liberalization package. The first hypotheses deal with the impact of *institutional opportunity structures* (a. *institutional agendas*, b. *institutional rules*, c. *office-holders*) on the formation of coalitions and the strategy choices made by the coalition members. According to Hypothesis 1.1 it is assumed that European associations and/or NGOs form coalitions only after the European Commission has included an issue on its agenda. For the example of the Alliance of Energy Intensive Industries this hypothesis was confirmed. In its first position paper on the internal energy market (Alliance of Energy Intensive Industries, 2006) the alliance directly referred to the European Commission's related green paper. This, however, does not imply that coalition members act only in response to political initiatives and never behave proactively, but as interview partners *EUAssoc1*[28] and *EUAssoc2* confirmed, coalition-formation is time-consuming. The process usually starts with each association formulating its own position on a topic and trying to influence the European Commission's agenda. Following this, compatible associations may discuss which common interests exist and whether joint action is appropriate. Therefore, coalitions would typically form during the decision-making rather than the agenda-setting phase. Concerning the influence of *institutional agendas* on the strategies pursued by coalition members, Hypothesis 1.2 assumes that if the topic has been placed high on the agenda of some nation states, coalition members (European associations) also advise their national member associations to seek access to national-level decision-makers. This hypothesis was generally confirmed. Interview partner *EUAssoc17*[29] stressed that including national member associations in the lobbying strategy was highly

---

28 Telephone interview with *EUAssoc1*, conducted 12 August, 2009, 02.00 pm.
29 Telephone interview with *EUAssoc17*, conducted 22 October 2010, 09.00 am.

important, especially with regard to the European Parliament and the Council as these institutions prefer to talk to industries with a national or even local background. However interview partner *EUAssoc7* emphasized that Eurogroups do not have the power to give orders to their national member associations as membership is voluntary and depends on the members' view of the organization's services and achievements. With regard to Hypothesis 1.3 on the impact of *institutional rules*, most interview partners consulted for this case study agreed that as a result of co-decision procedure, it has become more important to include the European Parliament in lobbying strategies. While the European Commission and the European Parliament are considered as the central addressees of lobbying, the Council was mainly addressed by national organizations. Considering Hypotheses 1.4 and 1.5, which deal with the variable *office-holders*, several respondents confirmed that these do indeed play an important role. While it seems to be less important for coalition-formation, institutional members can greatly influence a coalition's lobbying strategy. For example, after each election, new networks have to be established and institutional agendas may differ. Some office-holders are less industry-oriented than others and therefore more comprehensive lobbying strategies may have to be pursued in order to increase their receptiveness of industrial concerns.[30]

The second group of hypotheses deals with the variable *motivation* (a. *short-/long-term interests*, b. *long-established norms*). For the example of the Alliance of Energy Intensive Industries one can say that cooperation for the third liberalization package was clearly based on the long-term economic interest of obtaining internationally competitive electricity and gas prices that meet the needs of energy intensive industries:

> »In this non-functioning market, it is no longer possible for electricity customers to engage in true negotiations, nor to conclude long-term contracts as in other regions in the world, while in addition the price paid for electricity by European energy intensive industries is now much higher than in other regions in the world. As a consequence, the international competitive position of European industry has deteriorated sharply« (Alliance of Energy Intensive Industries, 2006: 2).

To realize this goal, the Alliance of Energy Intensive Industries, which was originally formed to influence the legislation on emissions trading, was reactivated and the coalition members issued a position paper expressing their concerns. Therefore, Hypothesis 2.1 was confirmed. Neither Hypothesis 2.2, which states that actors who share long-established norms tend to form a coalition that is more persistent over time and thus more likely to be formalized, nor Hypothesis 2.3, which assumes that formal coalitions also pursue voice strategies, could be tested for this case study. However, during the telephone interviews respondents were asked why

---

30 See, for example, telephone interviews with *EUAssoc2*, *EUAssoc4*, conducted 18 September 2009, 10.30 am; *EUAssoc17*.

they had decided against cooperation with others. As indicated already above, two reasons were provided for the absence of interest group coalitions between European associations and/or NGOs: The first was that interests between different associations had diverged to the extent that no common position on the topic can be agreed on. The second was that the formation of »visible« coalitions often depends on the reputation of potential coalition partners. Therefore, a common strategy is not to cooperate visibly, but in a way that is not obvious for outsiders, for example by agreeing on a specific strategy that is then pursued by each association on an individual basis.

This aspect directly leads to the fourth group of hypotheses dealing with the impact of the variable *reputation*. Hypothesis 4.1 assumes that if a European association or NGO can improve its reputation by cooperating with others, a coalition is more likely to be formed. In contrast, if its reputation will be damaged as a result of cooperation, it will decide against it. Here, reputation is defined as the representativity and credibility of the coalition members. For the members of the Alliance of Energy Intensive Industries, demonstrating representativity by speaking with one voice was considered to be important. Respondents assumed that the European institutions can be lobbied more effectively by sending a position paper signed by several associations sharing an opinion.[31] Hypothesis 4.2 states that coalition members with a bad reputation will experience difficulties in gaining access to the European institutions. For coalitions of European associations, however, voice strategies do not seem to be an alternative. As member associations of the Alliance of Energy Intensive Industries[32] explained, at the coalition level they prefer access strategies because, first of all, it is important to have direct contact with decision-makers, and, second, as a coalition they are missing an administrative body or a spokesperson that is authorized to speak on behalf of all coalition members. This made it unusual or even impossible to initiate media campaigns and as a consequence access to the European institutions was even more important. Interview partner *EC3*[33] from the European Commission emphasized that while access is generally given to all actors that contact the institution, the European Commission does not answer requests made by people who do not seem to be reasonable. Respondent *EC6*[34] added that especially with regard to questions of competitiveness, an association's (or coalition's) reputation is highly decisive as this is a very sensitive topic and the European Commission is dependent on what interest

---

31   See, for example, telephone interviews with *EUAssoc4* and *EUAssoc9*, conducted 19 March 2010, 11.00 am.
32   See, for example, telephone interviews with *EUAssoc17* and *EUAssoc4*.
33   Telephone interview with *EC3*, conducted 15 December 2010, 10.00 am.
34   Telephone interview with *EC6*, conducted 24 March 2011, 03.00 pm.

groups say. Against this background, the variable *credibility* was a decisive factor for not cooperating with the associations such as the fossil fuel industry.

The third group of hypotheses covers the role of the variables *information* and *expertise*. In order to be able to test these hypotheses, it must first be assessed if the members of the Alliance of Energy Intensive Industries, indeed, have the required information and expertise. With regard to information, all coalition members which signed the position paper on the third energy market package have representations in Brussels in order to represent the industry's interests at the EU level. Monitoring EU policy developments was described as an important task to successfully influence the policy process. With regard to expertise, all associations can be considered as experts for the industrial sector they represent, which they have proven by regularly publishing scientific reports and articles. Hypothesis 3.1 states that if European associations have information and expertise, they are more likely to be included in a coalition. This was not confirmed by the respondents consulted for this case study. Rather, they emphasized the existence of a similar goal - either interests or norms - as main driver for coalition-formation.[35] However, the interview partners confirmed Hypothesis 3.2 which assumes that if coalition members possess comprehensive information on the policy process as well as on the decision-makers concerned, the coalition is more likely to reformulate a position paper when sending it to several institutions. Interview partner *EUAssoc17* stressed that emphasizing different aspects in position papers with different addressees is an important strategic element. *EUAssoc2, EUAssoc9*, and *EUAssoc19*[36] added that position papers sent to the European Parliament often consist of more general political arguments, while those written to influence the (administrative level of the) European Commission include more technical details. In particular, as the DG Energy had in-depth knowledge of the subject, one could go into further detail.

However, the number of different position papers prepared for lobbying purposes also depends on the financial and human resources a coalition is equipped with, which leads to the fifth group of hypotheses dealing with the impact of *resources*. All respondents confirmed that the amount of resources an association possesses has no impact on whether it becomes member of a coalition ($\rightarrow$ H 5.1). On the one hand, it was considered helpful if several associations can share the work and costs required for comprehensive lobbying strategies. On the other hand, the formation of coalition is very time-consuming ($\rightarrow$ H 5.2). Concerning strategies, access strategies do not only include the submission of a position paper, but also the personal contact to the decision-makers in face-to-face meetings. In this

---

35   See, for example, telephone interview with *EUAssoc1, EUAssoc17* and *EUAssoc19*, conducted 28 October 2010, 11.30 am.
36   Telephone interview with *EUAssoc19*.

regard, some respondents, however, emphasized that, if they talk to decision-makers in face-to-face conversations, they only do so on behalf of their own association.

4.2.2 Interests and strategies regarding the inclusion of aviation in the EU ETS

Unhappy with the exclusion of international aviation activities from the Emissions Trading Scheme specified by the Kyoto Protocol, the European Commission initiated a public consultation process entitled *Reducing the climate change impact of aviation*, which took place from March to May 2005. The European Commission asked all participants to provide an opinion on three policy objectives:

1) to include »the air transport sector in efforts to mitigate climate change«;
2) to internalize »the external costs of climate change in the price of air transport«;
3) and to strengthen »the economic incentives for air transport operators to reduce their impact on the climate« (European Commission, 2005: 20 ff.).

The European Commission suggested a range of potential policy options which were expected to contribute to realizing the core objectives. Besides the inclusion of aviation activities in the EU ETS, these included further economic instruments, such as aircraft fuel taxes, en-route charges or taxes, departure and arrival taxes, and VAT on air transport. Additionally, non-economic incentives were proposed, consisting of raising passenger awareness for the climate change impact of aviation activities and resulting mitigation costs, reducing the growth of air transport, especially regarding leisure-based flights, restricting the access to EU airports for the most polluting aircrafts, improving air traffic management, higher investment in research and development of cleaner transport technologies, and voluntary commitments by the airlines to reduce emissions (European Commission, 2005). During the public consultation period, respondents were asked to indicate which of these options they considered to be most effective. The results are summarized in Figure 10 and Figure 11, the first illustrating the preferences regarding the economic instruments, and the second regarding the non-economic instruments. Concerning the economic instruments, 35.9 per cent of respondents selected aircraft fuel taxes as their first option, 31.5 per cent the inclusion of aviation in the EU ETS, and 26.1 per cent en-route charges or taxes. Only 4.9 per cent voted for departure and arrival taxes, and even less (1.6 per cent) for VAT. Concerning the non-economic instruments, most respondents supported the option to restrict ac-

Case studies

cess to EU airports for the most polluting aircraft. Secondly, they considered raising consumer awareness as most effective, and thirdly, investment in research and development. The improvement of air traffic management and voluntary commitments by the airlines to reduce emissions were only considered to be effective by 13.6 per cent and 4.3 per cent respectively.

In September 2005 the European Commission adopted the Communication *Reducing the climate change impact of aviation*, further emphasizing its intention to include aviation in the EU ETS:

»Having analyzed a number of options, the Commission considers that the best way forward, from an economic and environmental point of view, lies in including the climate impact of the aviation sector in the EU emissions trading scheme« (COM(2005)459 final: 10).

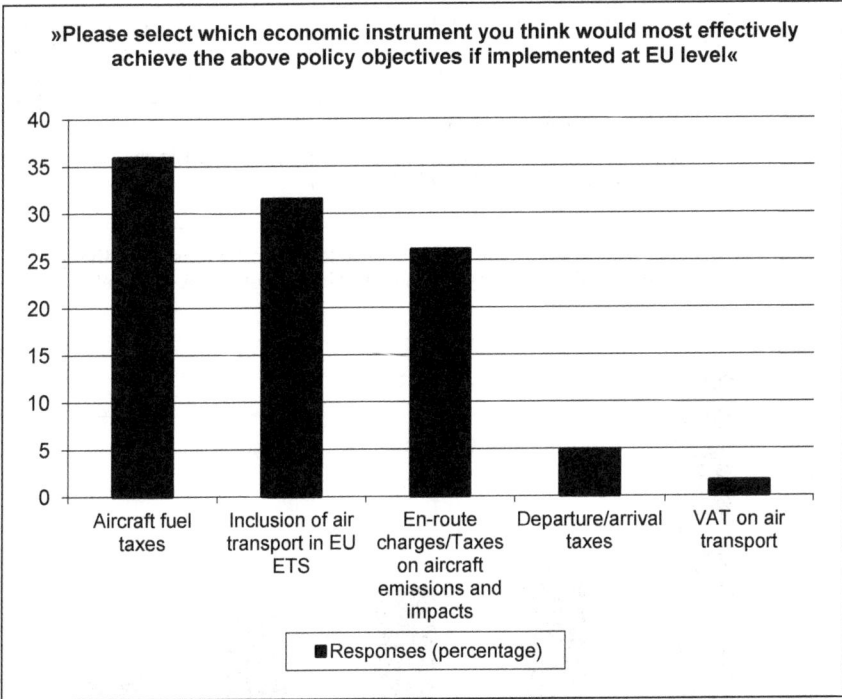

Figure 10: First choice of economic instruments (European Commission, 2005: 28)

In December 2006 this Communication was followed by the European Commission's *Proposal for a Directive so as to include aviation activities in the scheme for greenhouse gas emission allowance trading* (COM(2006)818 final). The key aspects of this proposal can be summarized as follows:

143

Research design and case studies

- »Aircraft operators will be the entities responsible for complying with the obligations imposed by the scheme«;
- »The scheme will cover all flights arriving at or departing from an airport in the Community as of 1 January 2012. Flights between EU airports will be covered from 1 January 2011«;
- »The total number of allowances to be allocated to the aviation sector will be determined at Community level by reference to average emissions from aviation in the years 2004-2006«;
- »A fixed percentage of the total quantity of allowances will be allocated free of charge on the basis of a benchmark to aircraft operators which submit an application (the earliest application relating to 2008 data)« [...];
- »Like other participants in the Community scheme, aircraft operators will have to monitor their emissions of carbon dioxide and report them to the competent authority of its administering Member State by 31 March each year« [...];
- »Aircraft operators will also be able to use project credits – so-called Emission Reduction Units (ERUs) and Certified Emission Reductions (CERs) - from the Joint Implementation or Clean Development Mechanisms (JI/CDM) up to a harmonized limit equivalent to the average of the limits prescribed by Member States in their national allocation plans for other sectors in the Community scheme«;
- »Domestic aviation will be included in the scheme and treated in the same way as international aviation« (COM(2006)818 final: 6-7).

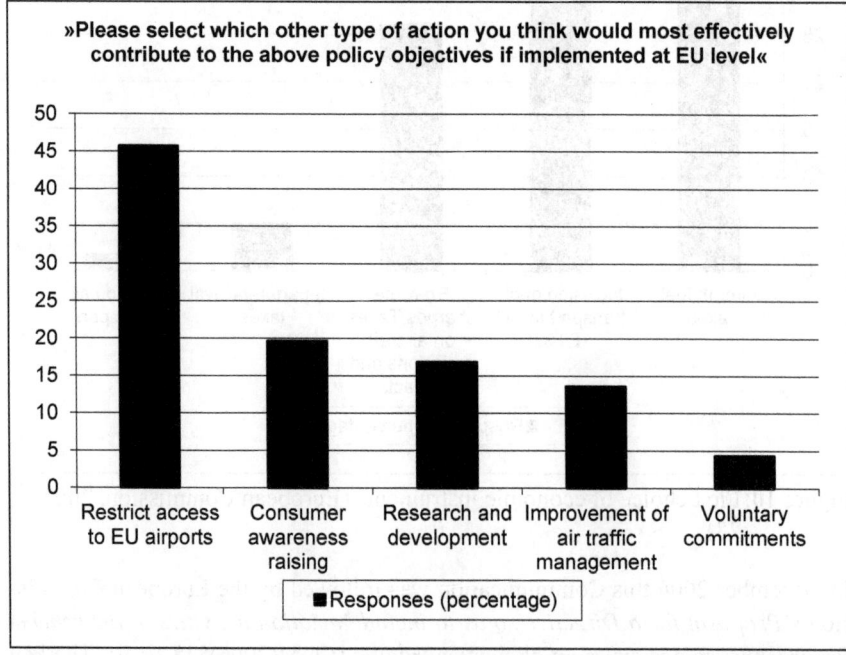

Figure 11: First choice of action other than economic instruments (European Commission, 2005: 28)

Case studies

Although no further official stakeholder consultation was initiated after 2005, energy actors nevertheless reacted to the European Commission's communication and its proposal by submitting their policy positions to the European decision-makers. Decisive for answering the research question here is which specific actors formed coalitions to influence the policy process and what kind of strategies they supported, either as a coalition member, or on behalf of an individual organization.

The energy actors who were concerned with the inclusion of aviation in the EU ETS can be categorized in two groups: a) NGOs concerned about the consequences of energy consumption, and b) intensive energy consumers/emission producers (especially the airline industry).

By analyzing the position papers submitted to European decision-makers between 2003 and 2008 in response to either Directive 2003/87/EC, the public consultation process, the Communication COM(2006)818 final, or the Proposal COM(2008)16 final, several European NGOs and industry associations could be identified. The NGOs, first of all, formulated positions on behalf of their individual organizations (see for example, T&E, 2005; WWF, 2006; FoE, 2007), in which they lobbied intensively in favor of the inclusion of aviation in the EU ETS. They argued that aviation is a fast growing industry sector and that emissions have increased drastically within the past five years. Furthermore, the aviation sector has failed to improve fuel-efficiency - although airline associations, such as the International Air Transport Association (IATA) or the European Low Fares Airline Association (ELFAA), claimed the opposite (T&E, 2005, ELFAA, 2005). In a position paper submitted by a European airline association it is stressed that »average fuel burn and carbon dioxide and water vapour emissions per passenger seat kilometer in modern aircraft are approximately 70 per cent lower than in the aircraft designed in the 1960s« (ELFAA, 2005: 2). As outlined in the same document later on, especially the average energy use of low fares airlines has decreased as these do not offer business class seating and catering and, thus, can configure their aircraft to accommodate more passengers than traditional airlines (ELFAA, 2005: 4). Although most European associations representing the airline industry generally supported the inclusion of aviation in the EU ETS as »the most environmentally efficient mechanisms« (AEA, 2008: 1), they nevertheless expressed their concern about whether the EU would ensure that »the European aviation industry's competitiveness and regional economic growth« will not be negatively affected compared to non-EU airlines (AEA, 2007: 1).

Further concerns were raised by industry sectors, such as the energy-intensive or the electricity industry, which raised quite different objections. They emphasized that, in contrast to other industry branches, airlines could add the costs of purchased allowances to product prices. Therefore, airlines would be a »net buyer in the CO_2 allowance market without this having a significant effect on their profits and losses« (IFIEC Europe, 2005: 2; see also EURELECTRIC, 2006). The International Federation of Industrial Energy Consumers (IFIEC) argued that, as a consequence of the inclusion of aviation in the EU ETS, »the cost-effectiveness of the existing system will deteriorate even further, with serious effects on the competitiveness of the participating sectors and all power intensive consumers« (IFIEC Europe, 2005: 1).

The individual associations and organizations submitted their position papers throughout the entire policy process, both individually and later jointly. When issuing joint position papers, the various NGOs and industry associations emphasized that they had formed a coalition in order to pursue common goals. Among the NGOs that formed coalitions were, for example, the European Environmental Bureau (EEB), the Climate Action Network Europe (CAN-E), the European Federation for Transport and Environment (T&E), Friends of the Earth Europe (FoEE), Greenpeace International, and the World Wide Fund for Nature (WWF). One of the early position papers regarding measures to mitigate the climate change impact of aviation was published by the EEB, together with FoEE, International Friends of Nature (IFN), and T&E in June 2005 (EEB, FoEE, IFN and T&E, 2005). These four NGOs stressed their common interest in a comprehensive framework to address the climate change impact of aviation. This should include various measures to be adopted at the EU, as well as at the national level (EEB, FoEE, IFN and T&E, 2005: 2), such as the inclusion of the aviation sector in any future international treaty dealing with the question of climate change, and the introduction of en-route emission charges or kerosene taxation. On September 22, 2005 the same NGOs cooperated with six other organizations within the Green 10 (Green 10, 2005) and formulated a joint letter concerning the European Commission's decision to publish the Communication *Reducing the climate change impact of aviation*, which was expected for September 27, 2005. The Green 10 is a group of ten large European environmental NGOs, which consists of: Birdlife International, CEE Bankwatch Network, Climate Action Network Europe (CAN-E), European Environment Bureau (EEB), Transport and Environment (T&E), Health and Environment Alliance, Friends of the Earth Europe (FoEE), Greenpeace, International Friends of Nature (IFN), and WWF European Policy Office (WWF-EPO)[37]. In its letter, the Green 10 asked the European Commission »to swiftly publish this important communication as a first and necessary step and to issue a concrete legislative proposal to tackle the impact of aviation as soon as possible thereafter« (Green 10, 2005: 1). In the following years, the Green 10 also cooperated on other environmental topics, such as emissions from light duty vehicles (Green 10, 2007) or the European Commission's general performance in meeting environmental challenges (Green 10, 2009).

---

37 See: http://www.green10.org/ [Accessed 19 July 2011].

Case studies

From 2006 onwards, some of the NGOs listed above formulated additional joint position papers, however without referring to their membership in the Green 10. For example, CAN-E and T&E revisited the topic of aviation emissions and formulated a position paper suggesting *Measures to curb the climate change impacts of aviation* (CAN-E and T&E, 2006). In this paper, most of the arguments emphasized by EEB, FoEE, IFN and T&E in 2005 were essentially adopted in their original form whilst taking into account subsequent political developments. It concludes by claiming that »EU action would not harm [the] competitiveness of EU carriers« (CAN-E and T&E, 2006: 4). This is in clear contrast to the description of energy- and export-intensive industries as »exposed sectors« and the potential of strict climate policies to »indeed harm the competitive position of these industries and give rise to re-location« (CAN-E and T&E, 2006: 4). In 2008 CAN-E, the WWF-EPO, FoEE, and T&E – all members of the Green 10 - cooperated with the Aviation Environment Federation (AEF), a UK-based association concerned about the environmental impacts of the aviation sector. In their position paper the organizations directly responded to the European Commission's draft proposal to include aviation in the EU ETS.

From the theoretical perspective of this work, the ad-hoc coalition between WWF International and Allianz Global Investors is also of great relevance. These actors published a joint report to »advance the debate in the financial community, and to propose solutions« to the climate change problem (WWF and Allianz Global Investors, 2005). The report outlines the risks and opportunities that have emerged for the financial services industry from the issue of climate change and the implementation of related European policies in the EU member states. Among other aspects the report calls for a »clear regulatory framework on climate policy« which banks and investors can »base their investment and lending decisions on« (WWF and Allianz Global Investors, 2005: 9). This example of coalition-formation is of particular interest as, in contrast to what Sabatier and his collaborators assume, this cooperation clearly does not rest on a joint belief or norm system that both actors share, but on common environmental and economic interests regarding future energy and climate change policies in the European Union.

Besides the NGOs, European airline associations also formed different coalitions to further their common interests. As interview partner *EUAssoc3*[38] emphasized, two types of coalitions have been created: On the one hand, during recent years several informal ad-hoc coalitions between European associations representing the aviation industry have been formed, especially with regard to the inclusion of aviation in the EU ETS. On the other hand, the Council for Environmentally Friendly Aviation (CEFA) was established in 1995 to create a forum for more permanent cooperation.

---

38 Telephone interview with *EUAssoc3*, conducted 2 September, 2009, 11.00 am.

Position papers indicating that informal ad-hoc coalitions have been formed to influence specific political issues were released especially between 2005 and 2008. In July 2005, the Association of European Airlines (AEA), the Aerospace and Defence Industries Association of Europe (ASD), the European Express Association (EEA), the European Business Aviation Association (EBAA), the European Regions Airline Association (ERA), and the International Air Carrier Association (IACA) reacted to the European Commission's announcement of a communication on aviation and climate change by jointly formulating a position paper. In this paper, the associations raised two concerns: 1) that the proposed timeframe »would not give the stakeholders enough time to make a meaningful contribution to the Commission's paper«, and 2) that »the scope of the Communication would be extremely limited and would fail to provide a solid foundation for future policy and subsequent legislation«, if it solely focused on economic instruments (AEA, ASD, EEA, EBAA, ERA and IACA; 2005: 1). In April 2006, the same associations wrote a letter commenting on the draft report of the working document *Reducing the climate change impact of aviation* by Caroline Lucas, a member of the Greens/European Free Alliance group and rapporteur for the ENVI[39] Committee of the European Parliament. In this letter, the associations claimed that the report was based on »erroneous facts and figures« which were accompanied by »unqualified general statements that have no substance or factual support« (AEA, ASD, EEA, EBAA, ERA and IACA; 2006: 1). Nevertheless, the report by Caroline Lucas was adopted by the ENVI Committee on May 30, 2006. As a consequence, several European associations representing the aviation industry once again addressed MEPs by sending a letter expressing their concerns about the measures suggested in the report. This second letter was signed not only by the six previously mentioned associations, but additionally by the International Air Transport Association (IATA), the Air Transport Action Group (ATAG), and the European Low Fares Airline Association (ELFAA) (AEA, ASD, EEA, EBAA, ERA, IACA; IATA, ATAG, and ELFAA, 2006). The letter to the MEPs was followed by a position paper formulated in October 2006 without the participation of IATA, EEA and ATAG (AEA, ASD, ECA, EBAA, ERA, IACA, and ELFAA, 2006).

Another coalition emerged in 2007 between six European aviation associations and the European Helicopter Association (EADS), the Safran Group, a high-technology group focusing on three related areas (aerospace, defense and security), and two multinational companies, namely Airbus and Boeing. The aviation associations requested a scientific study to be conducted by Ernst & Young and York Aviation on the effects of the European Commission's proposal to include the aviation industry in the EU ETS (Ernst & Young and York Aviation, 2007). This analysis was financially supported by Airbus, Boeing, the Safran Group, and

---

39 Committee on the Environment, Public Health and Food Safety (ENVI).

Case studies

EADS. In addition, the same aviation associations which requested the study submitted further position papers during the decision-making phase in which they suggested amendments to be considered by the European Parliament and the Council (AEA, ECA, EBAA, ELFAA, ERA and IACA, 2007; 2007a).

Compared to the ad-hoc coalitions listed above, CEFA was mentioned by interview partner *EUAssoc3* (→ see above) as a more permanent coalition. CEFA is chaired by ERA and, according to ERA's webpage, includes the following members: ERA, AEA, ASD, EBAA, EEA, ELFAA and IACA. As interview partner *EUAssoc3* stressed, hundreds of papers have been published by CEFA on different policy issues. However, these are difficult to identify on the internet, as CEFA is not always explicitly mentioned as an author (see for example AEA, ASD, EBAA, EEA, ELFAA, ERA and IACA, 2010, where it is only indicated that the Director General of ERA, who signed this paper, also chairs CEFA).

In the following section, the hypotheses developed in the previous section are applied to the case of the inclusion of aviation in the EU ETS. The first hypotheses were formulated concerning the impact of *institutional opportunity structures* (a. *institutional agendas*, b. *institutional rules*, c. *office-holders*) on the formation of coalitions and the strategies adopted by the coalition members. Here, the variable *institutional agendas* has emerged to be highly influential, especially regarding the dependent variable *coalition-formation* (→ H 1.1). As the quoted position papers illustrate, coalitions of European associations and/or NGOs reacted to the agenda of the European institutions. They formulated joint position papers in reply to the European Commission's public consultation, communication or proposal for directive, as well as after the rapporteur of the ENVI Committee of the European Parliament Caroline Lucas published her report. This was also confirmed by interview partner *EUNGO1*[40] who said that if NGOs act only on behalf their own organizations, they try to be proactive because they usually want the European Commission to further regulate an issue. However, as a coalition, the organizations would mostly react to the initiatives of the European Commission, simply because coalition-formation takes time. Interview partner *EUNGO5*[41] stressed that as soon as the organizations anticipated that the European Commission was going to come up with a proposal, everyone started to work on the issue. The cooperation between them intensified, however, after the European Commission had launched its initiative.

Regarding the impact of *institutional agendas* on the strategies adopted by the coalition members (→ H 1.2) it appears that coalitions of European associations and/or NGOs also advise their national members to seek access to those national-

---

40 Telephone interview with *EUNGO1*, conducted 26 November 2009, 11.30 am.
41 Telephone interview with *EUNGO5*, conducted 10 December 2010, 11.00 am.

Research design and case studies

level decision-makers that are similarly concerned with the topic. Interview partner *EUNGO2*[42] emphasized that the strategies pursued by a coalition are always developed in cooperation with the national member organizations. If the government of one nation state is particularly concerned about an EU policy initiative, the national organization of this country is asked to play a key role in refining the coalition's further strategy. One element of this strategy is typically to address national politicians through the national organization.

Hypothesis 1.3 states that if co-decision is applied, coalitions seek access to MEPs rather than to members of the Council. Since co-decision has become the norm for policy-making, European associations and NGOs increasingly address the European Parliament for lobbying purposes. The position papers that were sent to the European Parliament during the decision-making phase indicate the validity of this assumption. It was also confirmed, for example, by interview partner *EUNGO1* who explained that since the increasing relevance of co-decision, the European Parliament was much more important as a lobbying addressee. The Council was considered as equally important, however it would generally be addressed by the national member associations.

Hypothesis 1.4 deals with the impact of personal contacts between individual members of European associations and/or NGOs on the probability that a coalition is formed. As reported in the first case study, the respondents again emphasized the existence of common intentions as the main reason for coalition-formation. Interview partner *EUAssoc3* explained that as a first step every association formulates its own position and, second, other associations are contacted to find out if common goals exist. It is, of course, not a disadvantage if personal contacts between the individuals from different associations already exist, but it was not described as decisive. Closely related, Hypothesis 1.5 assumes that if office-holders alternate, coalition members will reconsider their strategies in order to increase the receptiveness of the new person in office. This assumption was confirmed by interview partner *EUNGO1*. She stressed that actors that attempt to influence the policy process constantly have to establish personal contacts with the members of the European institutions, especially the European Parliament. In the aftermath of parliamentary elections, it is even more important to contact the new office-holders to make them aware of the association's concerns.

The second group of hypotheses deals with the effect of the independent variable *motivation* on the formation of coalitions and the strategy choices of the coalition members. Most of the position papers referred to above resulted from the formation of ad-hoc coalitions between associations or organizations as indicated by their signatures (→ H 2.1). These ad-hoc coalitions especially served to represent a common interest regarding a specific aspect of a policy issue. The aspects

---

42   Telephone interview with *EUNGO2*, conducted 4 May 2010, 11.00 am.

which the coalition members disagreed on were presented in individual papers, as it was, for example, indicated by an airline coalition: »There are other vital areas on which details could not be agreed specifically. These areas will be covered by the individual airspace user associations« (AEA, ECA, EBAA, ELFAA, ERA and IACA, 2007: 1). The term *ad-hoc*, however, is not meant to imply that these coalitions have been formed only once. Instead, coalition-formation has taken place on different occasions depending on the agenda of the European institutions and the stage of the policy process. In contrast, cooperation within the Green 10 can be categorized as a formal coalition which seems to have emerged out of initially much looser cooperation between the organizations (→ H 2.2). The members of the Green 10 share a similar set of norms concerning environmental issues. Interview partner *EUNGO2* agreed that cooperation between the European NGOs was mainly based on common ideology. This is also reflected in the position papers and statutes of the member organizations. Regarding the degree of formality, the Green 10 have established their own website[43] in order to provide information on the group's activities. However, compared to an organization, the group does not have an administrative body. Instead, it is chaired by the Director or Secretary General of one of its member organizations, who is named as a contact person on the position papers or letters published by the Green 10. To make the cooperation public, the Green 10 have also set up a profile in the transparency register run by the European Commission and the European Parliament (identification number 70309834043-10). Hypothesis 2.3 assumes that formalized coalitions that are based on long-established norms also use voice strategies to complement their efforts to gain access to the decision-makers. Considering the example of the Green 10, a number of informative press releases are available on its website. Additionally, these explicitly provide a contact address for media inquiries (see for example Green 10, 2009). In contrast the strategies pursued by the informal ad-hoc coalitions clearly fall into the category of access strategies (→ H 2.3). The coalitions mainly relied on joint position papers, rather than on press releases. Interview partner *EUAssoc3* explained that informal coalitions do not approach the press because they lack a spokesperson.

The third group of hypotheses included assumptions on the impact of the independent variable *information and expertise*. The airline associations and NGOs mentioned above have established offices in Brussels in order to be able to monitor the policy process and proactively develop lobbying strategies. Furthermore, on their websites the associations and NGOs indicate that they work in close cooperation with the EU institutions. Therefore, it can be assumed that they have direct and early access to information on the EU policy process and the decision-makers involved. With regard to expertise, the associations and NGOs regularly conduct

---

43   See: http://www.green10.org/ [Accessed 19 July 2011].

research studies to support their arguments (see for example AEA, 2007a; CAN-E, 2011). Through their members they also have access to country-specific data. Hypothesis 3.1 states that if European associations and NGOs have information and expertise, they are more likely to be included in a coalition. *EUNGO5* and *EUAssoc3* confirmed that information-sharing is an important aspect of coalition-formation, and is especially important for NGOs as they must often confront strong industry lobbies. Concerning the impact information has on the strategy choices made by coalition members, Hypothesis 3.2 assumes that information on the decision-makers concerned enhances the likelihood that, depending on the addressee, a coalition will formulate several position papers stressing different arguments. *EUNGO2* emphasized that in order to efficiently influence the Directorates-General, the organization has to bring forward different arguments. Furthermore, the national venue is usually used to influence the Council, while influencing the European Commission requires technical expertise at the EU level. Therefore, specific information on the positions of the institutional members who are concerned with a topic is an important prerequisite.

The fourth group of hypotheses is concerned with the impact of the independent variable *reputation* - defined as *representativity* and *credibility* - on the formation of a coalition and its members' strategy choices. *EUNGO2* recalled an example where an international industry organization approached the NGO she represented. Although similar interests existed, the latter was seriously concerned about the effects a potential cooperation would have for its reputation, especially with regard to its credibility. Therefore, no coalition emerged between them. As pointed out by *EUNGO2*, reputation also played a role for the decision to form an invisible coalition, implying that strategies between the organizations were coordinated, but no joint position paper was submitted. *EUAssoc3* added that it is important to establish a »united front« to emphasize the representativity of a position. Concerning Hypothesis 4.2, *EUAssoc3* stressed that if an association wants to successfully influence the policy process, it is wise not to offend the legislator. Otherwise, gaining (personal) access to the decision-maker can become difficult.

The last group of hypotheses deals with the variable *resources*. Here the analysis of the empirical case showed that resources do not have a significant impact on the decision to form a coalition with other European associations and/or NGOs (→ H 5.1). In particular, the identified ad-hoc coalitions were mainly based on common (short-term) interests and not on the value added by human or financial resources. If resources would be a core argument for coalition-formation, consequently a coalition should include as many members as possible. This argument, however, was rejected by interview partner *EP1*[44] who stated that due to the variety of interests, it would be difficult for many associations to come to a consensus.

---

44 Telephone interview with *EP1*, conducted 21 March 2011, 01.30 pm.

Case studies

Thus, the position submitted by a coalition would often be watered down as a result of attempts to achieve compromise between too many signatories. Resources do however play a role in terms of the strategies adopted by the coalition members, as European associations often lack sufficient financial and human resources. Therefore, they usually cannot afford highly comprehensive lobbying strategies that include the services offered by international consultancies. The best example for the impact of resources on a coalition's strategy is the cooperation between a number of aviation associations and Airbus, Boeing, the European Helicopter Association, and the Safran Group. The coalition requested a scientific study to be conducted by Ernst & Young and York Aviation and, as indicated on the cover page of this analysis, could afford the study only because of the financial support of the bigger players (Ernst & Young and York Aviation, 2007).

4.2.3 Developments related to the directive on the energy performance of buildings

The first directive on the energy performance of buildings was adopted in 2002 (Dir. 2002/91/EC). The energy performance of buildings was defined as »the amount of energy actually consumed or estimated to meet the different needs associated with a standardised use of the building, which may include, inter alia, heating, hot water heating, cooling, ventilation and lighting« (Dir. 2002/91/EC, Art.4). The directive also outlined minimum energy performance requirements (Dir. 2002/91/EC, Art.4) that were to be met by new buildings and existing buildings »with a total useful floor area over 1000 m^2« (Dir. 2002/91/EC, Art.6) after undergoing major renovations. One further element of this directive was the introduction of energy performance certificates (EPCs)[45] to be made available by the

---

45 The energy performance certificate was introduced as a result of Directive 2002/91/EC. Article 7 says:
«1. Member States shall ensure that, when buildings are constructed, sold or rented out, an energy performance certificate is made available to the owner or by the owner to the prospective buyer or tenant, as the case might be. The validity of the certificate shall not exceed 10 years.[...]
2. The energy performance certificate for buildings shall include reference values such as current legal standards and benchmarks in order to make it possible for consumers to compare and assess the energy performance of the building. The certificate shall be accompanied by recommendations for the cost-effective improvement of the energy performance. [...]
3. Member States shall take measures to ensure that for buildings with a total useful floor area over 1 000 m2 occupied by public authorities and by institutions providing public services to a large number of persons and therefore frequently visited by these persons an energy certificate, not older than 10 years, is placed in a prominent place clearly visible to the public. [...]".

member states, which had to provide information on the exact energy performance of a building and give recommendations on how to improve it. In addition, Article 8 and 9 dealt with the inspection of boilers and air-conditioning systems.

In the following years, European decision-makers further reflected on how to save energy in the European Union. One of the core documents regarding energy efficiency was the *Green Paper on energy efficiency* (COM(2005)265 final) published in June 2005. It was based on the assumption that the EU could reduce energy consumption by at least 20 per cent in a way that is not exceedingly cost-intensive for the respective industries. Furthermore, it was expected that the increase in energy efficiency would contribute to the reduction of greenhouse gas emissions and the EU's dependence on energy imports. Finally, due to necessary investment, the creation of new jobs was expected. The European Commission made clear which measures were generally considered appropriate (COM(2005) 265 final: 21ff), with a huge potential again being seen in the building sector. In this instance it was suggested to apply the minimum energy performance requirements to all newly renovated buildings and not only those of more than 1000 m^2 (COM(2005)265 final: 21).

In October 2006 the *Action Plan for energy efficiency* was issued (COM (2006)545 final) and named the increase of energy efficiency in the building sector as a top priority:

»Partly because of its large share of total consumption, the largest cost-effective savings potential lies in the residential (households) and commercial buildings sector (tertiary sector), where the full potential is now estimated to be around 27% and 30% of energy use, respectively« (COM(2006)545 final: 5).

In residential buildings, the most promising opportunities were seen in wall and roof insulation, whereas in commercial buildings improved energy management systems were considered to be highly promising (ibid). Due to the large potential for energy savings identified in the building sector the European Commission announced its intention of expanding the scope of the *Directive on the energy performance of buildings* adopted in 2002 (Dir. 2002/91/EC) by 2009. By »lowering significantly the current threshold from 1000m^2 for minimum performance requirements for major renovations« (COM(2006)545 final: 12) the legislation to come would include many smaller buildings neglected in the directive of 2002.

Between April and June 2008 all parties concerned were invited to participate in the public consultation *Recasting of the energy performance of buildings directive*, organized by the DG Energy and Transport. In this way, the European Commission hoped to identify where and how obstacles could be overcome and savings realized. In total, the European Commission received and evaluated 246 online responses. Among those were 48 submissions from EU-wide organizations (DG Energy and Transport, 2008: 2). The central questions included in the questionnaire provided by the European Commission were concerned with a) the need to clarify complex definitions of the existing Directive 2002/91/EC, b) the thresholds within this directive, c) the necessity to strengthen the directive's requirements, for example regarding the energy performance certificate, and d) the role of the public sector (DG Energy and Transport, 2008). The main conclusions drawn from the public consultation were the following: A majority of 76 per cent voted for clarifications or simplifications of several articles of the existing directive in order to be able to fully realize the directive's objectives. Concerning the second aspect, the thresholds for energy performance requirements, again a majority of 75 per cent of the respondents were in favor of a reduction or even abolishment of this threshold. Support for this idea came especially from organizations but also from citizens, as indicated in Figure 12. Organizations clearly supported the reduction or abolishment of the threshold because many of them represented industrial interests and therefore expected new employment opportunities and economic benefits from stricter regulations that included also family houses of, for example, 100 to 200 m^2.

Concerning the third aspect, the strengthening of requirements especially with regard to the energy performance certificate, the respondents described the certification as a »crucial driver in energy efficiency improvement« and therefore supported a harmonization of national calculation methods in order to make it comparable between member states (DG Energy and Transport, 2008: 11). The parties involved in the public consultation also stressed the need to strengthen the role of the public sector (75 per cent). The public sector was expected to act as a leading example and in doing so raise broad awareness about the issue (DG Energy and Transport, 2008: 14).

The proposal for a new directive on the energy performance of buildings was presented by the European Commission in November 2008. The recast of the directive seemed particularly necessary because many member states, including some of the old member countries who were experiencing enormous problems caused by their highly inefficient building stock, had still not implemented the legislation (EurActiv, 2009). Acting upon the sentiment articulated in the public consultation, the 1000m^2 threshold for minimum energy performance requirements for buildings under major renovation was deleted because it excluded 72 per cent of all existing buildings (COM(2008)780 final: 8). To make the minimum energy performance requirements comparable between the member states, the European Commission intended to develop a comparative methodology member states were required to use. The results had to be reported to the European Commission for publication in a progress report (COM(2008)780 final: 7-8). To strengthen the role of energy performance certificates, certificates were to be provided »every time there is a property transaction« and measures were to be taken to ensure that »the prospective buyer or tenant is informed of the energy performance of the building (or its parts) at an early stage (for example in the sale/rent announcements)« (COM(2008)780 final: 9). In addition, a »requirement for an independent control system for the energy performance certificates and for the reports on the inspection of heating and air-conditioning systems, for example via random sampling checks of the quality« was introduced (ibid).

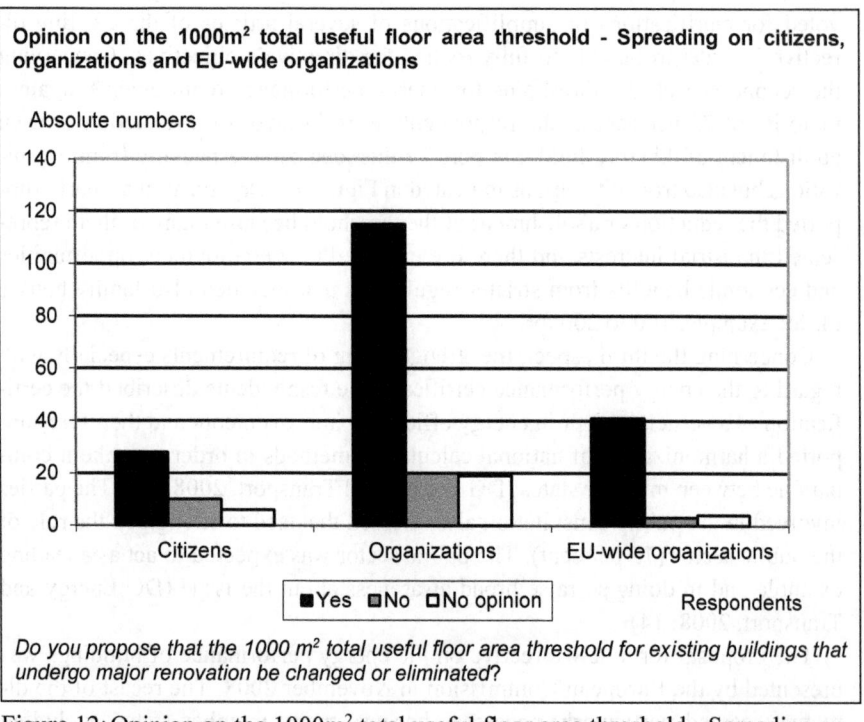

Figure 12: Opinion on the 1000m² total useful floor area threshold - Spreading on citizens, organizations and EU-wide organizations (DG Energy and Transport, 2008: 7)

In its first reading in April 2009 the European Parliament amended the European Commission's proposal by requiring that all new buildings have to be zero-energy buildings by 2020, meaning that they produce as much (renewable) energy as they need (EurActiv, 2009a). This, however, caused disagreement among some member states, who described the amendment as too ambitious. An agreement between the Council and the European Parliament was finally reached on the concept of a »nearly zero-energy building«, meaning a building in which »the nearly zero or very low amount of energy required should be covered to a very significant extent by energy from renewable sources, including energy from renewable sources produced on-site or nearby« (Dir. 2010/31/EU, Art.2.2). The proposal was finally adopted in May 2010.

Focusing on the question of which actors wished to influence the policy process leading to the recast the directive on the energy performance of buildings, one can identify four groups: a) European associations representing intensive energy consumers, b) European associations representing technologies/materials/ services related to energy consumption, c) European associations representing technologies/materials/services related to energy production/provision, and d) NGOs concerned with the consequences of energy consumption.

During the entire policy process, various European associations pursued individual lobbying strategies, which included the submission of position papers to EU decision-makers. For instance, the European Insulation Manufacturers Association (Eurima) in its response to the *Green Paper on energy efficiency* urged »MEPs to support all amendments which propose the rapid and full extension of the *Energy Performance of Buildings Directive (EPBD)*« (Eurima, 2006: 1) because according to a study commissioned by Eurima, this could save the EU up to 14.5 billion Euros by 2015 and create about 530,000 new jobs. In addition, as Eurima emphasized in 2008, the EPBD would help the EU to meet its climate and energy security objectives as adopted during the European Council summit in March 2007 (Eurima, 2008). Among other measures, the association suggested completely removing the threshold of 1000m^2 for buildings under major renovation in order to also include smaller houses, to establish, review and revise minimum performance requirements, to upgrade the directive's requirements with regard to the energy performance certificate, and to ensure that financing and further incentives are available in the member states (ibid). PU Europe[46], the EU association representing the polyurethane insulation industry, praised the plans presented by the European Commission as an opportunity to coherently further implementation of the EPBD in the member states and in its position paper supported similar measures to those suggested by Eurima (BING, 2008, PU Europe, 2009).

From the perspective of the European Builders Confederation (EBC), a professional organization which represents construction craftsmen and SMEs, the 1000m^2 total useful floor area threshold for existing buildings under major renovation should at least be lowered to 200m^2, while energy performance certificates »should be displayed in all public buildings, with no limitation of total useful area« (EBC, 2008). The European Association of Craft, Small and Medium-sized Enterprises (UEAPME) reacted more sceptically to the European Commission's suggestions and described some of its proposals as »unrealistic« (UEAPME, 2009). It criticized, for example, the intention to significantly increase the number of zero-energy buildings in the member states by 2020 as far too ambitious. Rather, member states should develop plans on how to realize this goal by 2030. These plans »might be accompanied by national, regional or local programmes to support

---

46   Formerly BING.

energy performance measures such as fiscal incentives, financial instruments or reduced VAT« (ibid). UEAPME justified its proposal with the difficulties some member states have faced so far in implementing Directive 2002/91/EC.

The European renewable energy industry sector raised its voice through the European Renewable Energy Council (EREC). In a declaration, EREC emphasized that the directive on the energy performance of buildings would not be »focused enough«, as it primarily supported energy efficiency measures, thereby neglecting the benefits renewable energy sources, especially for heating and cooling (EREC, 2005): »Huge amounts of renewable heating and cooling can be supplied by solar thermal, geothermal and biomass to satisfy the entire heating and cooling needs of many buildings and to satisfy in parts the needs of the industry in Europe« (ibid: 7). Similarly, EPIA, representing the European Photovoltaic Industry, requested the new directive to include that energy efficiency measures should be accompanied by the »integration of on-site renewable electricity«, which would correspond to the directive on the use of renewable energy sources (Dir. 2009/28/EC) (EPIA, 2009: 2).

In addition to the industry associations quoted above, several NGOs attempted to influence the policy process surrounding the recast of the directive on the energy performance of buildings. In response to the European Commission's *Green Paper on energy efficiency* (COM(2005)265 final), the WWF emphasized the need for incentives to reduce energy consumption in buildings. In 2009, the organization went further by stating that the European Commission's proposal to recast the directive on the energy performance of buildings was not ambitious enough. The WWF subsequently called for »zero net energy buildings as the construction standard for all new buildings after 2015« (WWF, 2009: 3) and also supported the proposal to apply minimum energy performance requirements to all buildings, irrespective of their size. Similar recommendations were made by the Climate Action Network Europe (CAN-E), arguing that »the energy consumption in buildings could be cut in half« if, for example, »all existing buildings were insulated up to current standards« as heating currently accounts for 66 per cent of energy use (CAN-E, 2006: 8). The European Environmental Bureau (EEB) added with regard to the threshold of 1000m^2 for buildings under major renovation that the European Commission should introduce strict standards instead of using the phrase »major renovations« in order to ensure that all parts of a building, such as heating and cooling systems, are included (EEB, 2009).

The individual European associations and NGOs quoted above, however, did not only submit papers on behalf of their own associations or organization but, in addition, acted as coalitions. For example, reacting to the April 2006 meeting in Vienna of members of the International Energy Agency (IEA), the European Commission, some EU member states, and several industry associations and NGOs on the potential for energy savings in the building sector, the European Insulation

Case studies

Manufacturers Association (Eurima), the European Alliance of Companies for Energy Efficiency in Buildings (EuroACE), and the Renewable Energy & Energy Efficiency Partnership (REEEP) formulated the *Vienna Statement* one month later, calling for intensified action in this field (Eurima, EuroACE and REEEP, 2006). In 2009 Eurima, together with EuroACE and the European Renewable Energy Council (EREC), submitted a common statement in response to the European Commission's proposal to recast the directive on the energy performance of buildings. As already done by Eurima in 2008, this coalition fully supported the European Commission's suggestions and called on the European Parliament and the Council to act in concert with the Commissioners (Eurima, EuroACE and EREC, 2009). Both coalitions can be categorized as rather informal, as they existed for a very limited time and therefore did not require either a spokesperson or an administrative body to coordinate the interaction between the coalition members. This was also confirmed by interview partner *EUAssoc12*[47] who emphasized that these coalitions were no »forever marriages« but rather »on-the-spot coalitions«. Eurima and EuroACE (a coalition of companies formed in 1998) did however participate in other coalitions that were more formal in nature.

The Energy Efficiency Industrial Forum (EEIF), which was founded in 2008, represents a semi-formal form of cooperation as the coalition has no administrative body, letterhead or profile in the transparency register. Its name, however, emphasizes the coalition members' common concerns:

> »The purpose of the EEIF is to provide one voice to represent a broad range of energy efficiency sectors on high-level messages, with the aim of increasing awareness of the strategic benefits of energy efficiency policy at European level and ensuring that energy efficiency measues remain the top priority for legislators«[48].

The coalition members have issued a number of position papers related to questions of how to save energy, thereby taking into account the specific needs of the industry associations supporting the position. These papers are based on the shared long-term interest in energy efficiency which is also indicated by the coalition's name. Importantly, the signatories have varied depending on the specific topic under consideration (see for example EEIF, 2008; 2009; 2010).

A quite formal example of coalition-formation is the Coalition for Energy Savings[49] which was officially formed between 19 European business, professional, and civil society associations in 2010[50], once again including Eurima and EuroACE. Its primary intention is to call on the European institutions to support the 20 per cent energy efficiency target by 2020 (Coalition for Energy Savings, 2010a).

---

47   Telephone interview with *EUAssoc12*, conducted 19 May 2010, 10.00 am.
48   See http://www.euroace.org/AboutUs/Partnerships.aspx [Accessed 05 November 2011].
49   See http://energycoalition.eu/ [Accessed 04 November 2011].
50   Until November 2011 the number of coalition members has increased to 23.

Research design and case studies

In order to realize this goal, the coalition issued a number of open letters and position papers between 2010 and 2011 emphasizing the common concerns of business and society (see for example Coalition of Energy Savings, 2010; 2010a; 2011; 2011a). With regard to the energy performance of buildings, the coalition was especially critical, stating that the proposed initiatives would not go far enough: »The Council's highlighting of public sector buildings as front-runners is welcome, but their proposal adds next to nothing to existing commitments. [...] What we need is a major retro-fitting programme for all buildings across the EU« (Coalition for Energy Savings, 2011). The formal nature of this coalition is also indicated in its profile in the transparency register (identification number 72911566925-69) by naming several spokespersons that are in charge of EU relations and have legal responsibility.

A predecessor of this coalition was the cooperation between the Architects' Council of Europe (ACE), BING, the Council of European Producers of Materials for Construction (CEPMC), EEB, the European Lamp Companies Federation (ELC), European Manufacturers of Expanded Polystyrene (EUMEPS), Eurima, EuroACE, the voice of European manufacturers of gypsum products (EUROGYPSUM), the European Extruded Polystyrene Insulation Board Association (EXIBA), the European Construction Industry Federation (FIEC), Glass for Europe, and the WWF. The associations, which represent industry and civil society interests, published a position paper in October 2008 highlighting the energy savings potential of buildings, thereby directly addressing the European Commission (ACE, BING, CEPMC, EEB, ELC, EUMEPS, Eurima, EuroACE, EUROGYPSUM, EXIBA, FIEC, Glass for Europe and WWF, 2008). As this coalition partly includes the same associations and NGOs as the more recent Coalition for Energy Savings, it can be assumed that the latter emerged from the success of previous cooperative arrangements.

Before the individual hypotheses guiding this work are tested for this case study, it is important to highlight the high degree of autonomy these coalition-members possess. As the example of Eurima and EuroACE shows, even members of formal coalitions are free to engage in other additional forms of cooperation. Eurima and EuroACE are not only members of the Coalition for Energy Savings, but also of the Energy Efficiency Industrial Forum and several other partnerships. This is also applicable to some NGOs, which, beside their membership in the Coalition for Energy Savings, engaged in further cooperation with other environmental organizations. CAN-E and the WWF also participated in an initiative within the framework of the Green 10 calling for progress on energy efficiency (Green 10, 2006), while the WWF formulated an additional joint paper with Friends of the Earth Europe (FoEE) and Greenpeace (FoEE, Greenpeace and WWF, 2006). In addition to these visible forms of cooperation, some of the European associations and NGOs concerned with the legislation on the energy performance of buildings also formed invisible coalitions, meaning that they coordinated their strategies but did not publish joint position papers or demonstrate cooperation in any other way. Interview partner *EUAssoc27*[51] stated that the association would often coordinate its strategies with others, however, without publishing a common statement. The main reason for not cooperating visibly was that some member associations perceived potential coalition partners as competitors and were therefore unwilling to agree to more formal cooperation. Respondents *EUAssoc13*[52] and *EUNGO5*[53] added that interests between different associations would sometimes not overlap enough for the formation of a informal, semi-formal or formal coalition. In this instance, cooperation would not go beyond coordination. This immense variety of forms of coalition-formation implies that European associations pursue comprehensive strategies through various venues in order to successfully influence the policy process.

In the following, the hypotheses are tested for the case of the energy performance of buildings. Hypothesis 1.1 concerning the time frame for coalition-formation was confirmed by analyzing the position papers referred to above and in the interviews with European associations and NGOs. Interview partners *EUAssoc13*, *EUAssoc24*[54] and *EUNGO1*[55] clearly verified the assumption that coalition-formation occurs in response to an initiative by the European Commission. *EUAssoc27* and *EUNGO5* added that at a minimum, something has to be »in the air« - it has to be obvious that the European Commission is going to release an initiative in the near future before cooperation between the European associations and/or NGOs is intensified. Hypothesis 1.2 states that a coalition of European associations and/or NGOs also advises its national members to seek access to the national-level decision-makers. *EUAssoc12* said that including the national member associations in the lobbying strategy is very important for the sector's potential success and *EUAssoc13* even assumed that at the national level there was a tendency for coalition-formation between national associations and politicians in order to pursue a common goal. With regard to Hypothesis 1.3, the assumption that if co-decision is applied, coalitions seek access to MEPs rather than to members of the Council could be confirmed. Most respondents (for example *EUAssoc12*, *EUAssoc13*, *EUAssoc25*[56], *EUNGO1*) emphasized that due to recent institutional reforms the European Parliament has gained more importance as a lobbying addressee. *EUNGO1* argued that the European Parliament was more accessible than

---

51 Telephone interview with *EUAssoc27*, conducted 12 January 2011, 05.00 pm.
52 Telephone interview with *EUAssoc13*, conducted 20 May 2010, 12.30 pm.
53 Telephone interview with *EUNGO5*, conducted 10 December 2010, 11.00 am.
54 Telephone interview with *EUAssoc24*, conducted 20 December 2010, 09.00 am.
55 Telephone interview with *EUNGO1*, conducted 26 November 2009, 11.30 am.
56 Telephone interview with *EUAssoc25*, conducted 21 December 2010, 10.30 am.

national ministers and therefore the latter would primarily be addressed by national members. Hypotheses 1.4 and 1.5 deal with the role of *office-holders*. While Hypothesis 1.4 claiming that personal contacts increase the likelihood of coalition-formation could not be confirmed because the interview partners emphasized other factors as being more important, Hypothesis 1.5 with regard to the impact of office-holders on the strategies pursued by the coalition members proved to be valid. All respondents stressed that when office-holders change, organizations have to reconsider their strategies in order to gain the attention of the new person in office. *EUNGO1* emphasized that depending on the political orientation of new office-holders, successful lobbying is often more difficult following elections.

The second group of hypotheses serves to analyze the impact of the independent variable *motivation*. Hypothesis 2.1 assumes that if actors share common short- or long-term interests, they are more likely to form an informal ad-hoc coalition in order to influence the policy process. In their position papers, the informal coalitions mentioned above (Eurima, EuroACE and REEEP, 2006; Eurima, EuroACE and EREC, 2009) argued on the basis of environmental norms, for example combating climate change, and economic interests, such as ensuring the security of energy supply and generating jobs. However, in its mission statement[57], Eurima focuses on economic concerns: »To create a favorable business environment for mineral wool insulation, by promoting the common interests of our industry and working for positive regulations and standards«. Similarly, EuroACE describes itself as a

> »grouping of like-minded companies working together to increase the uptake of energy-efficiency products, largely via specific legislative measures at EU level, as the most cost-effective route for the EU to reduce greenhouse gas emissions, enhance security of energy supply and increase competitiveness«[58].

Although EuroACE's members may, of course, also support environmental norms, it can be assumed that their primary intention is »to increase the uptake of energy-efficiency products«, meaning the promotion of the sector's economic development. Therefore, the informal coalitions formed by EuroACE and Eurima are perceived as cooperative agreements based on economic interests. Consequently, Hypothesis 2.1 was confirmed. Hypothesis 2.2 states that if actors share long-established norms, they tend to form a coalition that is more persistent over time and that it is likely that the informal coalition will be formalized. This assumption is clearly valid for the Coalition for Energy Savings which seems to have formed around economic interests, for example the increase of competitiveness

---

57 See: http://www.eurima.org/mission-statement/ [Accessed 10 November 2011].
58 See: http://www.euroace.org/AboutUs/MembershipCriteria.aspx [Accessed 10 November 2011].

Case studies

and the creation of new jobs, as well as long-established norms, such as environmental protection. The similar impact of norms and interests is also reflected in the coalition's membership structure, including industry associations and environmental NGOs. Therefore, it is assumed that the cooperation between the members of the Coalition for Energy Savings is not only based on economic interests, but also on shared environmental norms. As a consequence, the coalition was formalized as described above, which confirms Hypothesis 2.2. Concerning the strategies pursued by coalitions (→ H 2.3) the empirical analysis showed that members of formal coalitions, indeed, also pursue voice strategies in the form of information politics. The Coalition for Energy Savings issued several press releases (Coalition for Energy Savings, 2010b; 2011b) in order to inform the public about its ongoing activities. Similarly, the Green 10, which was also categorized as a formal coalition, published a press releases dealing not only with the question of energy efficiency, but also other environmental issues (see for example Green 10, 2009). Informal coalitions, in contrast, rely exclusively on access strategies, especially the submission of joint statements. This was confirmed by *EUAssoc27*, who explained that his association has also supported campaigns but that these have not been initiated in the context of one of the (informal) coalitions.

The third group of hypotheses deals with the impact of *information and expertise*. The question arises of whether the associations which are members of the coalitions analyzed in this case study possess information on the policy process and the positions of the actors concerned, as well as expertise on the subject. Associations representing the insulation industry, such as Eurima and PU Europe, have established offices in Brussels in order to »to establish relationships with main regulatory bodies so as to anticipate future regulatory requirements, exert a positive influence in shaping regulations, and exploit and measure effectiveness of regulations«[59]. They clearly express their interest in networking with the European institutions and like-minded European associations and have longstanding experience in lobbying, and thus it can be assumed that they have sufficient information on the policy process and the actors involved. EuroACE was founded in 1998 and also has representation in Brussels to cooperate with the European institutions. The same is valid for the environmental NGOs, such as CAN-E and the WWF. Concerning expertise, these associations employ experts for questions related to energy efficiency and, in particular, the energy consumption of buildings and potential technological alternatives to improve their energy performance. The expertise is also backed up by scientific reports and articles published by the NGOs. Hypothesis 3.1 states that if European associations or NGOs possess information and can provide expertise concerning a specific policy issue, they are more

---

59   See: http://www.eurima.org/mission-statement/ [Accessed 11 November 2011].

likely to be included in a coalition. This was not confirmed by the interview partners consulted for this case study. Rather, they considered joint interests or norms to be important. *EUAssoc25* emphasized that the main reason to form a coalition is to be able »to speak with one voice«. However, the interview partners confirmed Hypothesis 3.2 assuming that if coalition members possess comprehensive information on the policy process as well as on the decision-makers concerned, the coalition is more likely to reformulate a position paper when sending it to different political institutions. *EUAssoc13* said that interest groups actually have to formulate several position papers if both DG Energy and DG Environment are addressed because these have different responsibilities and thus focus on different aspects of the same legislative act. This does not mean that lobbying strategies generally vary but rather that positions are framed differently. *EUAssoc24* added that statements are adapted such that, for example, the European Parliament receives shorter papers including more political arguments, while the documents sent to the European Commission are longer (and probably more technical, if sent to the administrative level).

One further remark has to be made with regard to the strategies pursued by coalition members. Some coalition members, such as *EUAssoc25* and *EUAssoc27*, pointed out that the most typical element of access strategies pursued by coalitions is to send a joint position paper. On behalf of their associations, interview partners *EUAssoc25* and *EUAssoc27* would also seek personal contact with decision-makers in the form of face-to-face meetings, whereas as a coalition they would randomly talk directly to the EU institutions. However, *EUAssoc25* assumed that, in the future, the European Commission would also likely meet with coalitions which have successfully solved an internal conflict.

Hypotheses 4.1 and 4.2 discuss the role of the variable *reputation*, defined as *representativity* and *credibility*. Hypothesis 4.1 was confirmed by the interview partners, with the representativity of the position presented being particularly decisive. Therefore, speaking with one voice was considered to be highly important[60]. In addition, reputation in the sense of credibility was regarded as influential. *EUAssoc12* confirmed that for his association it was always better to act »hand in hand« with environmental organizations in order to improve the image of the industry. In contrast, however, reputation could also constitute a reason for environmental NGOs not to cooperate with certain industry branches. Hypothesis 4.2 states that coalition members with a bad reputation will experience difficulties in gaining access to the European institutions. This was confirmed, for example, by *EUAssoc12*, who said that in order to gain access, one has to be respected by the European institutions. Therefore, the association would ensure that position papers only include rational and solid arguments. European associations and/or

---

60 See, for example, telephone interview with *EUAssoc25, EUNGO5*.

Case studies

NGOs (or coalitions of these) that have, however, damaged their reputation may typically only use voice strategies, consisting primarily of media campaigns. Obviously voice strategies are not a suitable option for informal coalitions of European associations and/or NGOs as these lack an administrative body or spokesperson. In addition, voice strategies are not assumed to increase the interest groups' influence on the decision-makers. According to *EUNGO5* and *EUAssoc27*, campaigns only serve to gain public attention.

With regard to the last group of hypotheses dealing with the influence of (financial and human) *resources*, *EUAssoc13* stressed that coalition-formation is not financially driven. Rather coalition members are motivated by common strategic goals ($\rightarrow$ H 5.1). Resources, however, are valuable when it comes to the lobbying strategies: additional resources enable an association to commission expensive consultancies in order to expand lobbying efforts[61].

4.2.4 Coalition-formation concerning the role of biofuels in EU legislation

In order to increase the share of renewable energy in gross domestic consumption, European decision-makers have increasingly directed their attention to the transport sector. The *White Paper: European transport policy for 2010: time to decide* argued for the need to replace »20% of conventional fuels with substitute fuels« for road transport by 2020 (COM(2001)370 final: 87) - not only for environmental reasons, but also to reduce the Community's energy dependence. Directive 2003/30/EC of May 2003 on the promotion of the use of biofuels or other renewable fuels for transport (*biofuels directive*) was based on two basic assumptions: firstly, that the transport sector, upon the release of the directive already accountable for 30 per cent of the Community's energy consumption, would expand and consume an even greater amount of energy in the future, and secondly, that a 50 per cent increase in CO_2 emissions from transport could be expected over the period from 1990 to 2010 (COM(2001)370 final):

> »According to the latest estimates, if nothing is done to reverse the traffic growth trend, CO_2 emissions from transport can be expected to increase by around 50% to reach 1113 billion tonnes in 2010, compared with the 739 million tonnes recorded in 1990. Once again, road transport is the main culprit since it alone accounts for 84% of the CO2 emissions attributable to transport« (COM(2001)370 final: 10).

Therefore, Directive 2003/30/EC again called for a reduction of the consumption of oil in the transport sector in favor of alternative fuels (Dir. 2003/30/EC: 1). As one measure to achieve this goal, it was suggested that the member states should ensure that biofuels or other renewable fuels should account for a minimum of two

---

61 See, for example, telephone interview with *EUAssoc24*.

per cent of all fuels for transport on the market by the end of 2005. This proportion was to increase to 5.75 per cent by the end of 2010 (Dir. 2003/30/EC: Art. 3.1). To successfully implement the directive, member states, with prior authorization from the European Commission, were permitted to grant tax exemptions in favor of biofuels under certain condition (→ energy taxation directive, Dir. 2003/96/EC).

In 2005 the *Biomass Action Plan* was released. In this document, the European Commission expressed its concerns about the state of the biofuels directive's implementation. It emphasized that the targets set for 2005 would not be realized due to substantial variation in the achievements of the member states (COM (2005)628 final: 9). As a consequence, the European Commission developed a strategic approach in order to realize the full potential of biofuels, relying on seven policy axes (COM(2006)34 final):

1) To stimulate demand, for example by »setting national targets for the market share of biofuels, using biofuel obligations« (ibid: 7),
2) to realize the environmental benefits, while at the same time avoiding environmental damage resulting from biofuel production,
3) to expand feedstock supplies,
4) to further develop the production and distribution of biofuels by, for example, examining more closely the reasons for industrial barriers,
5) to enhance trade opportunities,
6) to support developing countries by assisting them in setting up sustainable biofuel action plans, and
7) to support research and development in order to strengthen the competitiveness of the sector.

In January 2007, the *Renewable Energy Roadmap* (COM(2006)848 final) proposed to set binding rules for the members states and in this way to abandon the indicative nature of the targets formulated in the biofuels directive. The European Commission extended its 2005 criticism of the biofuels sector to the whole renewable energy sector:

> »In 1997, the European Union started working towards a target of a 12% share of renewable energy in gross inland consumption by 2010 [...]. Current projections indicate that the 12% target will not be met. The EU looks unlikely to reach a contribution from renewable energy sources exceeding 10% by 2010. Even though the cost of most renewable energy sources is declining [...] at the current stage of energy market development renewable sources will often not be the short term least cost options. In particular, the failure to systematically include external costs in market prices gives an economically unjustified advantage to fossil fuels compared with renewables« (COM(2006)848 final: 4).

Case studies

In addition, the European Commission named administrative problems due to the complexity of renewable energy applications, information discrepancies, and discriminating rules for grid access as barriers to increase the share of renewable energy in consumption (ibid). For the biofuels sector, several reasons for the unsatisfactory progress were identified: a) the lack of adequate support systems in the member states, b) the reluctance of fuel suppliers to use bioethanol, and c) an insufficient regulatory framework at the EU level (ibid: 7).

In order to improve progress, it was suggested to set one overall target for the whole renewable energy sector, instead of individual targets for the electricity, transport and heating and cooling sectors (Howes, 2010). The benchmark of 20 per cent was suggested, which was later reflected in the *20-20-20 until 2020-* goals (COM(2008)19 final; COM(2008)30 final). In addition, a minimum binding target of ten per cent of biofuels in petrol and diesel consumption was fixed (to be realized by 2020).

From April to May 2007 stakeholders were asked to participate in public consultation on *Biofuel issues in the new legislation on the promotion of renewable energy*. This was already the second consultation on the issue as in 2006 stakeholders were asked to give their opinion on the *Review of EU biofuels directive* (DG Energy and Transport, 2006). For the 2007 consultation, DG Energy and Transport (2007) developed a questionnaire focussing on the following central issues (DG Energy and Transport, 2007: 3):

1) »How should a biofuel sustainability system be designed?«
2) »How should overall effects on land use be monitored?«
3) »How should the use of second-generation biofuels be encouraged?«
4) »What further action is needed to make it possible to achieve a 10% biofuel share?«

Environmental NGOs were especially critical of the production of 1st-generation biofuels (for example bioethanol and biodiesel), which are primarily produced from food crops and thus are assumed to have a negative impact on food security and prices, scarce water resources, deforestation, and biodiversity (IEA, 2008: 6). Meanwhile, the production of 2nd-generation biofuels seems to be much more promising. These (for example Biomass to Liquid (BtL) and cellulosic ethanol) are generally derived from cellulosic materials (lignocellulosic feedstocks) and are therefore considered as much more sustainable. However, due to the associated technological requirements and expected high costs, it is unlikely that 2nd-generation biofuels will be produced commercially before 2015 (IEA, 2008: 33).

These considerations were taken into account in the proposal for a directive on the use of energy from renewable sources (COM(2008)19 final) issued by the European Commission in January 2008. Concerning the role of biofuels in the legislation, the proposal confirmed the ten per cent target for the share of biofuels in petrol and diesel consumption to be achieved until 2020. In addition, it listed certain binding sustainability criteria for biofuels and other bioliquids to mitigate environmental damage (COM(2008)19 final, Art.15, 16, 17). These measures were also supported by the IEA, which stressed the need of sustainable biofuel production:

> »To be acceptable, biofuel feedstocks must be sustainably produced in terms of agricultural practices, forest management, protection of biodiverse ecosystems, responsible and efficient use of water, and free of exploitation of landowners« (IEA, 2008: 35).

The proposal amending and subsequently repealing Directives 2001/77/EC and 2003/30/EC was adopted in April 2009.

The following section analyzes the parties that attempted to influence the role of biofuels in the EU legislation on renewable energy sources. The following groups are considered: a) European associations representing energy consumers, b) European associations representing energy producers/providers, and c) NGOs concerned with the consequences of energy production and consumption. These energy actors pursued individual lobbying strategies, which included the submission of position papers to the EU decision-makers.

First of all, among the energy consumers, ACEA, the European Automobile Manufacturers' Association, contributed to the public consultation initiated by the DG Transport and Energy in 2007 by pointing out that it would be challenging to reach the 10 per cent target for the share of biofuels in petrol and diesel consumption by 2020: »10% biofuels by energy in 2020 may be reached only by introducing second-generation biofuels, the development of which remains the real challenge over the next decade« (ACEA, 2007: 4). In addition, with regard to the role of taxation it emphasized the need »to support biofuel use through financial incentives« (ibid). In a further statement of June 2008, ACEA furthermore asked the European Commission to ensure harmonized standards across Europe and appropriate lead-time for the automobile industry to realize these (ACEA, 2008).

Closely related to the scepticism raised by the association representing the automobile industry, deep concerns towards the plans proposed by the European Commission were expressed by EUROPIA, the European Petroleum Industry Association. In response to the Biomass Action Plan (COM(2005)628 final) and the EU strategy for biofuels (COM(2006)34 final) the association highlighted the disadvantages of biofuels compared to conventional fuels, such as high costs, insufficient availability and competing demands for food crops (EUROPIA, 2006). In January 2007, EUROPIA further criticized that these obstacles would »limit the rate of penetration of these fuels into the market« such that there was »no prospect of biofuels targets being achievable« (EUROPIA, 2007: 2-3).

In contrast, for AEBIOM, the European Biomass Association, the advantages of biofuels outweighed the negative effects. In its response to the public consultation on biofuels, AEBIOM stressed that limiting biofuels based on reasons related to land allocation or food prices would make things needlessly complicated as so far only a small proportion of agricultural land was used for non food crops and the impact of the price increase of, for example, wheat on food products was »negligible« (AEBIOM, 2007: 2-3). The criticism often articulated by NGOs with regard to the consequences of the production of 1st-generation biofuels (for example bioethanol and biodiesel) for food security and food prices was also rejected by the European Bioethanol Fuel Association (eBIO^{62}). The association argued that bioethanol production was sustainable in environmental and social terms because »biofuels produced and/or sold in the EU consume only a tiny proportion of the EU's (or the world's) agricultural supplies« (eBIO, 2008). The European Union of Ethanol Producers (U.E.P.A.) added that fuel ethanol would, in addition, contribute to reducing the EU's dependency on oil and mitigating the effects of global warming (U.E.P.A., 2006).

The European Natural Gas Vehicle Association (ENGVA), representing a variety of members ranging from gas associations and research institutes to companies producing vehicle components, also answered the questions raised throughout the public consultation period. The ENGVA generally criticized the proposed measures as too restrictive as they focussed almost exclusively on liquid biofuels, thereby ignoring the »the potential of biogas upgraded to biomethane as a vehicle fuel« (ENGVA, 2007).

Among the European NGOs, the European Federation for Transport & Environment (T&E) was one of the most concerned with the topic. In its response to public consultation in 2006, it criticized the promotion of biofuels, stating that this would not solve current environmental problems. Rather, the EU should adopt additional measures to reduce its overall fuel consumption: »Currently the EU is not ambitious in reduction of fuel use, and still strongly promotes more biofuels. In this policy context promotion of biofuels does in our view not make sense« (T&E, 2006: 1). Similarly, the WWF promoted »fuel efficiency standards for all vehicles and the development of an alternative, more environmentally sustainable, transport strategy as priorities« (WWF, 2007a: 4). Greenpeace was also critical of the European Commission's proposals stating that they would »not give an adequate level of assurance that biofuels will be produced in an ecological and socially responsible way. [..] The use of biofuels should therefore only be supported as part of a wider energy policy to reduce energy demand dramatically« (Greenpeace, 2007: 1). Furthermore, the NGO called on the European institutions to address environmental and social concerns as the production of biofuels would endanger many natural ecosystems (Greenpeace, 2008).

---

62 Meanwhile, eBIO and U.E.P.A. have merged. The name of the new association is ePURE: http://epure.org/aboutus/introduction [Accessed 14 November 2011].

Research design and case studies

The European associations and NGOs quoted above did not only submit papers on behalf of their own associations or organizations, but, in addition, acted in the context of coalitions. T&E joined forces with the European Environmental Bureau (EEB) and BirdLife International in order to respond to the public consultation in 2007, calling for the development of comprehensive sustainability criteria to accompany the legislation on biofuels (T&E, EEB and BirdLife International, 2007). In 2008, Greenpeace and Friends of the Earth Europe (FoEE) decided to cooperate with these three NGOs and together the group issued a position paper on the *Real impact of growing Biofuels* (T&E, EEB, BirdLife International, Greenpeace and FoEE, 2008). The cooperation between these NGOs can be categorized as an informal coalition because the coalition lacked a name, letterhead and website, and had no administrative body to coordinate the activities of the coalition members. The cooperation between T&E, EEB and BirdLife International was however reactivated several times, thereby also including other NGOs. In addition, to articulate their joint opinion on biofuel issues and on more general questions related to sustainability, the five NGOs cooperated within the framework of the Green 10, a formal coalition already mentioned in the previous case studies (see for example Green 10, 2006a; 2007).

From a theoretical point of view, another interesting informal coalition emerged between the WWF and CEPI, the Confederation of European Paper Industries. Although at first glance the NGO and the industry association do not seem to have much in common, with regard to the future role of renewable energy sources they obviously found common ground: »WWF and CEPI believe that biomass has an important role to play in providing sustainable energy for the future. However, the expansion needed to achieve this must be managed with great care for wider environmental concerns [...]« (WWF and CEPI, 2006: 1). Furthermore, in an attempt to draw the attention of European governments to their concerns, CEPI formulated a joint paper with AEBIOM, the European Biomass Association (AEBIOM and CEPI, 2007).

From the perspective of the European petroleum and automobile industries, it obviously seemed useful to join forces during the implementation phase of the directive. In their joint communication, ACEA and EUROPIA suggested a set of implementation guidelines in order to ensure that member states meet their obligations and harmonized rules are established (ACEA and EUROPIA, 2010).

To summarize, more informal coalitions were formed between NGOs concerned with the production and consumption of energy than between industry associations. One reason for this could be that the interests of the different industry sectors were too specific to be integrated into a common position.

In the next section, the hypotheses are tested for the case of the legislation on the future role of biofuels. Hypothesis 1.1, which assumes that European associations and/or NGOs form coalitions after an initiative was issued by the European

Case studies

Commission, was confirmed. The respondents consulted for this case study agreed that actors usually do not decide to cooperate before they can at least anticipate what is going to emerge from the EC. *EUAssoc5*[63] confirmed that associations only begin to cooperate once they become aware of a proposed initiative. *EUNGO8*[64] admitted that sometimes associations even did not cooperate before an initiative was actually published. Hypothesis 1.2 states that coalition members also include their national members in their lobbying strategies and advise them to seek access to national-level politicians, if this is expected to increase the coalition's influence. Interview partner *EUNGO2*[65] emphasized that when a lobbying strategy is developed, much time is spent identifying which national member associations are best suited to address the decision-makers in a given state. *EUNGO1*[66] explained that national organizations also often organize media campaigns to increase public awareness for an issue if they consider this to be helpful to influence national politicians. With regard to Hypothesis 1.3 concerning the importance of MEPs as lobbying addressees, *EUNGO1* confirmed that since the adoption of the Lisbon Treaty the European Parliament has become increasingly important. The Council, in contrast, is primarily contacted by the national members. *EUNGO8* said that the association addresses MEPs who are expected to ideologically support its interests and that in the meantime they have been able to establish close contact with some of these MEPs. As already mentioned in the previous case studies, Hypothesis 1.4 on the impact of personal contacts on coalition-formation was not confirmed. However, the respondents stressed the importance of personal contact with members of the European institutions (→ H 1.5). Especially after elections, establishing these contacts would often constitute a challenge rather than a promising opportunity (*EUNGO1*).

The second group of hypotheses deals with the impact of the independent variable *motivation*. Hypothesis 2.1 assumes that if actors share common short- or long-term interests, they are more likely to form an informal ad-hoc coalition. The informal coalitions identified above primarily formed around common interests with regard to a certain policy proposal. This is especially valid for the cooperation between CEPI and the WWF, which cooperated only once and did not submit any further joint statements. The coalition between T&E, EEB and BirdLife International was reactivated several times, indicating that the associations may also share a set of common norms, such as environmental protection. This seems to be even more likely if one considers that the three NGOs also regularly cooperate within the framework of the Green 10. Nevertheless, for the case of biofuels, transport-

---

63   Telephone interview with *EUAssoc5*, conducted 22 October 2009, 10.30 am.
64   Telephone interview with *EUNGO8*, conducted 1 February 2011, 10.00 am.
65   Telephone interview with *EUNGO2*, conducted 4 May 2010, 11.00 am.
66   Telephone interview with *EUNGO1*, conducted 26 November 2009, 11.30 am.

related interests, such as the use of specific methods to calculate greenhouse gas emissions resulting from the use of biofuels, the adoption of appropriate land-use rules, and the introduction of tax incentives, prevailed (T&E, EEB and BirdLife International, 2007). Hypotheses 2.2 and 2.3, which focus on the probability that coalitions sharing long-established norms are formalized and also pursue voice strategies in addition to access strategies, were unable to be tested for this case. The validity of these hypotheses for the formal coalition of the Green 10 has however already been demonstrated in the previous case studies.

The third group of hypotheses deals with the impact of *information and expertise*. First of all, it has to be evaluated if the associations and NGOs concerned indeed possess information on the policy process and the actors involved as well as expertise on the subject. All associations and NGOs referred to here have established an office in Brussels in order to maintain close contact with the European institutions and other stakeholders. ePURE, which resulted from the merger of eBIO and U.E.P.A., describes as one of its main intentions »[to] promote the beneficial uses of ethanol in Europe« by »representing our member's interests to the European institutions, industry stakeholders, the media and general public«[67]. In its statutes, T&E declares »[to] disseminate information to its Members, other organisations, the media, political institutions and the general public«[68]. And EUROPIA aims to strengthen the »industry's reputation as a positive and constructive contributor to the development of policies and legislation through a high quality and pro-active communication strategy«.[69] These examples illustrate that the associations and organizations referred to in this case study do indeed possess comprehensive information. Concerning their expertise, some represent a very specific sector and thus it can be assumed that they have detailed knowledge about the consequences of biofuel production and consumption. As T&E again indicates in its statutes, the organization intends to »promote, undertake and co-ordinate research and studies«.[70] Furthermore, all of them have published scientific reports and/or articles on the subject. Hypothesis 3.1 stating that if European associations or NGOs possess information and can provide expertise concerning a specific policy issue, they are more likely to be included in a coalition was not confirmed by the interview partners. Of course, it is advantageous if a coalition partner can provide additional information and expertise. However, the respondents considered

---

67 See: http://epure.org/aboutus/what_we_do [Accessed 14 November 2011].
68 See: http://www.transportenvironment.org/docs/statutes_english.pdf [Accessed 14 November 2011].
69 See: http://www.europia.com/content/default.asp?PageID=382 [Accessed 14 November 2011].
70 See: http://www.transportenvironment.org/docs/statutes_english.pdf [Accessed 14 November 2011].

Case studies

other factors, such as a common goal or the representativity of the position, to be more important. However, Hypothesis 3.2 which assumes that if coalition members possess comprehensive information on the policy process as well as on the decision-makers concerned, the coalition is more likely to reformulate a position paper when submitting it to different addressees was confirmed. Interview partner *EUAssoc9*[71] explained that although the strategies pursued to influence the positions of different institutions are broadly the same, the European Commissioners receive very detailed papers, while the MEPs are presented with more general versions.

The fourth group of hypotheses deals with the independent variable *reputation*. Hypothesis 4.1 states that if a European association or NGO can improve its reputation by cooperating with other actors, a coalition is more likely to be formed. This was confirmed by the empirical analysis. With regard to the representativity of a position, *EUAssoc9* pointed out that when it comes to the question of influence on the policy process a coalition speaking on behalf of ten associations has more weight than a single association. Concerning the credibility of an organization, *EUNGO2* admitted that in one instance the NGO had decided against cooperation with industry because they were afraid of losing credibility when submitting a joint paper. Hypothesis 4.2 assumes that if coalition members have a bad reputation, the coalition will experience difficulties in gaining access to the European institutions. This was again confirmed by respondent *EC1*[72] who emphasized that reputation is highly decisive for an association or a coalition of associations which intends to seek the attention of decision-makers. *EUAssoc9* stressed the importance of access strategies, stating that the best option was to talk to politicians face-to-face, especially when about technical details which cannot be explained in a campaign or press release. In this context, *EUNGO8* said that face-to-face meetings were, however, only held on behalf on his organization and not on behalf of a coalition.

Finally, the last set of hypotheses on the impact of *resources* on the formation of coalitions and their strategy choices was analyzed. Hypothesis 5.1 was confirmed: additional resources were not considered to be a decisive factor for joining a coalition[73]. However, resources do appear to play a role when it comes to the lobbying strategies pursued by the coalition members (→ 5.2). Due to the additional manpower, coalitions can be more efficient and address decision-makers at different levels individually[74]. In addition, consultancies can be commissioned to complement the lobbying efforts.

---

71 Telephone interview with *EUAssoc9*, conducted 19 March 2010, 11.00 am.
72 Telephone interview with *EC1*, conducted 26 November 2010, 10.30 am.
73 See, for example, interview with *EUNGO1*.
74 Telephone interview with *EUAssoc16*, conducted 15 October 2010, 03.00 pm.

Research design and case studies

4.2.5   The influence of coalitions on the receptiveness of the European institutions

In this section, the impact of coalitions and their strategy choices on the receptiveness of the European Commission, the European Parliament and the Council is assessed. This aspect has been included because although policy-makers seem to recognize the general need for further reforms in European energy policy, progress has only been mediocre at best. In the introduction, it was assumed that coalitions of energy actors exist that are able to increase the receptiveness of European institutions and in this way shape the outcome of the decision-making process.

Due to the expected difficulties in measuring a coalition's impact (see for example Dür, 2008), the question was only of secondary relevance for this work as a whole. Nevertheless, the tentative results gained on this issue are presented here. In order to assess this question, first of all, European associations and NGOs were asked to estimate their influence, either when acting on behalf of their own association/NGO or when acting in the context of a coalition. Next it was decided to conduct additional interviews with members of the European Commission, the European Parliament, and the Council. The interview partners from the institutions were asked to estimate the impact of different types of actors, such as national associations/NGOs, European associations/NGOs, coalitions of national or European associations and/or NGOs, multinational companies and consultancies on an ordinal scale: 1. actors are granted »direct access to the European institutions«, 2. actors are given »more time to directly present their positions«, 3. the actors' »position was partly adopted in the initiative/proposal/directive«, and 4. the actors' »position was completely adopted in the initiative/proposal/directive«.

The responses of the European associations and NGOs with regard to their degree of influence differed greatly from »not very successful in influencing the initiative/proposal/directive« to »successful in influencing large parts of the initiative/proposal/directive«. Some of the interview partners, however, admitted that for them it was virtually impossible to estimate if their position had had an impact on the decision-makers. *EUNGO2*[75] emphasized that while the European institutions are generally very open to all kinds of stakeholders, participating in public consultations and personal meetings does not necessarily imply that one also has influence. *EUAssoc5*[76] and *EUAssoc13*[77] stressed that even if an actor's interests are reflected in political decisions, it is difficult to judge whether, indeed, the po-

---

75   Telephone interview with *EUNGO2*, conducted 04 May 2010, 11.00 am.
76   Telephone interview with *EUAssoc5*, conducted 22 October 2009, 10.30 am.
77   Telephone interview with *EUAssoc13*, conducted 20 May 2010, 12.30 pm.

sition was adopted or whether the political decision was the result of another interest group's successful lobbying strategy or current global developments. This argument was also shared by some members of the European institutions. For example, interview partner *EC3*[78] admitted that for her it was almost impossible to say by whom she had actually been influenced. She described being influenced as an ongoing process which led to the formation of an opinion. She could not, however, remember a case when a single actor had changed her mind. In addition, the respondents representing the different institutions criticized the ordinal scale presented to assess the degree of influence. *EC2*[79] said that from his experience, influence« cannot be measured in terms of »access« and the »time« actors are given to present their ideas. Rather, other factors, such as the representativity of a position, are decisive.

This directly leads to the question of whether coalitions of European associations and/or NGOs have a greater chance to receive attention from the European institutions compared to European associations or NGOs acting alone. From the perspective of the associations and NGOs, *EUAssoc25*[80] pointed out that when acting in the context of a coalition the association had significantly more influence on the decision-makers' receptiveness than when acting alone. He even estimated that, based on his personal experience, coalition-formation will determine the future European policy process. *EUNGO5*[81] said that a »coalition spirit« exists at the EU level. Drawing on results from the interviews with the European Commission, the majority of respondents agreed that they generally preferred to talk to coalitions because these present a »complete picture«. *EC2* confirmed that if a whole sector is able to formulate a joint position, this position has much more weight than it would have if submitted by a single association. *EC3* added that, considering her workload, it was much easier to read one paper issued by a coalition of European associations and/or NGOs rather than ten individual positions on the same topic. In addition, especially during the early stages of the policy process, coalition papers serve to identify a sector's main interests. *EC5*[82] emphasized that the European Commission pays more attention if a coalition criticizes a policy initiative because this is a signal that serious problems exist that concern a whole industry.

However, despite its advantages, coalition-formation does not always seem to be suitable. *EC2* remarked that due to the diversity of existing interests, coalition

---

78   Telephone interview with *EC3*, conducted 15 December 2010, 10.00 am.
79   Telephone interview with *EC2*, conducted 02 December 2010, 11.30 am.
80   Telephone interview with *EUAssoc25*, conducted 21 December 2010, 10.30 am.
81   Telephone interview with *EUNGO5*, conducted 10 December 2010, 11.00 am.
82   Telephone interview with *EC5*, conducted 07 March 2011, 04.00 pm.

members often have difficulties in finding a joint position. As a result, the joint paper would sometimes only represent a minimum consensus. $EC4^{83}$ agreed that positions submitted by coalitions are often watered down. This can especially be the case if a paper is signed by too many European associations and NGOs representing quite different interests.

This perspective was also shared by the interview partners from the European Parliament. Although, due to time constraints it was helpful to receive one coalition paper^{84}, $EP1^{85}$ criticized that coalition papers often present a compromise reached between a variety of actors and therefore do not provide useful expertise. Consequently, it would be better to talk to the national associations and companies that are directly concerned with an issue.

The representatives of the Council interviewed over the course of the empirical analysis also stated that they are randomly contacted by coalitions of European associations and/or NGOs. Nevertheless, as $Council2^{86}$ emphasized, interest groups that seek contact must either represent a significant amount of members or a significant sector. Furthermore, one of the most decisive factors increasing the receptiveness of decision-makers was the quality of expertise provided in the papers or in conversations, as it was important to feel that the interest groups had »something to say«.

---

83 Telephone interview with *EC4*, conducted 12 January 2011, 10.00 am.
84 Telephone interview with *EP3*, conducted 24 March 2011, 02.00 pm.
85 Telephone interview with *EP1*, conducted 21 March 2011, 01.30 pm.
86 Telephone interview with *Council2*, conducted 02 May 2011, 12.00 pm.

Chapter 5. Empirical results

»Work with others – look for allies!« This recommendation was clearly expressed by the European Parliament in a document published on lobbying tactics at the EU level with the argument:

>»Officials, parliamentarians and Members of the Economic and Social Committee and Committee of the Regions, get very frustrated when more than one pressure group says more or less the same thing but in different words. It only leads to horrible confusion« (European Parliament, 2003: 22).

The quotation emphasizes the position of the European Parliament regarding the formation of coalitions between associations that have similar positions. Due to the vast amount of position papers submitted by various actors during the policy process, the European institutions are not always able to sift through all of them. Thus, the European Parliament recommends interest groups acting jointly.

The following section summarizes the main results drawn from the empirical analysis of the factors that lead to the formation of different kinds of coalitions by European associations and/or NGOs concerned with European energy policy and that determine the strategy choices made by the coalition members.

Table 18 categorizes the different types of coalitions that were identified as a result of the empirical research. In the first column, cases are covered in which coalition-formation was not intended or did not succeed. One methodological problem occurred with regard to this category: to identify cases in which no coalition was formed, the analysis depended on the willingness of the interview partners to provide information on such incidents. As a consequence, the results solely rely on the subjective perception of the respondents and could not be verified. As the interview partners named some convincing factors for the failure of coalition-formation, these are presented in this section, accompanied by a warning that they are not necessarily representative. One reason for the absence of a coalition was that a policy issue European associations and/or NGOs were concerned with was not included on the agenda of the European Commission ($\rightarrow$ H 1.1). As the analysis of the four case studies illustrated, coalitions usually did not emerge before members could anticipate that the European Commission was going to draft an initiative in the near future. If European associations and/or NGO were unsatisfied with the status quo and wanted to influence the agenda of the European Commission, they lobbied only on behalf of their own association or NGO, but not in the context of a coalition. The major reason for this reactive behavior of coalitions, as stated by the interview partners, was that coalition-formation is time-consuming. Lobbying usually begins with each association formulating its own position on a

Empirical results

topic and trying to influence the European Commission's agenda. This is often done in coordination with the national member associations. Following this, compatible associations may discuss which common interests exist and whether joint action is appropriate. Up until this point, however, the European Commission has typically issued an initiative in the form of an action plan or green paper. One exception may occur when coalitions submit a position paper to influence the European Commission's agenda: if coalitions have established formal structures and an administrative body to coordinate the interactions between the members, it can be assumed that each member association or NGO knows exactly what the others' positions on a variety of topics are. Under these circumstances, consensus-seeking is much easier and takes less time. However, the four case studies analyzed here did not provide evidence of such an exception. Concerning the impact of the independent variable *office-holders* (→ H 1.4) on the formation of coalitions, the assumption that personal animosities between, for example, two individuals representing different European associations may inhibit cooperation could not be confirmed. The interview partners contacted for the case studies denied that officeholders have a decisive impact on the decision to cooperate on a specific topic.

Hypotheses 2.1 and 2.2 deal with the effects of the variable *motivation*. For the category *no coalition* in Table 18 this variable implies that if no common norms or interests exist, no coalition will be formed. Most of the respondents emphasized that the main reason for coalition-formation is the existence of a common goal - either based on shared norms or interests. In the absence of a common goal, the formation of a coalition does not make sense. The independent variable *reputation* turned out to be especially decisive. According to Hypothesis 4.1 coalition-formation may not take place if a European association or NGO expects to damage its reputation by forming a coalition with another actor. This was generally confirmed by the respondents.

In the remaining four columns the variables determining the emergence of different kinds coalitions are specified. A coalition is defined as *invisible* if the actors involved decide to coordinate their strategies but do not want to demonstrate their cooperation to outsiders, for example by publishing a joint position paper. In doing so, they can ensure that they present the same arguments in favor or against a policy initiative and, at the same time do not emphasize certain aspects that could disadvantage other cooperating parties. Similar to the analysis of the category *no coalition*, the identification of an *invisible coalition* also depended on the interview partners' willingness to provide information. Furthermore, invisible coalitions were only formed if an issue was adopted on the European Commission's agenda (→ H 1.1). With regard to the impact of the independent variable *motivation*, common interests are much more decisive than common norms in the formation of invisible coalitions. Most decisive, however, is the impact of the variable reputation (→ H 4.1): as confirmed in the first two case studies (→ 4.2.1 and 4.2.2), if

European associations and/or NGOs have common interests but expect to damage their reputation through visible cooperation, it is likely that they will decide to cooperate invisibly.

The next category *visible coalition* was divided into three sub-categories. Depending on the degree of formalization it is possible to distinguish between *informal, semi-formal,* and *formal coalitions*. While informal coalitions between European associations and/or NGOs are usually formed to influence the political decision on one specific policy issue, they can however be reactivated in the future. Such coalitions neither have a name or letterhead, nor a spokesperson or an administrative body to coordinate the work between their members. As a result of cooperation, the coalition publishes a joint position paper or report. This work has especially shed light on the quite neglected phenomenon of informal coalitions. As was shown in the case study analysis, although these coalitions lack a formal organizational structure, they nevertheless constitute a decisive element of the European policy-making process. Semi-formal coalitions are formed to influence several political decisions on different topics. In contrast to informal arrangements, such a coalition has a name which emphasizes its members' common concerns (such as Alliance of Energy Intensive Industries), but no common administrative body. The last category, the formal coalition, can be characterized by having established an administrative body to coordinate the joint work. Usually, formal coalitions also set up a profile in the transparency register run by the European Commission and the European Parliament (for example Green 10). For all three categories, Hypothesis 1.1 dealing with the impact of *institutional agendas* was confirmed: European associations and/or NGOs formed coalitions after the European Commission adopted an issue on its agenda. In contrast, Hypothesis 1.4 on the role personal contacts between *office-holders* play in the process of coalition-formation could not be confirmed. In the four case studies the interview partners emphasized other factors as more decisive, although they admitted that personal contacts can be helpful. The second group of hypotheses deals with the influence of the variable *motivation*, denoting that actors intending to form a coalition are either primarily driven by (short- or long-term) interests or by long-established norms. This does not imply that those driven by short-term interests do not act in accordance with a normative framework, nor that those following normative beliefs do not also have short-term, at times perhaps quite material, interests. However, it is important to identify which characteristics prevail in a given situation. Hypothesis 2.1 assumes a causal relation between shared interests and the formation of informal coalitions. As the case studies demonstrated, informal coalitions could primarily be characterized by common short-term interests related to one specific policy issue. In contrast, the members of formal coalitions share a set of long-established norms which primarily determine their actions, such as environmental protection ($\rightarrow$ H 2.2). If coalition members share a very large set of

Empirical results

norms, the coalition is more likely to be persistent over time. Hypothesis 3.1 on the impact of information and expertise on coalition-formation was not confirmed for any of the three categories. Especially for those European associations and/or NGOs which are well established in Brussels, the information and expertise a potential coalition partner contributes is not overly decisive. The same is valid for the independent variable *resources* (→ H 5.1) the impact of which was also negligible. The variable *reputation* defined as representativity and credibility (→ H 4.1) turned out to be especially decisive for all categories of visible coalitions. In particular, the interview partners emphasized the importance of demonstrating a »united front« indicating the representativity of the presented position and the credibility of the actors involved. Table 18 summarizes the factors determining the formation of different types of coalitions.

At this point it should be noted that Table 18 does not necessarily imply that coalition-formation can be depicted on a continuum ranging from informal to formal. Nevertheless, a coalition which was originally intended to be informal can be formalized over time.

With regard to the strategies pursued by the different types of coalitions, the following results could be drawn from the empirical analysis. Hypothesis 1.2 states that coalition members will also advise their national members to seek access to the respective national-level decision-makers. As the interview partners emphasized, the strategies pursued by a coalition are always developed in cooperation with their national member organizations. If the government of one nation state is particularly concerned about an EU policy initiative, the national organization of this country is often asked to play a key role in refining the coalition's future strategy. Furthermore, concerning the impact of *institutional rules* (→ H 1.3) and *office-holders* (→ H 1.5) on the strategies pursued by coalition members, it was confirmed that since the adoption of the Lisbon Treaty the European Parliament has become increasingly important as lobbying addressee, particularly compared to the Council. However, whenever office-holders change, coalitions must reconsider their strategies to increase the receptiveness of the new person in office or to include additional institutions in a strategy.

Empirical results

Table 18: Categories of coalitions of European associations and/or NGOs

	Categories of coalitions of European associations and/or NGOs				
	No coalition	Invisible coalition	Informal	Visible coalition Semi-formal	Formal
Characteristics	a) Between the European associations and/or NGOs no coalition is formed.	a) European associations and/or NGOs cooperate on an informal basis without demonstrating this to others. b) Although they agree to coordinate their strategies, these are pursued by each actor alone.	a) European associations and/or NGOs form an informal coalition. E.g., they publish a joint statement, position paper, or report. b) While such a coalition is formed to influence a particular political decision regarding one specific policy issue, it can be reactivated in the future. c) The coalition has neither a name, nor an administrative body to coordinate the work of its members.	a) European associations and/or NGOs form a semi-formal coalition. E.g., they publish a joint statement, position paper, or report. b) This coalition is formed to influence several political decisions. c) The coalition has a name which emphasizes its members' common concerns, but no spokesperson or administrative body to coordinate the work between them.	a) European associations and/or NGOs form or join a formal coalition. b) This coalition is formed for an indefinite period of time. c) The coalition has a name which emphasizes its members' common concerns, a letterhead, a spokesperson and an administrative body to coordinate the work of its members. d) The coalition will set up a profile in the transparency register run by the European Commission and the European Parliament.
Factors that are most likely to determine if a certain type of coalition is (or is not) formed	a) A policy issue is not included on the European Commission's agenda. b) Neither common interests, nor common norms exist. c) European associations and/or NGOs expect to damage their reputation as a result of cooperation.	a) A policy issue is included on the European Commission's agenda. b) Common interests exist. c) European associations and/or NGOs expect visible cooperation to damage their reputation.	a) A policy issue is included on the European Commission's agenda. b) Common (short-term) interests exist. c) European associations and/or NGOs expect to improve their reputation through visible cooperation.	a) A policy issue is included on the European Commission's agenda. b) Common (short- and long-term) interests exist for a variety of topics. c) European associations and/or NGOs expect to improve their reputation through visible cooperation.	a) A policy issue is included on the European Commission's agenda. b) Common (short- and long-term) interests exist and, in addition, coalition members share a set of long-established norms. c) European associations and/or NGOs expect to improve their reputation through visible cooperation.

181

Hypothesis 2.3 assumes a causal relation between the establishment of a formal coalition and the use of voice strategies, such as press releases and media campaigns, to complement access strategies when seeking direct contact with decision-makers, either by sending position papers or reports, or by meeting members of the European institutions face-to-face. With regard to access strategies, first of all, it has to be stressed that coalitions only randomly meet decision-makers in person. This is especially valid for informal and semi-formal coalitions which do not have a spokesperson who is authorized to speak on behalf of all coalition members. Informal and semi-formal coalitions, therefore, concentrate on formulating position papers to be submitted to the EU institutions. However, when a coalition is formalized, its members also establish an administrative body and name a spokesperson to represent the interests of all actors involved. Consequently, formal coalitions also have the means to initiate media campaigns intended to increase public awareness for a topic and in this way can exert additional pressure on decision-makers.

Another common strategy pursued by coalition members as part of their access strategies is not to formulate a single position paper to be sent to all decision-makers, but to write several statements and each time reframe the position such that it directly refers to the main concerns of the addressee (→ H 3.2). As the interview partners explained, the European Commission, especially the administrative staff, usually receives papers which include many technical details, while the positions sent to the European Parliament are often shorter and more political. Similarly, different arguments are stressed when the DG Energy and the DG Environment are addressed. The number of position papers, however, also depends on the availability of human resources. Although resources were not considered as decisive for the decision on whether to cooperate with a potential coalition partner, they do play a role when it comes to the strategies pursued at a coalition level (→ H 5.2). The more interest groups work together on a specific topic, the more papers can be written and the more venues be used to communicate the position. Financial resources are especially critical when coalition members wish to develop a position using external consultancies or research institutions.

Hypothesis 4.2 states that if coalition members have a bad reputation, the coalition will have difficulties in gaining access to the European institutions. This assumption was confirmed by all interview partners, which directly leads to the factors determining the receptiveness of the European decision-makers. In this work, the question was raised if coalitions of European associations and/or NGOs are more likely to receive attention from the European institutions compared to European associations or NGOs acting alone. The interview partners representing the European institutions stressed several reasons why they preferred positions submitted by coalitions. First of all, a coalition is able to present a »complete picture« including the interests of different sectors. Second, a coalition can help to identify the shortcomings of a policy initiative: if several associations and/or NGOs jointly criticize a specific aspect, their concerns are considered to be a clear signal that major deficiencies exist. Third, it is less time-consuming to read one paper issued by a coalition instead of having to read individual papers from every association and NGO concerned.

These arguments in favor of lobbying by coalitions indicate that the variable *reputation* as defined in this work has a great impact on the receptiveness of the decision-makers. If the presented position is representative for a whole sector and if the coalition members are considered to be reliable players, then acting in the context of a coalition is potentially more influential than acting only on behalf of an individual association or NGO.

However, if coalitions want to be successful they have to fulfil a second condition: the coalition members have to be experts in the policy field they are concerned with and their joint position has to provide information on the common interest of the sectors involved, which can then be translated into clear guidelines for further policy developments. Consequently, it can be a disadvantage to include too many actors in a coalition as a joint paper is ultimately based on the consensus of all signatories. If they, however, disagree on crucial aspects, the joint position may be watered down to the extent that it is of little use for decision-makers.

To sum up, one can say that coalitions of European associations and/or NGOs have become important players in the field of European energy policy, but they are not per se better able to make the European Commission, the European Parliament and the Council receptive to their interests.

Chapter 6. Conclusions

In order to increase the transparency of European decision-making with regard to the actors involved in the policy process – both individuals and organizations – as well as the particular interests they pursue, various lobbying registers have been set up. Even with the variety of registers available, both the quantity of interest groups in existence and the quality of the data provided cannot be verified. The number of listed interest groups varies and although forms of collective activity, such as networks and platforms, are also expected to set up a profile, the information presented remains incomplete. Registering presupposes that the »form of collective activity« has reached a sufficient degree of formality such that an administrative body has been established and a spokesperson has been selected who is authorized to speak on behalf of all actors involved. As this work has demonstrated, this, however, is not always the case.

In recent years, the formation of different types of coalitions between European associations and/or NGOs has emerged as a new phenomenon characterizing EU policy-making. While formal coalitions are more persistent over time and have established an administrative body to coordinate the interactions between the coalition members, informal coalitions lack organizational structures, a letterhead and a spokesperson because they are usually formed to influence a single legislative initiative only. Therefore, they do not appear in any kind of register.

This work investigated why actors form different kinds of coalitions and which strategies the coalition members pursue to increase the receptiveness of the EU institutions. In doing so, the focus clearly was on European associations and/or NGOs because, compared to national associations, they are more likely to be consulted by the European institutions as they aggregate the EU-wide interests of a particular sector.

On the basis of these considerations, the central research questions were:
Firstly, what factors lead to the formation of interest group coalitions in European energy policy? And secondly, what determines the strategies pursued by the coalition members to influence the EU policy process?

From a theoretical perspective, the following approaches have guided this work: the Advocacy Coalitions Framework developed by Sabatier and Jenkins-Smith (1988; 1993; 1999; see also Sabatier and Weible, 2007) in order to explain policy change, the actor-centered institutionalism (Mayntz and Scharpf, 1995a; Scharpf, 1997), the concept of political opportunity structures (Kitschelt, 1986), and different approaches on interest groups' strategies (Baumgartner and Jones, 1991; Beyers, 2004; Mazey and Richardson, 1996). Although the ACF provides

Conclusions

valuable insights into actor constellations and interactions in the policy process, some aspects regarding the formation of coalitions and their strategies required more in-depth research:

1) According to Sabatier and his collaborators, the rationality of individuals is bounded by their limited cognitive abilities. As a consequence, joint belief systems are assumed to determine their decision to join a particular coalition. What, however, has been widely neglected from this perspective is the importance of interests as an explanatory variable for coalition membership. Therefore, this analysis investigated the role of short- and long-term interests regarding the decision to cooperate. As the empirical analysis demonstrated, these do have an impact on the formation of coalitions. The European associations and NGOs referred to in the four case studies did not only cooperate on the basis of a joint belief or norm system, but were also united by shared, sometimes very short-term, interests, especially when they intended to influence only a single policy initiative. In this regard, the assumptions of actor-centered institutionalism, which state that actors select the best strategies available to realize their preferences under the conditions determined by the institutional setting, better explained their interactions. Furthermore, it was investigated whether the dominance of interests or norms as central motivation has an impact on a coalition's persistence over time. Here the analysis showed that if coalition members share a large set of long-established norms, the coalition is more persistent.

2) The second aspect this work was concerned with was the role of informal and semi-formal coalitions in the field of European energy policy. In the social science literature on interest group politics the existence of informal relations is widely acknowledged, however, comprehensive studies that go beyond the recognition that informal contacts exist are rare. In the four case studies, different types of coalitions were identified, ranging from informal and semi-formal to formal arrangements. As the empirical analysis showed, informal and semi-formal coalitions emerged in response to all four legislative initiatives. Concerning the variables determining the degree of formality, especially shared short-term and, as in the case of the Alliance of Energy Intensive Industries and the Energy Efficiency Industrial Forum, also long-term interests turned out to be important for the formation of these types of cooperation. Although these coalitions lack formal organizational structures, they nevertheless are important players in the field of European energy policy. The Alliance of Energy Intensive Industries issued several position papers on a variety of topics. As the decision-makers interviewed confirmed, especially coalitions that unite actors from one industry or at least similar sectors and, there-

fore, can provide decisive information on the consequences of a policy initiative and expertise on the subject are welcomed – regardless of whether they have established organizational structures or cooperate on an informal basis.
3) The third crucial aspect was the question of why, under certain circumstances, a coalition is unable to be formed. In this regard, a set of variables responsible for the decision not to cooperate was identified. Reasons were: a) that simply no common interest or norms existed or that b) a policy issue the associations and/or NGOs were concerned with was not adopted on the European Commission's agenda and thus there was no need to act jointly. Another crucial factor was that some potential coalition partners expected that cooperation might damage their reputation.
4) This work attempted to analyze how coalitions of European associations and/or NGOs use resources, defined as human and financial resources, and different venues to lobby the European institutions. While resources turned out not to be decisive for the decision to form or join a coalition, they did have an impact on the strategies pursued by the coalition members. The more interest groups work together on a specific topic, the more papers can be written and the more venues be used to articulate the position. Financial resources are especially important when coalition members wish to commission studies by consultancies or research institutions.
5) Finally, this analysis contributed to the discussion on the role of institutions by testing the impact of institutional opportunity structures (Kitschelt, 1986; Tarrow, 1991), defined here as institutional agendas, institutional rules and office-holders, on the formation of coalitions and the strategy choices made by the coalition members. The empirical analysis showed that institutional agendas are highly influential, especially in regard to coalition-formation. Usually, coalitions formed after the European Commission included a topic on its agenda. Concerning the strategies adopted by the coalition members, all three variables had a decisive impact.

To summarize the results from a theoretical perspective, one can say that although the ACF provides valuable insights into the dynamics of actor constellations and interactions in the policy process, to explain 1) the process of the formation of coalitions, 2) the strategy choices of the coalition members, and 3) their impact on the receptiveness of the European Commission, the European Parliament and the Council, the ACF has to be complemented with further approaches adding a rational perspective to the discussion and focussing in-depth on the role of institutions.

Literature

Primary literature and policy positions

ABI, 2011. *Biofuels for transportation and electric vehicles. There is currently room for both.* Vienna, January 2011.

ACE, BING, CEPMC, EEB, ELC, EUMEPS, Eurima, EuroACE, EUROGYPSUM, EXIBA, FIEC, Glass for Europe and WWF, 2008. *Europe Biggest Strategic Energy Reserve - Its Buildings.* Position paper, 09 October 2008.

ACEA, 2007. ACEA input to the DG TREN public consultation on "Biofuel issues in the new legislation on the promotion of renewable energy". Position paper, 2007.

ACEA, 2008. *ACEA Statement on biofuels.* Position paper, 09 June 2008.

ACEA and EUROPIA, 2010. *ACEA-EUROPIA joint communication. Biofuels towards 2020.* Position paper, 18 June 2010.

Achen, Ch.H. and Snidal, D., 1989. Rational Deterrence Theory and Comparative Case Studies. *World Politics,* 41(2), pp.143-169.

Adam, S. and Kriesi, H., 2007. The Network Approach. In: P.A. Sabatier, ed. *Theories of the Policy Process.* 2nd ed. Boulder: Westview, pp.129-154.

Adcock, R. and Collier, D., 2001. Measurement Validity: A Shared Standard for Qualitative and Quantitative Research. *American Political Science Review,* 95(3), pp.529-546.

AEA, 2006. *General Comments on the working document of the rapporteur Caroline Lucas on reducing the climate change impact of aviation.* Position paper, 13 April, 2006.

AEA, 2007. AEA Position on the Inclusion of Aviation in the EU ETS. Position paper, 17 October, 2007.

AEA, 2008. *No full auctioning for aviation.* Position paper, 19 February 2008.

AEA, 2007a. *Summary Report. Operating Economy of AEA airlines.*

AEA, ASD, EEA, EBAA, ERA and IACA; 2005. *European Aviation Industry Joint Position Paper on Emission Containment Policy.* Position paper, 07 July, 2005.

AEA, ASD, EEA, EBAA, ERA and IACA, 2006. Letter regarding the Draft Report on Reducing the Climate Change Impact of Aviation by Dr. Caroline Lucas – Provisional 2005/2249 (INI). Letter, 13 April 2006.

AEA, ASD, ECA, EBAA, ERA, IACA, and ELFAA, 2006. *European Aviation Industry Joint Statement on Emission Trading Scheme.* Position paper, 13 October 2006.

AEA, ASD, EEA, EBAA, ERA, IACA; IATA, ATAG and ELFAA, 2006. *Letter to the Members of the European Parliament regarding the adoption of the Lucas report by the ENVI Committee in May 2006.* Letter, 23 June 2006.

AEA, ECA, EBAA, ELFAA, ERA and IACA, 2007. *Common Position Adopted by the Airspace User Associations on the Proposed Directive of the European Parliament and of the Council Amending Directive 2003/87/EC so as to Include Aviation Activities in the Scheme for Greenhouse Gas Emission Allowance Trading within the Community.* Position paper, 06 June 2007.

Literature

AEA, ECA, EBAA, ELFAA, ERA and IACA, 2007a. Common Position of the European Aviation Industry on Amendments to the Commission's Proposal to Include Aviation in the Current EU ETS. Position paper, 15 October 2007.

AEA, ASD, EBAA, EEA, ELFAA, ERA and IACA, 2010. Letter to Commissioner Hedegaard regarding the *Distortion in Allocation of ETS Permits Arising From Volcanic Ash Crisis.* Letter, 23 June 2010.

AEBIOM, 2007. *AEBIOM answers to Commission's consultation on transportation biofuels.* Position paper, 18 June 2007.

AEBIOM and CEPI, 2007. *European Governments developing national energy plans to fulfill binding targets for renewable energy sources should focus on mobilisation, sustainability and efficient use of biomass.* Position paper, December 2007.

Alliance of Energy Intensive Industries, 2006. *Urgent Measures are required to improve the functioning of electricity and gas markets.* Position paper, 22 September 2006.

Alliance of Energy Intensive Industries, 2007. *Emission trading scheme for NO_x and SO_2.* Position paper, March 2007.

Alliance of Energy Intensive Industries, 2010. *Treatment of New Entrants: No auctioning for growth but equal treatment of new entrants and incumbents.* Position paper, 10 June 2010.

Almond, G.A., 1983. Corporatism, pluralism, and professional memory. *World Politics*, 35(2), pp.245-60.

Aspinwall, M.D. and Greenwood, J. eds., 1998. *Collective Action in the European Union. Interests and the New Politics of Associability.* London, New York: Routledge.

Aspinwall, M.D. and Greenwood, J., 1998a. Conceptualizing collective action in the European Union: an introduction. In: M.D. Aspinwall and J. Greenwood, eds. *Collective Action in the European Union. Interests and the New Politics of Associability.* London, New York: Routledge, pp.1-30.

Aspinwall, M.D. and Schneider, G., 2000. Same Menu, Separate Tables: The Institutionalist Turn in Political Science and the Study of European Integration. *European Journal of Political Research*, 39(1), pp.1–36.

Bache, I., 2008. Europeanization and Multilevel Governance. Lanham et al.: Rowman & Littlefield.

Bache, I. and Flinders, M., 2004. *Multi-level Governance.* Oxford: Oxford University Press.

Barroso, J.M., 2009. *Political guidelines for the next Commission.* Brussels: European Commission.

Baumgartner, F.R. Berry, J.M. Hojnacki, M. Kimball, D,C. and Leech, B., 2009. *Lobbying and Policy Change. Who Wins, Who Loses, and Why.* Chicago: University of Chicago Press.

Baumgartner, F.R. and Jones, B.D., 1991. Agenda Dynamics and Policy Subsystems. *Journal of Politics*, 53(4), pp.1044-1074.

Baumgartner, F.R. and Jones, B.D., 1993. *Agendas and Instability in American Politics.* Chicago: University of Chicago Press.

Baumgartner, F.R. and Jones, B.D., 2009. *Agendas and Instability in American Politics.* 2nd ed. Chicago: University of Chicago Press.

Baumgartner, F.R. and Mahoney, C., 2008. The Two Faces of Framing. Individual-Level Framing and Collective Issue Definition in the European Union. *European Union Politics*, 9(3), pp.435-449.

Bavelas, A. 1950. Communication Patterns in Task-Oriented Groups. *Journal of the Acoustical Society of America* 22(6), pp.725-730.

Literature

Bennett, A. and Elman, C., 2007. Case Study Methods in the International Relations Subfield. *Comparative Political Studies*, 40(2), pp.170-195.

Benz, A. Lütz, S. Schimank, U. and Simonis, G., 2007. *Handbuch Governance. Theoretische Grundlagen und empirische Anwendungsfelder*. Wiesbaden: VS Verlag.

Benz, A. ed., 2010. *Governance – Regieren in komplexen Regelsystemen. Eine Einführung*. 2nd ed. Wiesbaden: VS-Verlag.

Behrens, M., 2010. Global Governance. In: A. Benz, ed. *Governance – Regieren in komplexen Regelsystemen. Eine Einführung*. 2nd ed. Wiesbaden: VS-Verlag, pp.93-108.

Benson, J.K., 1978. The Interorganizational Network as a Political Economy. In: L. Karpik, ed. *Organization and Environment: Theory, Issues and Reality*. Beverly Hills: Sage, pp.69-102.

Benz, A., 1998. Mehrebenenverflechtung in der Europäischen Union. In: M. Jachtenfuchs and B. Kohler-Koch, eds. *Europäische Integration*. Opladen: Leske & Budrich: pp.317-351.

Benz, A., 2006. Governance in Mehrebenensystemen. In: G.F. Schuppert, ed. *Governance-Forschung. Vergewisserung über Stand und Entwicklungslinien*. 2nd ed. Baden-Baden: Nomos, pp.95-120.

Berkhout, J. and Lowery, D., 2008. Counting organized interests in the European Union: a comparison of data sources. *Journal of European Public Policy* 15(4), pp.489-513.

Berry, J., 1989. *The Interest Group Society*. 2nd ed. Boston: Little Brown.

Beyers, J., 2002. Gaining and seeking access: The European adaptation of domestic interest associations. *European Journal of Political Research* 41(5), pp.585–612.

Beyers, J., 2004. Voice and Access: Political Practices of European Interest Associations. *European Union Politics*, 5(2), pp. 211-240.

Beyers, J. and Kerremans, B., 2004. Bureaucrats, Politicians, and Societal Interests. How is European Policy Making Politicized? *Comparative Political Studies*, 37(10), pp. 1119-1150.

Beyers, J. Eising, R. and Maloney, W., 2008. Much We Study, Little We Know? The Study of Interest Group Politics in Europe and Elsewhere. *West European Politics*, 31(6), pp.1103-1128.

BING, 2008. *Comments of BING on the recast of Directive 2002/91/EC on the Energy Performance of Buildings*. Position paper, 25 March 2008.

Birkland, T.A., 2004. Learning and Policy Improvement after Disaster: The Case of Aviation Security. *American Behavioral Scientist*, 48(3), pp.341-364.

Blaisdell, D.C., 1941. *Economic Power and Political Pressures*. Washington, D.C.: US Government Printing Office.

Börzel, T.A, 1997. What's So Special About Policy Networks? – An Exploration of the Concept and Its Usefulness in Studying European Governance. *European Integration online Papers (EIoP)*, 1(16), [online] Available at: <http://eiop.or.at/eiop/texte/1997-016a.htm> [Accessed 14 April 2010].

Börzel, T.A., 2011. Networks: Reified Metaphor or Governance Panacea? *Public Administration* 89(1), pp.49-63.

Börzel, T.A. and Heard-Lauréote, K., 2009. Networks in EU Multi-level Governance: Concepts and Contributions. *Journal of Public Policy*, 29(1), pp.135-152.

Bogason, P., 2006. Networks and Bargaining in Policy Analysis. In: G. Peters and J. Pierre, eds. *Handbook of Public Policy*. London, Thousand Oaks, New Delhi: Sage, pp.97-114.

Bouwen, P., 2002. Corporate lobbying: towards a theory of access, *Journal of European Public Policy*, 9(3), pp.365-390.

Literature

Breakthrough Institute, 2011. *Energy Emergence. Rebound and backfire as emergent phenomena*, [online] Available at: <http://thebreakthrough.org/blog/Energy_Emergence.pdf> [Accessed 30 March 2011].

Broscheid, A. and Coen, D., 2003. Insider and Outsider Lobbying of the European Commission: An Informational Model of Forum Politics. *European Union Politics*, 4(2), pp. 165-189.

Brunnengräber, A., 2007. Multi-Level Climate Governance. Strategische Selektivitäten in der internationalen Politik. In: A. Brunnengräber and H. Walk, ed. *Multi-Level Governance. Klima-, Umwelt- und Sozialpolitik in einer interdependenten Welt*. Baden-Baden: Nomos, pp.207-228.

Brunnengräber, A. and Walk, H., 2007. Der Mehrwert der Mehrebenenbetrachtung. In: A. Brunnengräber and H. Walk, ed. *Multi-Level Governance. Klima-, Umwelt- und Sozialpolitik in einer interdependenten Welt*. Baden-Baden: Nomos, pp.17-32.

Bundesregierung, 2007. *Historical agreement on climate protection*, [press release], 09 March 2007, Berlin.

Burns, T.R., Baumgartner, T. and Deville, P., 1985. *Man, Decision, Society: The Theory of Actor-System Dynamics for Social Scientists*. New York: Gordon and Breach.

CAN-E, 2006. *CAN Europe response to public consultation on green paper on energy efficiency*. Position paper, 27 January 2006.

CAN-E, 2011. *Why Europe should strengthen its 2020 climate target*, [online] Available at: <http://www.greenpeace.org/eu-unit/Global/eu-unit/reports-briefings/2011%20pubs/2/yes-we-should-2011-2-17.pdf> [Accessed 01 November 2011].

CAN-E and T&E, 2006. *Measures to curb the climate change impacts of aviation*. Position paper, October 2006.

CEER, 2006. *CEER response to the Energy Green Paper*. Position paper, 28 July 2006.

Cefic, 2006. *Comments on the Green Paper on a European strategy for sustainable, competitive and secure energy*. Position paper, September 2006.

CEPI, 2007. *Energy markets – The need for fully liberalised and well-functioning markets in Europe*. Position paper, 01 March 2007.

Chalmers, A.W., 2011. Interests, Influence and Information: Comparing the Influence of Interest Groups in the European Union. *Journal of European Integration*, 33(4), pp.471-486.

Christiansen, T. and Piattoni, S. eds., 2003. *Informal Governance in the European Union*. Cheltenham: Edward Elgar.

Christiansen, T., Føllesdal, A. and Piattoni, S., 2003. Informal Governance in the European Union: an introduction. In: T. Christiansen and S. Piattoni, eds. *Informal Governance in the European Union*. Cheltenham: Edward Elgar, pp.1-21.

Coalition of Energy Savings, 2010. *An Open Letter to: Members of the European Council, European Council President Van Rompuy, European Commission President Barroso, European Parliament President Buzek*. Position paper, 09 February 2010.

Coalition for Energy Savings, 2010a. *Business and NGOs Unite to Urge Energy Ministers to Triple Efforts on Energy Savings and Efficiency*. Position paper, 06 September 2010.

Coalition for Energy Savings, 2010b. *Coalition for Energy Savings calls for action on energy efficiency*, [press release], 06 December 2010.

Coalition for Energy Savings, 2011. *EU leader recognise importance of energy efficiency, but fail to fix 2020 target shortfall*. Position paper, 04 February 2011.

Coalition for Energy Savings, 2011a. *The Coalition Portfolio: Financial Issues for EnergyEfficiency*. Position paper, 07 April 2011.

Coalition for Energy Savings, 2011b. *Energy Efficiency: a missed opportunity. Commission's proposed Directive falls short of Europe's energy efficiency ambitions*, [press release], 22 June 2011.

Cobb, R.W. and Elder, Ch.D., 1972. *Participation in American Politics. The Dynamics of Agenda-Building*. Baltimore: Johns Hopkins University Press.

Coen, D., 1999. The impact of U.S. lobbying practice on the European business - government relationships. *California Management Review*, 41 (4), pp.27-44.

Coen, D., 2007. *Lobbying in the European Union. Briefing Paper*. Brussels: European Parliament, Directorate-General Internal Policies, [online] Available at: <http://www.europarl.europa.eu/activities/committees/studies/download.do?file=18208> [Accessed 06 December 2010].

Coen, D. and Thatcher, M., 2008. Network Governance and Multi-level Delegation: European Networks and Regulatory Agencies. *Journal of Public Policy*, 28(1), pp.49-71.

Corbetta, P., 2003. *Social Research: Theory, Methods and Techniques*. London: Sage Publications.

Council of the European Union, 2007. *Presidency Conclusions*.

Dahl, R.A., 1957. The concept of power. *Behavioral Science*, 2(3), pp.201-15.

Della Porta, D. and Caiani, M., 2009. *Social Movements and Europeanization*. Oxford: Oxford University Press.

DG Energy, 2011. *Registration of Crude Oil Imports and Deliveries in the European Union (EU27) (1) (Intra + Extra EU)*, Brussels.

DG Energy, 2011a. *Energy 2020. A Strategy for Competitive, Sustainable, and Secure Energy*, Brussels.

DG Energy and Transport, 2006. *Review of EU biofuels directive*. Public consultation exercise, April-July 2006, Brussels.

DG Energy and Transport, 2007. *Biofuel issues in the new legislation on the promotion of renewable energy*. Public consultation exercise, April-May 2007, Brussels.

DG Energy and Transport, 2008. *Results of the Public Consultation on the Recast of the Energy Performance of Buildings Directive*, Brussels.

DG Environment, 2005. *Questions and answers on Emissions Trading and National Allocation Plan*, [press release], Brussels.

DG Environment, 2006. *Questions and answers on national allocation plans for 2008 – 2012*, [press release], 09 January 2006, Brussels.].

DG Environment, 2007. *Climate change: IPCC report confirms EU call for deep cuts in global greenhouse gas emissions*, [press release], 04 May 2007, Brussels.

Diani, M., 1992. The Concept of Social Movement. *Sociological Review*, 40(1), pp.1-25.

Diani, M. and Bison, I., 2004. Organizations, coalitions, and movements. *Theory and Society* 33, pp. 281-309.

Dowding, K., 1995. Model or Metaphor? A Critical Review of the Policy Network Approach. *Political Studies*, 43(1), pp. 136-158.

Downs, A., 1957. *An Economic Theory of Democracy*. New York: Harper &. Row.

Dür, A., 2008. Interest Groups in the European Union: How Powerful Are They? *West European Politics*, 31(6), pp. 1212 - 1230.

Literature

Dür, A. and de Bièvre, D., 2007. The question of interest group influence. *Journal of Public Policy*, 27(1), pp.1-12.

Eberlein, B., 2007. The Making of the European Energy Market: The Interplay of Governance and Government. *Journal of European Public Policy*, 28(1), pp.73-92.

Ebbinghaus, B., 2006. Qualitativer oder quantitative Vergleich? Herausforderungen für die sozialwissenschaftliche Europaforschung. *Zeitschrift für Staats- und Europawissenschaften*, 4(3), pp.388-404.

EBC, 2008. *EBC's reply to the Commission consultation on the Recasting of the Energy Performance of Buildings Directive EPBD (2002/91/EC)*. Position paper, 23 June 2008.

eBIO, 2008. *Proposal for a Directive on the Promotion of the use of Energy from Renewable Sources. Position Paper of the European Bioethanol Fuel Association (eBIO)*. Position paper, 31 March 2008.

EEB, 2009. *EEP Working Position on the Recast of the Energy Performance of Buildings Directive*. Position paper, July 2009.

EEB, FoEE, IFN and T&E, 2005. *Measures to Curb the Climate Change Impacts of Aviation*. Position paper, June 2005.

EEIF, 2008. *Energy Efficiency Industrial Forum Position Paper: energy efficiency – a vital component of energy security*. Position paper, 23 September 2008.

EEIF, 2009. *Energy Efficiency Industrial Forum (EEIF) Discussion Document on the consultation on Energy Efficiency Action Plan (EEAP) 2006*. Position paper, 03 August 2009.

EEIF, 2010. 5Css for *Energy Efficiency. The cornerstone o a viable Energy Policy for Europe*. Position paper, June 2010.

Eikeland, P.O., 2011. The Third Internal Energy Market Package: New Power Relations among Member States, EU Institutions and Non-state Actors? *Journal of Common Market Studies*, 49(2), pp.243-263.

Eising, R., 2000. *Liberalisierung und Europäisierung. Die regulative Reform der Elektrizitätsversorgung in Großbritannien, der Europäischen Gemeinschaft und der Bundesrepublik Deutschland*. Opladen: Leske & Budrich.

Eising, R., 2002. Policy Learning in Embedded Negotiations: Explaining EU Electricity Liberalization. *International Organization*, 56(1), pp.84-120.

Eising, R., 2003. Europäisierung und Integration. Konzepte in der EU-Forschung. In: M. Jachtenfuchs and B. Kohler-Koch, eds. *Europäische Integration*. 2nd ed. Opladen: Leske & Budrich, pp.387-416.

Eising, R., 2005. The access of business interests to European Union institutions: notes towards a theory. *Arena Working Paper* 29, University of Oslo, Centre for European Studies.

Eising, R., 2007. Institutional context, organizational resources and strategic choices: Explaining interest group access in the European Union. *European Union Politics*, 8(3), pp.329-362.

Eising, R., 2008. Interest groups in EU policy-making. *Living Reviews in European Governance* 3(4), [online] Available at: <http://europeangovernance.livingreviews.org/Articles/lreg-2008-4/> [Accessed 10 December 2010].

Eising, R., 2009. *The Political Economy of State-Business Relations in Europe. Interest mediation, capitalism and EU policy-making*. Abingdon, New York: Routledge.

Eising, R. and Kohler-Koch, B., 1999. Introduction: network governance in the European Union. In: B. Kohler-Koch and R. Eising, eds. *The Transformation of Governance in the European Union*. London, New York: Routledge, pp.3-13.

Literature

Eising, R. and Kohler-Koch, B. eds., 2005. *Interessenpolitik in Europa*. 1st ed. Baden-Baden: Nomos.

Eising, R. and Kohler-Koch, B., 2005a. Interessenpolitik im europäischen Mehrebenensystem. In: R. Eising and B. Kohler-Koch, eds. *Interessenpolitik in Europa*. 1st ed. Baden-Baden: Nomos, pp.11-78.

Eisinger, P.K., 1973. The Conditions of Protest Behavior in American Cities. *American Political Science Review*, 67, pp.11-28.

ENGVA, 2007. *ENGVA Reaction to: Public Consultation Exercise*. Position paper, June 2007.

Environmental News and Data Services, 2003. Wallström Warms to Role for Aviation in EU Emissions Trading. *The Environmental Industry Online*, [online] 1 January 2003. Available at: <http://www.environmental-expert.com/articles/wallstroem-warms-to-role-for-aviation-in-eu-emissions-trading-3000> [Accessed 15 March 2011].

ELFAA, 2005. *Low Fares Airlines and the Environment*. Position paper, June 2005.

EPIA, 2009. *Recast of the Energy Performance of Buildings Directive (EPBD) – Turn buildings into energy producers*. Position paper, 27 January 2009.

EREC, 2005. Joint Declaration for a European Directive to Promote Renewable Heating and Cooling. 25% of the EU heating & cooling supply by renewables in 2020. Position paper, 18 July 2005.

EREC, 2006. *Make Europe the most energy import independent region of the world - Renewables for security of energy supply, competitiveness and environmental protection*. Position paper, 02 April 2006.

EREC, 2007. *European Heads of States back the Commission strategy to set binding targets for renewable energy*: Position paper, 09 March 2007.

Ernst & Young and York Aviation, 2007. *Analysis of the EC Proposal to Include Aviation Activities in the Emission Trading Scheme*. Brussels, Ernst & Young and York Aviation.

ETSO, 2006. *ETSO comments on EC the Green Paper for a European strategy for sustainable, competitive and secure energy*. Position paper, 1 September 2006.

ETSO, 2007. *Key message on the EC 3rd legislative package*. Position paper, November 2007.

EURACOAL, 2006. *Contribution to the fossil fuels forum working group on coal as well as on the Green paper A European strategy for sustainable, competitive and secure energy*. Position paper, 2006.

EurActiv, 2008. *Energy ministers agree to disagree on liberalization*, [press release] 29 February 2008.

EurActiv, 2008a. *Eight states oppose unbundling, table 'third way'*, [press release] 01 February 2008.

EurActiv, 2008b. *Commission rebuffs Franco-German energy proposals*, [press release] 15 February 2008.

EurActiv, 2008c. *Energy ministers clinch deal on liberalization*, [press release] 13 October 2008.

EurActiv, 2009. *Obstacles pile up for EU's 'green buildings' law*. [press release] 08 July 2009.

EurActiv, 2009a. *MEPs push back deadline for zero-energy buildings*, [press release] 01 April 2009.

EurActiv, 2009b. *Liberalising the EU energy sector*, [press release] 07 July 2009.

EURELECTRIC, 2006. *Comments on the Inclusion of aviation in the EU Emissions Trading Scheme*. Position paper, March 2006.

Literature

EURELECTRIC, 2006a. *EURELECTRIC comments, European Commission Green Paper on "A European strategy for sustainable, competitive and secure energy"*. Position paper, June 2006.

EURELECTRIC, 2007. *EURELECTRIC Views on Unbundling DSOs*. Position paper, July 2007.

Eurima, 2006. *Capturing the potential from buildings is urgent and cost-effective*. Position paper, 20 April 2006.

Eurima, 2008. *Eurima's position on the recast of the EPBD*. Position paper, 17 June 2008.

Eurima, EuroACE and REEEP, 2006. *The Vienna Statement. From Words to Action – A call to policy makers to accelerate measures to improve energy efficiency in buildings*. Position paper, 30 May 2006.

Eurima, EuroACE and EREC, 2009. *Common Statement on the Recast of the Directive on the Energy Performance of Buildings*. Position paper, 09 March 2009.

Eurogas, 2006. *The European gas market: Eurogas views on the way forward*. Position paper, 14 July 2006.

Eurogas, 2006a. *Eurogas views on the Green Paper "A European strategy for sustainable, competitive and secure energy"*. Position paper, 14 July 2006.

EUROMETAUX, 2006. *The Green paper for sustainable, competitive and secure energy. Urgent measures are required for functioning electricity markets*. Position paper, July 2006.

European Alliance of Energy Intensive Industries, 2004. *Energy Intensive Industries' Position on the amendments to be voted by the EP's Environment Committee on 15 March 2003 on the Emission Trading linking Directive*. Position paper, 11 March 2004.

European Alliance of Energy Intensive Industries, 2010. *Interservice consultation on the EU Emission Trading System draft Allocation Rules and Benchmarks*. Position paper, 15 October 2010.

European Commission, 2005. *Reducing the Climate Change Impact of Aviation, Report on the Public Consultation March-May 2005*, Brussels.

European Commission, 2006. Commission Staff Working Document: Summary report on the analysis of the debate on the green paper "A European Strategy for Sustainable, Competitive and Secure Energy", Brussels.

European Commission, 2008. *Questions and Answers on the Commission's proposal to revise the EU Emissions Trading System*, [press release], 23 January 2008, Brussels.

European Commission, 2008a. *Report to the 5th EU-OPEC Ministerial meeting*, Brussels.

European Commission, 2009. *Evaluation and revision of the Action Plan for Energy Efficiency, Report on the Public Consultation June–August 2009*, Brussels.

European Commission, 2009a. *EU energy trends to 2030, Update 2009*, Brussels.

European Commission, 2010. *EU Guidance on wind energy development in accordance with the EU nature legislation*, Brussels.

European Environment Agency, 2008. *Greenhouse gas emission trends and projections in Europe 2008. Tracking progress towards Kyoto targets*, [online] Available at: <http://www.eea.europa.eu/publications/eea_report_2008_5/Trends_and_projections_2008_executive_summary.pdf> [Accessed 07 November 2009].

European Environment Agency, 2010. *Annual European greenhouse gas inventory 1990-2008 and inventory report 2010. Submission to the UNFCCC Secretariat, EEA Technical Report No 6/2010*, [online] Available at: <http://www.eea.europa.eu/publications/european-union-greenhouse-gas-inventory-2010> [Accessed 24 March 2011].

Literature

European Parliament, 2003. *Lobbying in the European Union: Current Rules and Practices, Constitutional Affairs Series AFCO 104 EN.*

European Parliament, 2008. *MEPs give first reactions to climate change and energy package*, [press release].

European Parliament, 2008a. *Report on the development of the framework for the activities of interest representatives (lobbyists) in the European institutions (2007/2115(INI)).*

EUROPIA, 2006. *EUROPIA position on the Biomass Action Plan COM(2005)628 and the EU Strategy on Biofuels COM(2006)34.* Position paper, March 2006.

EUROPIA, 2007. EUROPIA's *Position on the CEN Gasoline, Diesel Norms and Maximum Biofuel Limits.* Position paper, January 2007.

Eurostat, 2010. *Energy production and imports.*

Fairbrass, J. and Jordan, A., 2003. The informal governance of EU environmental policy: the case of biodiversity protection. In: T. Christiansen and S. Piattoni, eds. *Informal Governance in the European Union.* Cheltenham: Edward Elgar, pp.94-113.

Fairbrass, J. and Jordan, A., 2004. Multi-level Governance and Environmental Policy. In: I. Bache and M. Flinders, eds. *Multi-level Governance.* Oxford: Oxford University Press: pp.147-164.

Fearon, J. and Wendt, A., 2001. Rationalism v. Constructivism? A Skeptical View. In: W. Carlsnaes, T. Risse, and B. Simmons, eds. *Handbook of International Relations.* Thousand Oaks, CA: Sage Publications, pp. 52-72.

Festinger, L., 1954. A Theory of Social Comparison Processes. *Human Relations* 7(2), pp.117-140.

Festiner, L. Schachter, S. and Back, K., 1963. *Social Pressures in Informal Groups.* Stanford, CA: Stanford University Press.

Finer, S. E., 1958. *Anonymous Empire. A Study of Lobby in Great Britain.* London: Pall Mall Press.

Follesdal, A. and Hix, S., 2005. Why there is a Democratic Deficit in the EU: A Response to Majone and Moravcsik. *European Governance Papers*, No. C-05-02, [online] Available at: <http://www.connex-network.org/eurogov/pdf/egp-connex-C-05-02.pdf > [Accessed 21 February 2011].

Fraunhofer ISI et al., 2009: *Study on the Energy Savings Potential in EU Member States, Candidate Countries, and EEA Countries.* Final report for the European Commission, Directorate-General Energy and Transport, 15 March 2009.

Freeman, L.C., 1979. Centrality in Social Networks – Conceptual Clarifications. *Social Networks* 1(3), pp.215-239.

FoE, 2007. *Aviation in a low-carbon EU: how the aviation Emissions Trading Scheme proposal must be improved.* Report, September 2007.

FoEE, Greenpeace and WWF, 2006. *Joint Statement. Plugged in at last: Europe pledge to stop wasting energy.* Position paper, 19 October 2006.

Garrett, G. and Weingast, B. 1993. Ideas, Interests and Institutions: Constructing the European Community's Internal Market. In: J. Goldstein and R. Keohane, eds. *Ideas and Foreign Policy.* Ithaca: Cornell University Press, pp.173–206.

George, A. and Bennett, A., 2005. *Case Studies and Theory Development in the Social Science.* Cambridge, MA: MIT Press.

Gerring, J., 2001. *Social Science Methodology. A Critical Framework.* Cambridge: Cambridge University Press.

Gerring, J., 2004. What Is a Case Study And What Is It Good for? *American Political Science Review*, 98(2), pp.341-354.

Gerring, J. 2007. *Case Study Research. Principles and Practices*. Cambridge: Cambridge University Press.

Goldstein, J. and Keohane, R., eds., 1993. *Ideas and Foreign Policy*. Ithaca: Cornell University Press.

Granovetter, M.S., 1973. The Strength of Weak Ties. *American Journal of Sociology* 78(6), pp.1360-1380.

Green 10, 2005. *Letter to the European Commission regarding its forthcoming communication Reducing the climate change impact of aviation*. Letter, 22 September 2005.

Green 10, 2006. *Making Progress on Energy Efficiency*. Position paper, 28 September 2006.

Green 10, 2006a. The *EU's renewed sustainable development strategy. Green 10 briefing for MEPs*. Letter, March 2006.

Green 10, 2007. *Reducing CO_2 emissions from light duty vehicles*. Letter, 23 January 2007.

Green 10, 2009. *Green groups: European Commission off target*, [press release] 10 June 2009, Available at: <http://green10.org/> [Accessed 10 November 2011].

Greenpeace, 2007. *Greenpeace responses to the public consultation "Biofuel issues in the new legislation on the promotion of renewable energy"*. Position paper, 18 June 2007.

Greenpeace, 2008. *Position on Bioenergy*. Position paper, June 2008.

Greenwood, J. and Aspinwall, M. eds., 1998. *Collective Action in the European Union: interests and the new politics of associability*. London, New York: Routledge.

Greven, M.Th., 2005. Informalization of Transnational Governance – A threat to Democratic Government. In: E. Grande and L.W. Pauly, eds. *Complex Sovereignty: Reconstituting Political Autonomy in the 21st Century*. Toronto: Toronto University Press, pp.35-62.

Haas, E.B., 1958. *The Uniting of Europe: Political, Social and Economic Forces 1950-1957*. Notre Dame: University of Notre Dame Press.

Haas, E.B., 1968. *The Uniting of Europe. Political, Social and Economic Forces, 1950-1957*. 2nd ed. Stanford: Stanford University Press.

Haas, E.B., 1975. *The Obsolescence of Regional Integration Theory*. Berkeley: University of California Press.

Hall, P.A. and Taylor, R.C.R., 1996. Political Science and the Three New Institutionalism. *MPIfG Discussion Paper*, 96(6), [online] Available at: <http://www.mpifg.de/pu/mpifg_dp/dp96-6.pdf> [Accessed 13 April 2011].

Hall, P.A., 2003. Aligning Ontology and Methodology in Comparative Research. In: J. Mahoney and D. Rueschemeyer, eds. *Comparative Historical Analysis: New Approaches and Methods*. New York: Cambridge University Press, pp.373-406.

Hancké, B., 2009. *Intelligent Research Design. A guide for beginning researchers in the Social Sciences*. Oxford: Oxford University Press.

Heclo, H. and Wildavsky, A.B., 1975. *The Private Government of Public Money: Community and Policy Inside British Politics*. London: Macmillan.

Hedstroem, P. and Swedberg, R. eds., 1998. *Social Mechanisms: An Analytical Approach to Social Theory*. Cambridge: Cambridge University Press.

Heisenberg, D., 2005. The institution of 'consensus' in the European Union: Formal versus informal decision-making in the Council. *European Journal of Political Research*, 44(1), pp. 65-90.

Héritier, A. ed., 2002. *Common Godds. Reinventing European and International Governance*. Lanham: Rowman & Littlefield.

Héritier, A., 2002a. New Modes of Governance in Europe: Policy-Making without Legislating. In: A. Héritier, ed. *Common Godds. Reinventing European and International Governance*. Lanham: Rowman & Littlefield, pp.185-206.

Herring, E.P., 1929. *Group Representation before Congress*. Washington, DC: Brookings.

Hoffmann, S., 1966. Obstinate or Obsolete? The Fate of the Nation-State and the Case of Western Europe. *Daedalus*, 95(3), pp. 862–915.

Hooghe, L. and Marks, G., 2003. Unraveling the Central State, but How? Types of Multi-level Governance. *American Political Science Review*, 97(2), pp. 233-243.

Howes, T., 2010. The EU's New Renewable Energy Directive (2009/28/EC). In: S. Oberthür and M. Pallemaerts, eds. *The New Climate Change Policies of the European Union*. Brussels: VUB, pp. 117-150.

IEA, 2008. *From 1st- to 2nd-Generation Biofuel Technologies. An Overview of Current Industry and RD&D Activities*, [online] Available at: <http://www.iea.org/papers/2008/-2nd_Biofuel_Gen.pdf> [Accessed 25 May 2011].

IEA, 2010. *Energy Efficiency Governance*, [online] Available at: <http://www.iea.org/papers/2010/eeg.pdf> [Accessed 30 March 2011].

IFEU, 2004. *Co$_2$ Mitigation through Biofuels in the Transport Sector*, [online] Available at: <http://www.ifeu.de/landwirtschaft/pdf/co2mitigation.pdf> [Accessed 25 May 2011].

IFIEC Europe, 2005. *Inclusion of Aviation into the EU Emission Trading Scheme – Serious concerns about the consequences*. Position paper, 19 December 2005.

IPCC, 1990. *IPCC First Assessment Report*, [online] Available at: <http://www.ipcc.ch/-publications_and_data/publications_and_data_reports.shtml> [Accessed 30 October 2010].

IPCC, 1995. *Climate Change: A Glossary by the Intergovernmental Panel on Climate Change*, [online] Available at: <http://www.ipcc.ch/pdf/glossary/ipcc-glossary.pdf> [Accessed 30 October 2010].

IPCC, 1999. *Aviation and the Global Atmosphere – Summary for Policymakers*, [online] Available at: <http://www.grida.no/publications/other/ipcc_sr/> [Accessed 13 May 2010].

IPCC, 2007. *IPCC Fourth Assessment Report - Climate Change 2007. Synthesis Report*, [online] Available at: <http://www.ipcc.ch/pdf/assessment-report/ar4/syr/ar4_syr.pdf> [Accessed 30 October 2010].

Imig, D. and Tarrow, S. eds., 2001. *Contentious Europeans: Protest and Politics in an Emerging Polity*. Lanham, MD: Rowman & Littlefield.

Jachtenfuchs, M. and Kohler-Koch, B. eds., 1996. *Europäische Integration*. Opladen: Leske & Budrich.

Jachtenfuchs, M. and Kohler-Koch, B., 1996a. Regieren im dynamischen Mehrebenensystem. In: M. Jachtenfuchs and B. Kohler-Koch, eds. *Europäische Integration*. 1st ed. Opladen: Leske & Budrich, pp.15-46.

Jachtenfuchs, M. and Kohler-Koch, B. eds., 2003. *Europäische Integration*. 2nd ed. Opladen: Leske & Budrich.

Jamasb, T. and Pollitt, M., 2005. Electricity Market Reform in the European Union: Review of Progress toward Liberalization & Integration. *The Energy Journal*, 26(Special Edition), pp.11-41.

Jenkins, J.C. and Klandermans, B. eds., 1995. *The Politics of Social Protest. Comparative Perspectives on States and Social Movements*, London: UCL Press.

Literature

Jenkins, C. and Perrow, C., 1977. Insurgency of the powerless: Farm workers movements, 1946–1972. *American Sociological Review*, 42(2), pp.249 - 268.

Jenkins-Smith, H. and St. Clair, G., 1993. The Politics of Offshore Energy: Empirically Testing the Advocacy Coalition Framework. In: P.A. Sabatier and H. Jenkins-Smith, eds. *Policy Change and Learning*, Boulder: Westview Press, pp.149-176.

Jordan, G., 1998. What drives associability at the European level? The limits of the utilitarian explanation. In. J. Greenwood and M. Aspinwall, eds. *Collective Action in the European Union. Interests and the new politics of associability*, London, New York: Routledge, pp.31-62.

Karpik, L. ed., 1978. *Organization and Environment: Theory, Issues and Reality*. Beverly Hills: Sage.

Kelman, S., 1987. *Making Public Policy: A Hopeful View of American Government*. New York: Basic Books.

King, G. Keohane, R.O. and Verba, S., 1994. *Designing Social Inquiry: Scientific Inference in Qualitative Research*. Princeton: Princeton University Press.

Kitschelt, H.P., 1986. Political Opportunity Structures and Political Protest: Anti-Nuclear Movements in Four Democracies. *British Journal of Political Science*, 16(1), pp.57-85.

Klein, D.A. Gupta, M.J. Cooper, P. and Jansson, A.F.R., 2007. Carbon dioxide production by benthic bacteria: the death of manmade global warming theory? *Journal of Geoclimatic Studies*, 23: pp.273-275.

Klüver, H., 2010. Europeanization of lobbying activities: When national interest groups spill over to the European level. *Journal of European Integration*, 32(2), pp.175-191.

Klüver, H., 2011. Lobbying in coalitions: Interest group influence on European policy-making. *Nuffield's Working Papers Series in Politics*, [online] Available at: <http://www.nuff.ox.ac.uk/Politics/papers/2011/Heike%20Kluever_working%20paper_2011_04.pdf> [Accessed 10 June 2011].

Kohler-Koch, B., 1999. The evolution and transformation of European governance. In: B. Kohler-Koch and R. Eising, eds. *The Transformation of Governance in the European Union*, London: Routledge, pp.14-35.

Kohler-Koch, B. and Eising, R. eds., 1999. *The Transformation of Governance in the European Union*. London: Routledge.

Kohler-Koch, B. and Rittberger, B., 2006. Review Article: The 'Governance Turn' in EU Studies. *Journal of Common Market Studies*, 44(1), pp.27-49.

Kriesi, H., 1995. The Political Opportunity Structure of New Social Movements: Its Impact on Their Mobilization. In: J.C. Jenkins and B. Klandermans, eds. *The Politics of Social Protest. Comparative Perspectives on States and Social Movements*, London: UCL Press, pp.167-198.

Kriesi, H. and Jegen, M., 2000. Decision-making in the Swiss Energy policy Elite. *Journal of Public Policy* 20(1), pp.21-53.

Kübler, D., 2001. Understanding policy change with the advocacy coalition framework: an application to Swiss drug policy. *European Union Politics*, 8(4), pp.623–641.

Lahusen, C. and Jauß, C., 2001. *Lobbying als Beruf*. Baden-Baden: Nomos.

Lahusen, C., 2002. Commercial consultancies in the European Union: the shape and structure of professional interest intermediation. *Journal of European Public Policy*, 9(5), pp.695-714.

Lazer, D., 2011. Networks in Political Science: Back to the Future. *Political Science and Politics* 44(1), pp.61-68.

Literature

Lehmann, W., 2007. Soft law or no law? The European Parliament's new role in the management of organized interests. In: *10th EUSA Meeting*. Montreal, Canada 17-19 May, [online] Available at: <http://aei.pitt.edu/7948/1/lehmann-w-08d.pdf> [Accessed 29 June 2011].

Library of the European Parliament, 2013. *Lobbying the EU institutions*, Library Briefing, 18/06/2013.

Lijphart, A., 1999. *Patterns of Democracy: Government Forms and Performance in Thirty-Six Countries*. New Haven, CT: Yale University Press.

Lindberg, L., 1963. *The Political Dynamics of European Integration*, Stanford: Stanford University Press.

Lipsky, M., 1968. Protest as a Political Resource. *American Political Science Review*, 62, pp.1144-1158.

Mahoney, C., 2004. The Power of Institutions. State and Interest Group Activity in the European Union. *European Union Politics*, 5(4), pp.441-466.

Mahoney, C., 2007. Lobbying Success in the United States and the European Union. *Journal of Public Policy*, 27(1), pp.35-56.

Mahoney, C., 2008. *Brussels versus the Beltway. Advocacy in the United States and the European Union*. Washington: Georgetown University Press.

Mahoney, J., 2008. Toward a Unified Theory of Causality. *Comparative Political Studies* 41(4/5), pp.412-436.

Mahoney, J. and Goertz, G., 2006. A Tale of Two Cultures: Contrasting Quantitative and Qualitative Research. *Political Analysis*, 14(3), pp.227-249.

March, J.G. and Simon, H.A., 1993. *Organizations*. 2nd ed. Cambridge, MA: Blackwell.

March, J.G. and Olsen, J.P., 1996. Institutional Perspective on Political Institutions. *Governance*, 9(3), pp.247-264.

Marks, G., 1992. Structural Policy in the European Community. In: A. Sbragia, ed. *Europolitics: Institutions and Policymaking in the "New" European Community*. Washington: The Brookings Institute, pp.191-225.

Marsh, D. ed., 1998. *Comparing Policy Networks*. Buckingham, Philadelphia: Open University Press.

Marsh, D., 1998a. The development of the policy network approach. In: D. Marsh, ed. *Comparing Policy Networks*. Buckingham, Philadelphia: Open University Press, pp.3-20.

Marsh, D. and Rhodes, R.W.A. eds., 1992. *Policy Networks in British Government*. Oxford: The Clarendon Press.

Marx, G.T. and McAdam, D., 1994. *Collective Behavior and Social Movements. Process and Structure*. Upper Saddle River, NJ: Prentice Hall.

Mayntz, R., 2004. Governance Theory as fortentwickelte Steuerungstheorie? In: G.F. Schuppert, ed. *Governance-Forschung. Vergewisserung über Stand und Entwicklungslinien*. 2nd ed. Baden-Baden: Nomos, pp.11-20.

Mayntz, R. and Scharpf, F.W., 1995. *Gesellschaftliche Selbstregelung und politische Steuerung*. Frankfurt a.M.: Campus.

Mayntz, R. and Scharpf, F.W., 1995a. Der Ansatz des akteurzentrierten Institutionalismus. In: R. Mayntz and F.W. Scharpf, eds. *Gesellschaftliche Selbstregelung und politische Steuerung*. Frankfurt a.M.: Campus, pp.39-72.

Mazey, S. and Richardson, J., 1996. Interest Groups and EU policy-making: organisational logic and venue shopping. In: J. Richardson, ed. *European Union. Power and policy-making*. 2nd ed. London, New York: Routledge, pp.217-238.

Literature

Mazey, S. and Richardson, J., 1997. Policy framing: Interest groups and the lead up to 1996 inter-governmental conference. *West European Politics*, 20(3), pp.111 - 133.

McCarthy, J.D. and Zald, M.N., 1977. Resource Mobilization and Social Movements: A Partial Theory. *American Journal of Sociology*, 82(6), pp.1212-1241.

McGowan. L., 2007. Theorising European Integration: revisiting neofunctionalism and testing its suitability for explaining the development of EC competition policy. *European Integration online Papers (EIoP)*, 11 (3), [online] Available at: <http://eiop.or.at/eiop/index.php/-eiop/article/viewFile/2007_003a/50> [Accessed 11 December 2010].

McPherson, M. Smith-Lovin, L. And Cook, J.M., 2001. Birds of a Feather: Homophily in Social Networks. *Annual Review of Sociology* 27(1), pp.415-444.

Messner, D. and Nuscheler, F., 2003. Das Konzept Global Governance – Stand und Perspektiven. *INEF-Report*, 67/2003, [online] Available at: <http://inef.uni-due.de/cms/files/report67.pdf> [Accessed 25 February 2011].

Michalowitz, I., 2005. Assessing Conditions for Influence of Interest Groups in the EU. IHS *Political Science Series*, 106, [online] Available at: <http://www.ihs.ac.at/vienna/IHS-Departments-2/Political-Science-1/Publications-18/Political-Science-Series-2/Publications-19/publication-page:2.htm> [Accessed 07 June 2011].

Michalowitz, I., 2007. What determines influence? Assessing conditions for decision-making influence of interest groups in the EU. *Journal of European Public*, Policy 14(1), pp. 132-151.

Moravcsik, A., 1993. Preferences and Power in the European Community: A Liberal Intergovernmentalist Approach. *Journal of Common Market Studies* 31(4), pp. 473–524.

Moravcsik, A., 1997. Taking Preferences Seriously: A Liberal Theory of International Politics. *International Organization* (51)4, pp: 513-553.

Moravcsik, A., 1998. *The choice for Europe: Social purpose and state power from Messina to Maastricht.* Ithaca, NY: Cornell University Press.

Moravcsik, A., 2002. In Defence of the 'Democratic Deficit': Reassessing Legitimacy in the European Union. *Journal of Common Market Studies*, 40(4), pp.603–24.

Morales, L., 2009. *Joining Political Organizations. Institutions, Mobilisation and Participation in Western Democracies.* Colchester: ECPR Press.

Mulford, C.L. and Rogers, D.L., 1982. Definitions and models. In: D.L. Rogers and D.A. Whetten, eds. *Interorganizational Coordination: Theory, Research, and Implementation.* Ames: Iowa State University Press, pp.9-31.

Naurin, D. and Lindahl, R., 2010. Out in the cold? Flexible integration and the political status of Euro opt-outs. *European Union Politics*, 11(4), pp.485-509.

Nohrstedt, D., 2005. External shocks and policy change: Three Mile Island and Swedish nuclear energy policy. *Journal of European Public Policy*, 12(6), pp.1041-1059.

North, D.C., 1990. *Institutions, Institutional Change, and Economic Performance.* Cambridge: Cambridge University Press.

Olson, M., 1965. *The Logic of Collective Action: Public Goods and Theory of Groups.* Cambridge, London: Harvard University Press.

OFID, 2009. *Biofuels and Food Security. Implications of an accelerated biofuels production*, [online] Available at: <http://www.ofid.org/publications/PDF/pamphlet/ofid_pam38_-Biofuels.pdf> [Accessed 25 May 2011].

Ostrom, E., 2007. Institutional Rational Choice: An Assessment of the Institutional Analysis and Development Framework. In: P.A. Sabatier, ed. *Theories of the Policy Process.* 2nd ed. Boulder: Westview Press, pp.21-64.

Peters, G., 1998. Policy networks: myth, metaphor and reality. In: D. Marsh, ed. *Comparing Policy Networks*. Buckingham, Philadelphia: Open University Press, pp.21-32.

Peters, G. and Pierre, J. eds., 2006. *Handbook of Public Policy*. London, Thousand Oaks, New Delhi: Sage.

Pijnenburg, B., 1998. EU lobbying by ad hoc coalitions: an exploratory case study. *Journal of European Public Policy*, 5(2), pp.303-321.

Pointvogel, A., 2009. Perceptions, realities, concessions – What is driving the integration of European energy policies? *Energy Policy*, 37, pp.5704-5716.

Pollak, J., 2007. *Repräsentation ohne Demokratie. Kollidierende Systeme der Repräsentation in der Europäischen Union*. Wien, New York: Springer.

Pollak, J. Schubert, S. and Slominski, P., 2010. *Die Energiepolitik der EU*. Wien: WUV/facultas (UTB).

Praetorius, B. and Schumacher, K., 2009. Greenhouse gas mitigation in a carbon constrained world: The role of carbon capture and storage. *Energy Policy*, 37: pp.5081-8093.

Princen, S., 2007. Advocacy Coalitions and the Internationalization of Public Health Policies. *Journal of Public Policy*, 27(1), pp.13-33.

Princen, S., 2007a. Agenda-setting in the European Union: A Theoretical Exploration and Agenda for Research. *Journal of European Public Policy*, 14(1), pp.21-38.

Princen, S., 2009. *Agenda-setting in the European Union*. Basingstoke: Palgrave Macmillan.

Princen, S. and Kerremans, B., 2008. Opportunity Structures in the EU Multi-Level-System. *West European Politics*, 31(6), pp.1129-1146.

Przeworski, A. and Teune, H., 1970. *The Logic of Comparative Social Inquiry*. New York: Wiley.

PU Europe, 2009. *Recast of Directive 2002/91/EC. Second reading position of the European Parliament – Focussing on key elements*. Position paper, 17 September 2009.

Putnam, R., 1988. Diplomacy and Domestic Politics: The Logic of Two-level Games. *International Organization*, 42(3), pp.427-460.

Rhodes, R.W.A., 1997. *Understanding Governance. Policy Networks, Reflexivity and Accountability*. Buckingham: Open University Press.

Rhodes, R.W.A. and Marsh, D. 1992. Policy Network in British Politics. In: D. Marsh and R.W.A. Rhodes, eds. *Policy Networks in British Government*. Oxford: The Clarendon Press.

Richardson, J.J., 1993. *Pressure Groups*. Oxford: Oxford University Press.

Richardson, J. ed., 1996. *European Union. Power and policy-making*. 2nd ed. London, New York: Routledge.

Richardson, J.J. ed., 2006. *European Union: Power and Policy-making*. 3rd ed. Abingdon: Routledge.

Richardson, J.J., 2006a. Policy-making in the EU: Interests, Ideas and Garbage Cans of Primeval Soup. In: J.J. Richardson, ed. *European Union: Power and Policy-making*. 3rd ed. Abingdon: Routledge, pp. 1-30.

Riker, W.H., 1962. *The Theory of Political Coalitions*. New Haven: Yale University Press.

Risse, T., 2004. Social constructivism and European integration. In: A. Wiener and T. Diez, eds. *European Integration Theory*. Oxford: Oxford University Press, pp. 159-176.

Rogers, D.L. and Whetten, D.A., eds., 1982. *Interorganizational Coordination: Theory, Research, and Implementation*. Ames: Iowa State University Press.

Literature

Rosenau, J.N. and Czempiel, E.-O. eds., 1992. *Governance without Government: Order and Change in World Politics.* Cambridge: Cambridge University Press.

Sabatier, P.A., ed, 2007. *Theories of the Policy Process.* 2nd ed. Boulder: Westview Press.

Sabatier, P.A and Jenkins-Smith, H.C., 1988. The Advocacy Coalition Model of Policy Change and the Role of Policy Orientated Learning Therein. *Policy Sciences* 21: pp.129-168.

Sabatier, P.A. and Jenkins-Smith, H.C., 1993. *Policy Change and Learning: An Advocacy Coalition Approach.* Boulder: Westview Press.

Sabatier, P.A and Jenkins-Smith, H.C., 1999, The Advocacy Coalition Framework: An Assessment. In: P.A. Sabatier, ed. *Theories of the Policy Process.* 1st ed. Boulder: Westview Press: pp.117-166.

Sabatier, P.A. and Weible, C.M., 2007. The Advocacy Coalition Framework – Innovations and Clarifications. In: P.A. Sabatier, ed. *Theories of the Policy Process.* 2nd ed. Boulder: Westview Press, pp.189-220.

Salisbury, R.H., 1992. *Interests and Institutions: Substance and Structure in American Politics.* Pittsburg, PA: University of Pittsburgh Press.

Samuelson, P., 1954. The Pure Theory of Public Expenditure. *The Review of Economics and Statistics*, 36(4), pp.387-389.

Sandholtz, W. and Zysman, J., 1989. 1992: Recasting the European Bargain. *World Politics*, 42(1), pp.95-128.

Sbragia, A. ed., 1992. *Europolitics: Institutions and Policymaking in the "New" European Community.* Washington: The Brookings Institute.

Schäfer, A. and Streeck, W., 2008. Korporatismus in der Europäischen Union. In M. Höpner and A. Schäfer, eds. *Die Politische Ökonomie der europäischen Integration*, Frankfurt a.M.: Campus, pp.203-240.

Scharpf, F.W., 1970. *Demokratietheorie zwischen Utopie und Anpassung.* Konstanz: Universitätsverlag.

Scharpf, F.W., 1978. Interorganizational Policy Studies: Issues, Concepts and Perspectives. In F.W. Scharpf and K.I. Hanf, eds. *Interorganizational Policy Making: Limits to Coordination and Central Control.* London: Sage, pp.57-112.

Scharpf, F.W., 1997. *Games Real Actors Play. Actor-centered Institutionalism in Policy Research.* Boulder: Westview Press.

Schmidt, V. A., 1997. European Integration and Institutional Change: The Transformation of National Patterns of Policy-making. In: G. Göhler, ed. *Institutionenwandel.* Opladen: Westdeutscher Verlag, pp.143-180.

Schuppert, G.F., 2006. *Governance-Forschung. Vergewisserung über Stand und Entwicklungslinien.* 2nd ed. Baden-Baden: Nomos.

Seale, C., 1998. Qualitative Interviewing. In: C. Seale, ed. *Researching Society and Culture.* London: Sage, pp. 202-16.

Sewell, G.C., 2005. *Actors, Coalitions, and the Framework Convention on Climate Change.* Ph.D. Massachusetts Institute of Technology, [online] Available at: <http://dspace.mit.edu/handle/1721.1/33743> [Accessed 12 March 2010].

Stewart, J.D., 1958. *British Pressure Groups: Their Role in Relation to the House of Commons.* Oxford: Oxford University Press.

Streeck, W. and Schmitter, W., 1991. From National Corporatism to Transnational Pluralism: Organized Interests in the Single European Market. *Politics & Society*, 19(2), pp.133-164.

T&E, 2005. *Report shows fifty-year failure of aviation industry to improve fuel efficiency*. Press release, 07 December 2005.

T&E, 2006. *Response of the European Federation for Transport and Environment (T&E) to the consultation of the European Commission on the review of the biofuels directive*. Position paper, 10 July 2006.

T&E, EEB and BirdLife International, 2007. *Biofuel issues in the new legislation on the promotion of renewable energy. Public consultation exercise, April-June 2007. Response from BirdLife International, the European Environmental Bureau and the Transport and Environment Network*. Position paper, 2007.

T&E, EEB, BirdLife International, Greenpeace and FoEE, 2008. *The real impact of growing biofuels. Calculating indirect land-use change*. Position paper, October 2008.

Tarrow, S., 1991. Struggle, Politics, and Reform: Collective Action, Social Movements, and Cycles of Protest. *Western Societies Program Occasional Paper No. 21*. Ithaca, NY: Cornell University.

Thatcher, M., 1998. The Development of Policy Network Analyses. *Journal of Theoretical Politics*, 10(4): pp.389-416.

Tilly, C., 1984. Social Movements and National Politics. In: C. Bright and S. Harding, eds. *Statemaking and Social Movements*. Ann Arbor: University of Michigan Press, pp.297–317.

Truman, D.B., 1951. *The governmental process*. New York: Alfred A. Knopf.

UEAPME, 2009. *UEAPME's position paper on the recast of the Energy Performance of Buildings Directive*. Position paper, 13 March 2009.

U.E.P.A., 2006. *About the competitiveness of the present and future EU ethanol industry*. Position paper, 14 February 2006.

UNFCCC, 2007. *Uniting on Climate*, [online] Available at: <http://unfccc.int/resource/docs/-publications/unitingonclimate_eng.pdf> [Accessed 25 May 2011]

Walker, J.L., 1983. The Origins and Maintenance of Interest Groups in America. *The American Political Science Review*, 77(2), pp.390-406.

Weber, M., 1922. *Wirtschaft und Gesellschaft*.Frankfurt a.M.: Zweitausendeins.

Weible, C. and Sabatier, P.A., 2007. A Guide to the Advocacy Coalition Framework. In: F. Fischer, G. Miller and M.S, Sidney, eds. *Handbook of Public Policy Analysis: Theory, Politics, and Methods*. Boca Raton: Taylor & Francis, pp.123-13.

Weiss, R.S., 1994. *Learning from Strangers. The Art and Method of Qualitative Interview Studies*. New York: The Free Press.

Wendt, A., 1999. *Social Theory of International Politics*. Cambridge: Cambridge University Press.

Wiener, A. and Diez, T. eds., 2004. *European Integration Theory*. Oxford: Oxford University Press.

Woll, C., 2006. Lobbying in the European Union: From sui generis to a comparative perspective. *Journal of European Public Policy*, 13(3): pp.456-469.

Woll, C., 2007. Leading the Dance? Power and political resources of business lobbyists. *Journal of Public Policy*, 27(1): pp.57-78.

Wonka, A. Baumgartner, F.R. Mahoney, C. and Berkhout, J., 2009. Measuring the Size and Scope of the EU Interest Group Population. In: ECPR, *General Conference*. Potsdam, Germany 10-12 September, [online] Available at: <http://www.unc.edu/~fbaum/papers/ECPR-2009-IG-Population.pdf> [Accessed 27 September 2011].

Literature

Wuppertal Institute for Climate, Environment and Energy and the Government Institute for Economic Research (VATT), 2006. *Security of Energy Supply. Potentials and Reserves of Various Energy Sources; Technologies Furthering Self-Reliance, and the Impact of Policy Choices*, [online] Available at: <http://www.wupperinst.org/uploads/tx_wibeitrag/security-energy-supply.pdf> [Accessed 25 May 2011].

WWF, 2006. *Including aviation into the EU Emission Trading Scheme – WWF position statement.* Position paper, October 2006.

WWF, 2007. *Climate Solutions: WWF's vision for 2050*, [online] Available at: <http://wwf.panda.org/what_we_do/footprint/water/dams_initiative/dams/energy/> [Accessed 02 April 2011].

WWF, 2007a. *WWF Contribution to the European Commission – Energy & Transport Directorate Public Consultation on the Review of the EU Biofuels Directive*. Position paper, 19 June 2007.

WWF, 2009. *WWF's Position Paper on the Recast of the EPBD*. Position paper, January 2009.

WWF and Allianz Group, 2005. *Climate Change and the Financial Sector: An Agenda for Action*, [online] Available at: <http://www.wwf.org.uk/filelibrary/pdf/allianz_rep_0605.pdf> [Accessed 05 April 2014].

WWF and CEPI, 2006. *WWF and CEPI recommendations for an effective implementation of European Renewable Energy Sources (RES) policies*. Position paper, August 2006.

Zürn, M., 2006. Global Governance. In: G.F. Schuppert, ed. *Governance-Forschung. Vergewisserung über Stand und Entwicklungslinien*. 2nd ed. Baden-Baden: Nomos, pp. 121-125.

Treaties and agreements

Agreement on the European Economic Area (EEA) (OJ No L 1, 3.1.1994), [online] Available at: <http://www.efta.int/eea/eea-agreement> [Accessed 05 April 2014].

Johannesburg Renewable Energy Coalition, 2002. *Declaration on The Way Forward on Renewable Energy*.

Kyoto Protocol to the United Nations Framework Convention on Climate Change, [online] Available at: <http://unfccc.int/resource/docs/convkp/kpeng.pdf> [Accessed 05 April 2014].

Treaty of Amsterdam amending the treaty on European Union, the treaties establishing the European Communities and certain related acts (97/C 340/01), [online] Available at: <http://europa.eu/eu-law/decision-making/treaties/index_en.htm> [Accessed 08 March 2014].

Treaty on European Union (TEU) and Treaty on the Functioning of the European Union (TFEU) (2010/C 83/01) (consolidated versions), [online] Available at: <http://europa.eu/eu-law/decision-making/treaties/index_en.htm> [Accessed 22 March 2014].

Treaty of Nice amending the treaty on the European Union, the treaties establishing the European Communities and certain related acts (2001/C 80/01). [online] Available at: <http://europa.eu/eu-law/decision-making/treaties/index_en.htm> [Accessed 08 March 2014].

Treaty of Lisbon amending the Treaty on European Union and the treaty establishing the European Community (2007/C 306/01), [online] Available at: <http://europa.eu/eu-law/decision-making/treaties/index_en.htm> [Accessed 08 March 2014].

United Framework Convention on Climate Change (UNFCCC), [online] Available at: <http://unfccc.int/resource/docs/convkp/conveng.pdf> [Accessed 05 April 2014].

Literature

Directives, Decisions, Regulations, and Resolutions (in chronological order)

Council Dir. 68/414/EEC of 20 December 1968 imposing an obligation on Member States of the EEC to maintain minimum stocks of crude oil and/or petroleum products.

Council Dir. 72/425/EEC of 19 December 1972 amending the Council Directive of 20 December 1968 imposing an obligation on Member States of the EEC to maintain minimum stocks of crude oil and/or petroleum products.

Council Resolution of 16 September 1986 concerning new Community energy policy objectives for 1995 and convergence of the policies of the Member States.

Council Dir. 90/377/EEC of 29 June 1990 concerning a Community procedure to improve the transparency of gas and electricity prices charged to industrial end-users.

Council Dir. 90/547/EEC of 29 October 1990 on the transit of electricity through transmission grids.

Council Dir. 91/296/EEC of 31 May 1991 on the transit of natural gas through grids.

Council Dir. 92/42/EEC of 21 May 1992 on efficiency requirements for new hot-water boilers fired with liquid or gaseous fuels.

Council Dir. 92/75/EEC of 22 September 1992 on the indication by labelling and standard product information of the consumption of energy and other resources by household appliances.

Council Dir. 93/76/EEC of 13 September 1993 to limit carbon dioxide emissions by improving energy efficiency (SAVE).

Dir. 96/57/EC of the European Parliament and of the Council of 3 September 1996 on energy efficiency requirements for household electric refrigerators, freezers and combinations thereof.

Council Dir. 96/61/EC of September 24, 1996 concerning integrated pollution prevention and control.

Dir. 96/92/EC of the European Parliament and of the Council of 19 December 1996 concerning common rules for the internal market in electricity.

Dir. 98/30/EC of the European Parliament and of the Council of 22 June 1998 concerning common rules for the internal market in natural gas.

Council Dir. 98/93/EC of 14 December 1998 amending Directive 68/414/EEC imposing an obligation on Member States of the EEC to maintain minimum stocks of crude oil and/or petroleum products.

Dir. 2000/55/EC of the European Parliament and of the Council of 18 September 2000 on energy efficiency requirements for ballasts for fluorescent lighting.

Dir. 2001/77/EC of the European Parliament and of the Council of 27 September 2001 on the promotion of electricity produced from renewable energy sources in the internal electricity market.

Dir. 2002/91/EC of the European Parliament and of the Council of 16 December 2002 on the energy performance of buildings.

Dir. 2003/30/EC of the European Parliament and of the Council of 8 May 2003 on the promotion of the use of biofuels or other renewable fuels for transport.

Dir. 2003/54/EC of the European Parliament and of the Council of 26 June 2003 concerning common rules for the internal market in electricity and repealing Directive 96/92/EC.

Literature

Dir. 2003/55/EC of the European Parliament and of the Council of 26 June 2003 concerning common rules for the internal market in natural gas and repealing Directive 98/30/EC.

Regulation (EC) No 1228/2003 of the European Parliament and of the Council of 26 June 2003 on conditions for access to the network for cross-border exchanges in electricity.

Dir. 2003/87/EC of the European Parliament and of the Council of October 13, 2003 establishing a scheme for greenhouse gas emission allowance trading within the Community and amending Council Directive 96/61/EC.

Council Dir. 2004/67/EC of 26 April 2004 concerning measures to safeguard security of natural gas supply.

Dir. 2004/8/EC of the European Parliament and of the Council of 11 February 2004 on the promotion of cogeneration based on a useful heat demand in the internal energy market and amending Directive 92/42/EEC.

Council Dir. 2004/67/EC of 26 April 2004 concerning measures to safeguard security of natural gas supply.

Dir. 2004/101/EC of the European Parliament and of the Council of October 27, 2004 amending Directive 2003/87/EC establishing a scheme for greenhouse gas emission allowance trading within the Community, in respect of the Kyoto Protocol's project mechanism.

Regulation (EC) No 1775/2005 of the European Parliament and of the Council of 28 September 2005 on conditions for access to the natural gas transmission networks.

Dir. 2005/89/EC of the European Parliament and of the Council of 18 January 2006 concerning measures to safeguard security of electricity supply and infrastructure investment.

Dir. 2006/32/EC of the European Parliament and of the Council of 5 April 2006 on energy end-use efficiency and energy services and repealing Council Directive 93/76/EEC.

Council Dir. 2006/67/EC of 24 July 2006 imposing an obligation on Member States to maintain minimum stocks of crude oil and/or petroleum products.

Dir. 2008/92/EC of the European Parliament and of the Council of 22 October 2008 concerning a Community procedure to improve the transparency of gas and electricity prices charged to industrial end-users (recast).

Dir. 2008/101/EC of the European Parliament and of the Council of November 19, 2008 amending Directive 2003/87/EC so as to include aviation activities in the scheme for greenhouse gas emission allowance trading within the Community.

Commission Regulation (EC) No 244/2009 of 18 March 2009 implementing Directive 2005/32/EC of the European Parliament and of the Council with regard to ecodesign requirements for non-directional household lamps.

Commission Regulation (EC) No 245/2009 of 18 March 2009 implementing Directive 2005/32/EC of the European Parliament and of the Council with regard to ecodesign requirements for fluorescent lamps without integrated ballast, for high intensity discharge lamps, and for ballasts and luminaires able to operate such lamps, and repealing Directive 2000/55/EC of the European Parliament and of the Council.

Dir. 2009/28/EC of the European Parliament and of the Council of April 23, 2009 on the promotion of the use of energy from renewable sources and amending and subsequently repealing Directive 2001/77/EC and Directive 2003/30/EC.

Dir. 2009/29/EC of the European Parliament and of the Council of April 23, 2009 amending Directive 2003/87/EC so as to improve and extend the greenhouse gas emission allowance trading scheme of the Community.

Dir. 2009/72/EC of the European Parliament and of the Council of 13 July 2009 concerning common rules for the internal market in electricity and repealing Directive 2003/54/EC.

Literature

Dir. 2009/73/EC of the European Parliament and of the Council of 13 July 2009 concerning common rules for the internal market in natural gas and repealing Directive 2003/55/EC.

Regulation (EC) No 713/2009 of the European Parliament and of the Council of 13 July 2009 establishing an Agency for the Cooperation of Energy Regulators.

Regulation (EC) No 714/2009 of the European Parliament and of the Council of 13 July 2009 on conditions for access to the network for cross-border exchanges in electricity and repealing Regulation (EC) No 1228/2003.

Regulation (EC) No 715/2009 of the European Parliament and of the Council of 13 July 2009 on conditions for access to the natural gas transmission networks and repealing Regulation (EC) No 1775/2005.

Council Dir. 2009/119/EC of 14 September 2009 imposing an obligation on Member States to maintain minimum stocks of crude oil and/or petroleum products.

Dec. 406/2009/EC of the European Parliament and of the Council of April 23 2009 on the effort of Member States to reduce their greenhouse gas emissions to meet the Community's greenhouse gas emission reduction commitments up to 2020.

Dir. 2010/30/EU of the European Parliament and of the Council of 19 May 2010 on the indication by labelling and standard product information of the consumption of energy and other resources by energy-related products (recast).

Dir. 2010/31/EU of the European Parliament and of the Council of 19 May 2010 on the energy performance of buildings.

Regulation (EU) No 994/2010 of the European Parliament and of the Council of 20 October 2010 concerning measures to safeguard security of gas supply and repealing Council Directive 2004/67/EC.

European Commission Communications, Green/White Papers, Proposals for Directives (in chronological order)

COM(85)310 final: White Paper from the Commission to the European Council of June 14, 1985 "Completing the Internal Market.

COM(97)599 final: White Paper for a Community Strategy and Action Plan of 26 November 1997. Energy for the Future: Renewable Sources of Energy.

COM(1999)230: Commission Communication to the Council and the Parliament "Preparing for Implementation of the Kyoto Protocol".

COM(2000)87 final: Green Paper on greenhouse gas emissions trading within the European Union (presented by the Commission).

COM(2000)247 final: Communication form the Commission to the Council, the European Parliament, the Economic and Social Committee and the Committee of the Regions: Action Plan to Improve Energy Efficiency in the European Community.

COM(2000)769 final: Green Paper - Towards a European strategy for the security of energy supply.

COM(2001)370 final: White Paper - European transport policy for 2010: time to decide.

COM(2001)428 final: White Paper European Governance.

COM(2001)581: Proposal for a Directive of the European Parliament and of the Council establishing a scheme for greenhouse gas emission allowance trading within the Community and amending Council Directive 96/61/EC.

Literature

COM(2002)680: Amended Proposal for a Directive of the European Parliament and of the Council establishing a scheme for greenhouse gas emission allowance trading within the Community and amending Council Directive 96/61/EC.

COM(2005)265 final: Green Paper on Energy Efficiency or Doing More With Less.

COM(2005)459 final: Communication from the Commission to the Council, the European Parliament, the European Economic and Social Committee and the Committee of the Regions. Reducing the Climate Change Impact of Aviation.

COM(2005)628 final: Communication from the Commission, Biomass Action Plan.

COM(2006)34 final: Communication from the Commission: An EU Strategy for Biofuels.

COM(2006)105 final: Green Paper: A European Strategy for Sustainable, Competitive and Secure Energy.

COM(2006)194 final: Green Paper European Transparency Initiative.

COM(2006)545 final: Communication from the Commission, Action Plan for Energy Efficiency: Realising the Potential.

COM(2006)583 final: Communication from the Commission to the Council and the European Parliament, Mobilising public and private finance towards global access to climate-friendly, affordable and secure energy services: The Global Energy Efficiency and Renewable Energy Fund.

COM(2006)818 final: Proposal for a Directive of the European Parliament and of the Council amending Directive 2003/87/EC so as to include aviation activities in the scheme for greenhouse gas emission allowance trading within the Community.

COM(2006)841 final: Communication from the Commission to the Council and the European Parliament: Prospects for the internal gas and electricity market.

COM(2006)848 final: Communication from the Commission to the Council and the European Parliament: Renewable Energy Road Map. Renewable energies in the 21st century: building a more sustainable future.

COM(2007)1 final: Communication from the Commission to the European Council and the European Parliament. An Energy Policy for Europe.

COM(2007)354 final: Green Paper from the Commission to the Council, the European Parliament, the European Economic and Social Committee and the Committee of the Regions: Adapting to climate change in Europe – options for EU action.

COM(2007)528 final: Proposal for a Directive of the European Parliament and of the Council amending Directive 2003/54/EC concerning common rules for the internal market in electricity.

COM(2007)529 final: Proposal for a Directive of the European Parliament and of the Council amending Directive 2003/55/EC concerning common rules for the internal market in natural gas.

COM(2008) Communication from the Commission to the European Parliament, the Council, the European Economic and Social Committee and the Committee of the Regions: Facing the challenge of higher oil prices.

COM(2008)16 final: Proposal for a Directive of the European Parliament and of the Council amending Directive 2003/87/EC so as to improve and extend the greenhouse gas emission allowance trading system of the Community.

COM(2008)19 final: Proposal for a Directive of the European Parliament and of the Council on the promotion of the use of energy from renewable sources.

Literature

COM(2008)30 final: Communication from the Commission to the European Parliament, the Council, the European Economic and Social Committee and the Committee of the Regions: 20 20 by 2020. Europe's climate change opportunity.

COM(2008)221 final: Communication from the Commission to the European Parliament pursuant to the second subparagraph of Article 251 (2) of the EC Treaty concerning the common position of the Council on the adoption of a Directive of the European Parliament and of the Council amending Directive 2003/87/EC so as to include aviation activities in the scheme for greenhouse gas emission allowance trading within the Community.

COM(2008)772 final: Communication from the Commission, Energy efficiency: delivering the 20% target.

COM(2008)778 final: Proposal for a Directive of the European Parliament and of the Council on the indication by labelling and standard product information of the consumption of energy and other resources by energy-related products.

COM(2008)780 final: Proposal for a Directive of the European Parliament and of the Council on the energy performance of buildings (recast) (presented by the Commission).

COM(2008)781 final: Communication from the Commission to the European Parliament, the Council, the European Economic and Social Committee and the Committee of the Regions, Second Strategic Energy Review: an EU energy security and solidarity action plan.

COM(2009)115 final: Communication from the Commission to the Council and the European Parliament, Report on progress in creating the internal gas and electricity market.

COM(2009)192 final: Communication from the Commission to the Council and the European Parliament, The Renewable Energy Progress Report: Commission Report in accordance with Article 3 of Directive 2001/77/EC, Article 4(2) of Directive 2003/30/EC and on the implementation.

COM(2009)519 final: Communication from the Commission to the European Parliament, the Council, the European Economic and Social Committee and the Committee of the Regions, Investing in the Development of Low Carbon Technologies (SET-Plan).

COM(2009)612 final: Communication from the Commission to the European Parliament and the Council: the Register of Interest Representatives, one year after.

COM(2010)639 final: Communication from the Commission to the European Parliament, the Council, the European Economic and Social Committee and the Committee of the Regions, Energy 2020: A strategy for competitive, sustainable and secure energy.

COM(2011)31 final: Communication from the Commission to the European Parliament and the Council, Renewable Energy: Progressing towards the 2020 target.

COM(2011)109 final: Communication from the Commission to the European Parliament, the Council, the European Social and Economic Committee and the Committee of the Regions, Energy Efficiency Plan 2011.

COM(2011)112 final: Communication from the Commission to the European Parliament, the Council, the European Economic and Social Committee and the Committee of the Regions. A Roadmap for moving to a competitive low carbon economy in 2050.